How to Start a Business in Michigan

Third Edition

Edward A. Haman
Mark Warda
Attorneys at Law

SPHINX® PUBLISHING
AN IMPRINT OF SOURCEBOOKS, INC.®
NAPERVILLE, ILLINOIS

DEC   2002

Third Edition, 2002

Published by: **Sphinx® Publishing, An Imprint of Sourcebooks, Inc.®**

<u>Naperville Office</u>
P.O. Box 4410
Naperville, Illinois 60567-4410
630-961-3900
Fax: 630-961-2168
http://www.sourcebooks.com
http://www.sphinxlegal.com

This publication is designed to provide accurate and authoritative information in regard to the subject matter covered. It is sold with the understanding that the publisher is not engaged in rendering legal, accounting, or other professional service. If legal advice or other expert assistance is required, the services of a competent professional person should be sought.

From a Declaration of Principles Jointly Adopted by a Committee of the
American Bar Association and a Committee of Publishers and Associations

This product is not a substitute for legal advice.

Disclaimer required by Texas statutes.

Library of Congress Cataloging-in-Publication Data
Haman, Edward A.
    How to start a business in Michigan / Edward A. Haman, Mark Warda.--3rd ed.
        p. cm.-- (Legal survival guides)
    Includes bibliographical references and index.
    ISBN 1-57248-183-8 (alk. paper)
      1. New business enterprises--Law and legislation--Michigan--Popular works. I.
Warda, Mark. II. Title. III. Series.

KFM4407.Z9 H36 2002
346.774'065--dc21

                                                                                        2001048351

Printed and bound in the United States of America.

VHG Paperback — 10 9 8 7 6 5 4 3 2 1

CONTENTS

USING SELF-HELP LAW BOOKS

Before using a self-help law book, you should realize the advantages and disadvantages of doing your own legal work and understand the challenges and diligence that this requires.

THE GROWING TREND

Rest assured that you won't be the first or only person handling your own legal matter. For example, in some states, more than seventy-five percent of divorces and other cases have at least one party representing him or herself. Because of the high cost of legal services, this is a major trend and many courts are struggling to make it easier for people to represent themselves. However, some courts are not happy with people who do not use attorneys and refuse to help them in any way. For some, the attitude is, "Go to the law library and figure it out for yourself."

We at Sphinx write and publish self-help law books to give people an alternative to the often complicated and confusing legal books found in most law libraries. We have made the explanations of the law as simple and easy to understand as possible. Of course, unlike an attorney advising an individual client, we cannot cover every conceivable possibility.

COST/VALUE ANALYSIS

Whenever you shop for a product or service, you are faced with various levels of quality and price. In deciding what product or service to buy, you make a cost/value analysis on the basis of your willingness to pay and the quality you desire.

When buying a car, you decide whether you want transportation, comfort, status, or sex appeal. Accordingly, you decide among such choices as a Neon, a Lincoln, a Rolls Royce, or a Porsche. Before making a decision, you usually weigh the merits of each option against the cost.

When you get a headache, you can take a pain reliever (such as aspirin) or visit a medical specialist for a neurological examination. Given this choice, most people, of course, take a pain reliever, since it costs only pennies; whereas a medical examination costs hundreds of dollars and takes a lot of time. This is usually a logical choice because it is rare to need anything more than a pain reliever for a headache. But in some cases, a headache may indicate a brain tumor and failing to see a specialist right away can result in complications. Should everyone with a headache go to a specialist? Of course not, but people treating their own illnesses must realize that they are betting on the basis of their cost/value analysis of the situation. They are taking the most logical option.

The same cost/value analysis must be made when deciding to do one's own legal work. Many legal situations are very straight forward, requiring a simple form and no complicated analysis. Anyone with a little intelligence and a book of instructions can handle the matter without outside help.

But there is always the chance that complications are involved that only an attorney would notice. To simplify the law into a book like this, several legal cases often must be condensed into a single sentence or paragraph. Otherwise, the book would be several hundred pages long and too complicated for most people. However, this simplification necessarily leaves out many details and nuances that would apply to special or unusual situations. Also, there are many ways to interpret most legal questions. Your case may come before a judge who disagrees with the analysis of our authors.

Therefore, in deciding to use a self-help law book and to do your own legal work, you must realize that you are making a cost/value analysis. You have decided that the money you will save in doing it yourself outweighs the chance that your case will not turn out to your satisfaction. Most people handling their own simple legal matters never have a problem, but occasionally people find that it ended up costing them more to have an attorney straighten out the situation than it would have if they had hired an attorney in the beginning. Keep this in mind if you decide to handle your own case, and be sure to consult an attorney if you feel you might need further guidance.

LOCAL RULES   The next thing to remember is that a book which covers the law for the entire nation, or even for an entire state, cannot possibly include every procedural difference of every county court. Whenever possible, we provide the exact form needed; however, in some areas, each county, or even each judge, may require unique forms and procedures. In our *state* books, our forms usually cover the majority of counties in the state, or provide examples of the type of form that will be required. In our *national* books, our forms are sometimes even more general in nature but are designed to give a good idea of the type of form that will be needed in most locations. Nonetheless, keep in mind that your *state*, county, or judge may have a requirement, or use a form, that is not included in this book.

You should not necessarily expect to be able to get all of the information and resources you need solely from within the pages of this book. This book will serve as your guide, giving you specific information whenever possible and helping you to find out what else you will need to know. This is just like if you decided to build your own backyard deck. You might purchase a book on how to build decks. However, such a book would not include the building codes and permit requirements of every city, town, county, and township in the nation; nor would it include the lumber, nails, saws, hammers, and other materials and tools you would need to actually build the deck. You would use the book as your guide, and then do some work and research involving such matters as whether you need a permit of some kind, what type and grade of wood are available in your area, whether to use hand tools or power tools, and how to use those tools.

Before using the forms in a book like this, you should check with your court clerk to see if there are any local rules of which you should be aware, or local forms you will need to use. Often, such forms will require the same information as the forms in the book but are merely laid out differently, use slightly different language, or use different color paper so the clerks can easily find them. They will sometimes require additional information.

CHANGES IN THE LAW
Besides being subject to state and local rules and practices, the law is subject to change at any time. The courts and the legislatures of all fifty states are constantly revising the laws. It is possible that while you are reading this book, some aspect of the law is being changed or that a court is interpreting a law in a different way. You should always check the most recent statutes, rules and regulations to see what, if any changes have been made.

In most cases, the change will be of minimal significance. A form will be redesigned, additional information will be required, or a waiting period will be extended. As a result, you might need to revise a form, file an extra form, or wait out a longer time period; these types of changes will not usually affect the outcome of your case. On the other hand, sometimes a major part of the law is changed, the entire law in a particular area is rewritten, or a case that was the basis of a central legal point is overruled. In such instances, your entire ability to pursue your case may be impaired.

Again, you should weigh the value of your case against the cost of an attorney and make a decision as to what you believe is in your best interest.

INTRODUCTION

Each year thousands of new corporations are registered in Michigan and thousands more partnerships and proprietorships open for business. Michigan is booming. Nationwide, the 1990s were called the "Decade of the entrepreneur," and that trend is continuing into the twenty-first century.

The best way to take part in this boom is to run your own business. Be your own boss and be as successful as you dare to be. But, if you do not follow the laws of the local, state, and federal governments, your progress can be slowed or stopped by fines, civil judgments, or even criminal penalties.

This book is intended to give you the framework for legally opening a business in Michigan. It also includes information on where to find special rules for various types of businesses. If you have legal questions or problems that are not covered by this book, you should seek out an attorney who can be available for your ongoing needs.

Chapters 1 and 2 will help you decide if you really want to start your own business, and what type of business entity would be best for you. Chapter 3 will discuss naming your business. Chapter 4 will explore financing options. Chapter 5 covers the location of your business. Chapter 6 considers possible licensing requirements, while Chapter 7 gives an overview of the law of contracts. Chapter 8 explains various types of insurance to consider. Chapter 9 covers legal issues relating to doing business on the Internet.

Chapters 10 through 12 discuss legal requirements relating to health and safety, employment relations, and advertising. Chapter 13 relates to payment and collection matters, while Chapter 14 explains various laws regarding business relations. Chapter 15 covers various miscellaneous legal issues. Chapter 16 explores bookkeeping and accounting matters. Chapters 17 through 19 cover federal, state, and out-of-state taxes.

You will also find a glossary, and references for further reading. Appendix A is a business start-up checklist. Appendix B contains sample filled in forms, and blank forms are found in Appendix C.

In order to cover all of the aspects of any business you are thinking of starting, you should read through this entire book, rather than skipping to the parts that look most important. There are many laws that may not sound like they apply to you but that do have provisions that will affect your business.

In recent years the government bureaucracies have been amending and lengthening their forms regularly. The forms included in this book were the most recent version available at the time of publication. It is possible that some may be revised at the time you read this book, but in most cases they will be similar and require the same information.

References to Michigan laws are to the *Michigan Compiled Laws Annotated* (abbreviated by lawyers and judges as M.C.L.A., but in this book as Mich. Comp. Laws Ann.). The symbol "§" means section, however section is abbreviated as "Sec." in this book.

NOTE: *Outside of this book you may come across references to Michigan laws designated* Michigan Statutes Annotated *(abbreviated "M.S.A." or "MSA"). This is an alternative set of books containing Michigan laws, which is being phased out. The M.S.A. uses a different numbering system, however, no M.S.A. numbers are being assigned to new laws as they are passed. If all you can find is a set of* Michigan Statutes Annotated, *the set includes a volume of tables which cross-references the M.S.A. numbers and* Michigan Compiled Laws Annotated *numbers.*

DECIDING TO
START A BUSINESS

1

If you are reading this book you have probably made a serious decision to take the plunge and start your own business. Hundreds of thousands of people make the same decision each year and many of them become very successful. Some merely eke out a living, others become billionaires. But a lot of them also fail. Knowledge can only help your chances of success. Some of what follows may seem obvious, but to someone wrapped up in a new business idea, some of this information is occasionally overlooked.

KNOW YOUR STRENGTHS

The last thing a budding entrepreneur wants to hear is that he is not cut out for running his own business. Those "do you have what it takes" quizzes are ignored with the fear that the answer might be one the entrepreneur doesn't want to hear. But even if you lack some skills, you can be successful if you know where to get them.

You should consider all of the skills and knowledge that running a successful business means and decide whether you have what it takes. If you do not, it does not necessarily mean you are doomed to be an employee all your life. Perhaps you just need a partner who has the skills you lack. Perhaps you can hire someone with the skills you need.

Or, you can structure your business to avoid areas where you are weak. If those do not work, maybe you can learn the skills.

For example, if you are not good at dealing with employees (either you are too passive and get taken advantage of, or are too tough and scare them off) you can:

- handle product development yourself and have a partner or hired manager deal with employees;

- take seminars in employee management; or,

- structure your business so you do not need employees, use independent contractors, or become an independent contractor.

Here are some of the factors to consider when planning your business:

- If it takes months or years before your business turns a profit, do you have the resources and emotional ability to hold out? Businesses have gone under or have been sold just before they were about to take off. Some people just give up too easily if their business does not take off rapidly. Staying power is an important ingredient to success.

- Are you willing to put in a lot of overtime to make your business a success? Owners of businesses do not set their own hours; the business sets them for the owner. Many business owners work long hours, seven days a week. But they enjoy running their business more than family picnics or fishing.

- Are you willing to do the dirtiest or most unpleasant work of the business? Emergencies come up and employees are not always dependable. You might need to mop up a flooded room, spend a weekend stuffing 10,000 envelopes or work Christmas if someone calls in sick.

- Do you know enough about the product or service? Are you aware of the trends in the industry and what changes new technology might bring? Think of the people who started typesetting or printing businesses just before type was replaced by laser printers.

- Do you know enough about accounting and inventory? Do you have a good "head for business?" Some people naturally know how to save money and do things profitably. Others are in the habit of buying the best and the most expensive of everything, which can be fatal to a struggling new business.

- Are you good at managing employees?

- Do you know how to sell your product or service? You can have the best product on the market but people do not beat a path to your door. If you are a wholesaler, shelf space in major stores can be hard to get, especially for a new company without a record, a large line of products, or a large advertising budget.

- Do you know enough about getting publicity? The media receive thousands of press releases and announcements each day and most are thrown away. Don't count on free publicity to put your name in front of the public.

KNOW YOUR BUSINESS

You do not only need to know the concept of a business, you need the experience of working in the type of business you intend to operate. Maybe you always dreamed of running a bed and breakfast or having your own pizza place, and now that you are laid off you think it is time to use your savings to fulfill your dream. Have you ever worked in such a business? If not, you may have no idea of the day-to-day headaches and problems of the business. For example, do you really know how much to allow for theft, spoilage, and returns from unhappy customers? Or, what can you expect in the way of employee turnover?

You might feel silly taking an entry level job at a pizza place when you would rather start your own, but it might be the most valuable preparation you could have. A few weeks of seeing how a business operates could mean the difference between success and failure.

Working in a business as an employee is one of the best ways to be a success at running such a business. New people with new ideas who work in old stodgy industries have been known to revolutionize them with obvious improvements that no one before dared to try.

DO THE MATH

Conventional wisdom says you need a business plan before committing yourself to a new venture, but lots of businesses are started successfully without the owner even knowing what a business plan is. They have a great concept, put it on the market, and it takes off. But you at least need to do some basic calculations to see if the business can make a profit. Below are some examples.

- If you want to start a retail shop, figure out how many people are close enough to become customers, and how many other stores will be competing for those customers. Visit some of those others and see how busy they are. Without giving away your plans to compete, ask some general questions like "how's business?" and maybe they will share their frustrations or successes.

- Whether you sell a good or a service, do the math to find out how much profit is in it.

    Example: If you plan to start a house painting company, find out what you will have to pay to hire painters; the cost of paint, brushes and rollers, thinner, rags, drop cloths, and other supplies; the cost for all of the insurance, bonding and licensing you will need; and the cost of advertising. Figure out how many jobs you can do per month and what other painters are charging.

    Depending upon such things as the industry and the area of the country, there may be a large margin of profit or there may be almost no profit.

- Find out if there is a demand for your product or service. Suppose you have designed a beautiful new kind of candle and your friends all say you should open a shop because "everyone will want them." Before making a hundred of them and renting a store, bring a few to craft shows or flea markets and see what happens.

- Figure out what the income and expenses would be for a typical month of your new business. List monthly expenses such as rent, salaries, utilities, insurance, taxes, supplies, advertising, services, and other overhead. Then figure out how much profit you will average from each sale. Next, figure out how many sales you will need to cover your overhead and divide by the number of business days in the month. Can you reasonably expect that many sales? How will you get those sales?

Most types of businesses have trade associations, which often have figures on how profitable its members are. Some even have start-up kits for people wanting to start businesses. One good source of information on such organizations is the *Encyclopedia of Associations* published by Gale Research Inc., and available in many library reference sections. Producers of products to the trade often give assistance to small companies getting started, to win their loyalty. Contact the largest suppliers of products your business will be using and see if they can be of help.

SOURCES FOR FURTHER GUIDANCE

The following offices offer free or low cost guidance for new businesses.

SMALL BUSINESS ADMINISTRATION

The Small Business Administration (SBA) is a federal government agency set up to provide assistance to small businesses. The SBA offers educational programs for small businesses through Small Business Development Centers at many Michigan colleges and universities. You should see if they have any that could help you in any weak areas. To find the SBA office nearest to you, check in your local phone directory under the U.S. Government listings. The SBA is a good place to check for licensing requirements, financing information, and general assistance with what you need to start and run a successful business. If you cannot find a local listing, try the following:

Small Business Administration
477 Michigan Ave.
Suite 515, McNamara Building
Detroit, MI 48226
313-226-6075
313-226-4769 (fax)
email: michigan@sba.gov

Small Business Development Center
Grand Valley State University
Seidman School of Business
510 W. Fulton Street
Grand Rapids, MI 49504
616-336-7480
616-336-7485 (fax)
website: http://www.mi-sbdc.org/

SCORE

The Service Corps of Retired Executives (SCORE) is an organization of retired business people who volunteer their time to help people starting new businesses. SCORE is sponsored by the Small Business Administration. They also sponsor loan information clinics for a small fee (usually about $5.00).

To contact your nearest SCORE organization, check in your local phone directory under the U.S. Government listings (SCORE will be listed under the heading for the Small Business Administration). If you cannot find it in the phone directory, call one of the phone number listed above for the SBA and ask them for the phone number of the SCORE office nearest you. Or check the SCORE website:

http://www.score.org

Choosing the Form of Your Business 2

One of the first decisions you will need to make in relation to setting up a business is how you will structure your business. Will you be in business alone, in a relatively loose association with one or more others, or will you use one of the more formal statutory organizations such as a corporation or limited liability company. This chapter will explore the various forms of organizing a business to help you determine which is best for you.

Basic Forms of Doing Business

Traditionally, the four most popular forms for a business in Michigan have been proprietorship, partnership, corporation, and limited partnership. In 1993, a law was passed which allowed creation of a new type of enterprise, a *limited liability company*, which is becoming the preferred form for many, especially among lawyers, doctors, CPAs, and other professionals. (Mich. Comp. Laws Ann., beginning with Sec. 450.4101.) The characteristics, advantages, and disadvantages of each are as follows:

PROPRIETORSHIP   ***Characteristics.*** One person does business in his or her own name or under an assumed name.

Advantages. Proprietorships are simple. There is no organizational expense, and no partners to potentially come into conflict with in making business decisions.

Disadvantages. There is personal liability for all debts and obligations, and no continuation after death. All profits are directly taxable, and business affairs easily mix with personal affairs.

PARTNERSHIP

Characteristics. Two or more people carry on a business together and share the profits and losses. Laws covering partnerships are found in the Michigan Uniform Partnership Act. (Mich.Comp. Laws Ann., beginning with Sec. 449.1.)

Advantages. Partners can combine expertise and assets. Liability may be spread among more persons. Business can be continued after the death of a partner if bought out by a surviving partner, and there is relatively little regulation.

Disadvantages. Each partner is personally liable for acts of himself and other partners within the scope of the business. All profits are taxable, even if left in the business. Control is shared by all parties, and death of a partner may result in liquidation. Also, it is often hard to get rid of a bad partner.

CORPORATION

Characteristics. A corporation is a "person" created by the law that carries on business through its officers for its shareholders. (In Michigan one person may form a corporation and be the sole shareholder and officer.) Laws covering corporations are contained in the Michigan Business Corporation Act. (Mich. Comp. Laws Ann., beginning with Sec. 450.1101.)

An *S corporation* is a corporation that has filed **IRS FORM 2553** choosing to have all profits taxed to the shareholders, rather than to the corporation. An S corporation files a tax return but pays no federal or state tax. The profit shown on the S corporation tax return is reported on the owners' tax returns.

A C *corporation* is any corporation that has not elected to be taxed as an S corporation. A C corporation pays income tax on its profits. The effect of this is that when dividends are paid to shareholders they are taxed twice, first as income to the corporation and second when they are paid to the shareholders.

A *professional service corporation* is a corporation formed by a licensed professional such as a doctor or accountant. Michigan has special rules for professional service corporations that differ slightly from those of other corporations. These are included in the Michigan Professional Service Corporation Act. (Mich. Comp. Laws Ann., beginning with Sec. 450.221.) There are also special tax rules for professional service corporations.

A *nonprofit corporation* is usually used for such organizations as churches and condominium associations. However, with careful planning some types of businesses can be set up as nonprofit corporations and save in taxes. While a nonprofit corporation cannot pay dividends, it can pay its officers and employees fair salaries. Some of the major American nonprofit organizations pay their officers well over $100,000 a year. Michigan's special rules for nonprofit corporations are covered in the Michigan Nonprofit Corporation Act.(Mich. Comp. Laws Ann., beginning with Sec. 450.2101.)

Advantages. If properly organized, shareholders have no liability for corporate debts and lawsuits, and officers usually have no personal liability for their corporate acts. Existence of a corporation may be perpetual, and there are tax advantages allowed only to corporations. There is prestige in owning a corporation. Capital may be raised by issuing stock, and it is easy to transfer ownership upon death. A small corporation can be set up as an S corporation to avoid corporate taxes but still retain corporate advantages. Some types of businesses can be set up as nonprofit corporations, which provide significant tax savings.

Disadvantages. There are start-up costs for forming a corporation, as well as certain formalities such as annual meetings, separate bank accounts, and tax forms. Unless a corporation registers as an S corporation, it must pay income tax separate from the tax paid by the owners.

LIMITED
PARTNERSHIP

Characteristics. A limited partnership has characteristics similar to both a corporation and a partnership. There are two types of partners in a limited partnership: *general partners* who have the control and liability; and *limited partners* who put up money, but have no control over the business, and whose liability is limited to what they paid for their share of the partnership (like corporate stock). See the Michigan Uniform Limited Partnership Act. (Mich. Comp. Laws Ann., beginning with Sec. 449.1101.)

Advantages. Capital can be contributed by limited partners who have no control of the business or liability for its debts.

Disadvantages. General partners are personally liable for partnership debts and for the acts of each other. There are high start-up costs, and an extensive partnership agreement is required.

LIMITED
LIABILITY
COMPANY

Characteristics. In 1993, Michigan enacted the Michigan Limited Liability Company Act. (Mich. Comp. Laws Ann., Secs. 450.4101 to 450.5200.) This is a fairly new invention that has characteristics of both a corporation and a partnership. None of the partners (called *members*) have personal liability and all can have some control.

Advantages. The limited liability company offers the tax benefits of a partnership (if structured properly) with the protection from liability of a corporation. It offers more tax benefits than an S corporation because it may pass through more depreciation and deductions, it may have different classes of ownership, an unlimited number of members and may have aliens as members. It is similar to a Latin-American "Limitada" or a German "GmbH & Co. K.G." A name can also be reserved with the Department of Commerce.

Disadvantages. There are start-up costs, and because it is a fairly new invention there may not be a definite answer to some legal questions that may arise. However, the courts will probably rely on corporation and limited partnership law. As the IRS has not ruled that all Michigan LLCs automatically receive partnership tax treatment, an attorney or tax accountant should be consulted to be sure documents are phrased in such a manner to assure the desired tax treatment.

NOTE: *Michigan no longer has limited liability partnerships. It just recognizes limited liability companies.*

CHOOSING THE
FORM FOR YOUR
BUSINESS

The selection of a form of doing business is best made with the advice of an accountant and an attorney. If you were selling harmless objects by mail, a proprietorship would be the easiest way to get started. But if you own a taxi service, it would be important to incorporate or form a limited liability company. That way, you avoid losing your personal assets if one of your drivers were to injure someone in an accident where the damages could exceed your insurance.

If you can expect a high cash buildup the first year, then a corporation may be the best way to keep taxes low. If you expect the usual start-up losses, then a proprietorship, partnership or S corporation would probably be best.

START-UP PROCEDURES

In this section we will explain how to go about setting up each type of business organization.

PROPRIETORSHIP

There are no formal procedures to set up a sole proprietorship. This is the most simple and basic form of business operation. All bank accounts, and any necessary licenses, are in the name of the owner. If you wish to use a name other than your own, you will need to register that business name. See Chapter 3 for more information about using an assumed name.

PARTNERSHIP

To form a partnership, a written agreement should be prepared to spell out the rights and obligations of the partners. You must also file a *copartnership certificate* with the county clerk, although an assumed name certificate will meet this requirement. (Mich. Comp. Laws Ann., Sec. 449.101.) See Chapter 3 for information about using an assumed name.

CORPORATION

To form a corporation, *articles of incorporation* must be filed with the Department of Consumer and Industry Services in Lansing, along with a $10 filing fee. An organizational meeting is then held at which officers are elected, stock issued, and other formalities are complied with to avoid the corporate entity being later declared invalid. Licenses and accounts are titled in the name of the corporation. Also see Chapter 3 for information about selecting a corporate name and about using an assumed name.

LIMITED
PARTNERSHIP

To start a limited partnership, a written *certificate of limited partnership* must be filed with the Department of Consumer and Industry Services in Lansing, and a lengthy disclosure document must be given to all prospective limited partners. Because of the complexity of securities laws and the criminal penalties for violation, it is advantageous to have an attorney organize a limited partnership.

LIMITED
LIABILITY
COMPANY

Two or more persons may form a limited liability company by filing *articles of organization* with the Department of Consumer and Industry Services in Lansing, and paying a $50 filing fee. Licenses and accounts are in the name of the company. It is similar to filing for a corporation.

SECURITIES LAWS

Both the state and federal governments have long and complicated laws dealing with the sales of *securities* (interests in businesses sold to investors, such as shares of stock, corporate bonds, or certain limited partnership interests). There are also hundreds of court cases attempting to explain what these laws mean. A thorough explanation of this area of law is beyond the scope of this book.

Basically, securities exist whenever a person provides money with the expectation that he will get a profit through the efforts of another person. This can apply to any situation where someone buys stock in, or makes a loan to your business. What the laws require is disclosure of the risks involved, and, in some cases, registration of the securities with the government. There are some exemptions such as for small amounts of money and for a limited numbers of investors.

Penalties for violation of securities laws are severe, including triple damages and prison terms, so you should consult a specialist in securities laws before issuing any security. You can often get an introductory consultation at a reasonable rate to have your options explained.

A copy of Michigan's securities law (known as the *Blue Sky Law*) may be obtained from:

> Department of Consumer and Industry Services
> Bureau of Commercial Services
> P.O. Box 30054
> Lansing, MI 48909
> 517-241-6470
> email: bcsinfo@cis.state.mi.us
> Website: http://www.cis.state.mi.us/bcs/corp/home.htm
> Website to download brochure:
> http://cis.state.mi.us/ofis/pubs/guides/sec/guide.pdf

Federal securities laws are enforced by the Securities and Exchange Commission.

FOREIGN NATIONALS

Persons who are not citizens nor legal permanent residents of the United States are free to start any type of business organization in Michigan. The type that would be most advantageous would be the LLC because it allows foreign owners (unlike an S corporation) and it avoids corporate taxation (unlike a C corporation).

Two legal issues that foreign persons should be concerned with when starting a business in Michigan are their immigration status and the proper reporting of the business's foreign owners.

IMMIGRATION STATUS
The ownership of a U.S. business does not automatically confer rights to enter or remain in the United States. Different types of visas are available to investors and business owners and each of these has strict requirements.

A visa to enter the United States may be permanent or temporary. *Permanent visas* for business owners usually require investments of from $500,000 to $1,000,000 that result in the creation of new jobs. However, there are ways to obtain visas for smaller investments if structured right. For more information on this area you should consult an immigration specialist or a book on immigration.

Temporary visas may be used by business owners to enter the U.S., however, these are hard to get because in most cases the foreign person must prove that there are no U.S. residents qualified to take the job.

REPORTING   U.S. businesses that own real property and are controlled by foreigners are required to file certain federal reports under the International Investment Survey Act, the Agricultural Foreign Investment Disclosure Act, and the Foreign Investment in Real Property Tax Act (FIRPTA). If these laws apply to your business you should consult an attorney who specializes in foreign ownership of U.S. businesses.

Naming Your Business 3

One early consideration is naming your business. In addition to being important from a marketing standpoint, you also need to be aware of certain legal issues relating to business names.

Preliminary Considerations

Before deciding upon a name for your business you should be sure that it is not already being used by someone else. Many business owners have spent thousands of dollars on publicity and printing and then had to throw it all away because another company owned the name. A company that owns a name can take you to court and force you to stop using that name.

If you will be running a small local shop with no plans for expansion, you should at least check out whether the name has been trademarked. If someone else is using the same name anywhere in the country and has registered it as a federal trademark, they can sue you. If you plan to expand or to deal nationally, then you should do a thorough search of the name.

The first places to look are the local phone books and official records of your county. Next, you should check with the Department of Consumer and Industry Services in Lansing to see if another company is using the name you have chosen, or a name that would be confusingly similar. Their number is 517-241-6470.

To do a national search you should check trade directories and phone books of major cities. These can be found at many libraries and are usually reference books that cannot be checked out. The *Trade Names Directory* is a two volume set of names compiled from many sources and is published by Gale Research Co.

If you have a computer with Internet access, you can use it to search all of the yellow pages listings in the U.S. at a number of sites (at no charge). One of the sites that offers free yellow pages searches of all states at once (at the time of publication of this book) is:

http://www.infoseek.com

A thorough search would include a check of all trademarks registered in the U.S. Patent Office in Washington. Some public libraries can do a preliminary search with their computers. There may be a fee for such a search. There are also companies that do such searches for a fee, usually under $100. One such company is:

> Government Liaison Services, Inc.
> P. O. Box 10648
> Arlington, VA 22210
> 703-524-8200

They also offer searches of 100 trade directories and 4800 phone books.

No matter how thorough your search, there is no guarantee that there is not a local user somewhere with rights to the mark.

Example: You register a name for a new chain of restaurants and later find out that someone in Winnemucca, Nevada, has been using the name longer than you. That person will still have the right to use the name, but just in his local area. If you do not want his restaurant to be confused with your chain, you can try to buy him out.

Similarly, if you are operating a small business under a unique name, and a law firm in New York writes and offers to buy the right to your business name, you can assume that some large corporation wants to start a major expansion under that name.

The best way to make sure a name you are using is not already owned by someone else is to make up a name. Names such as Xerox, Kodak, and Exxon were made up and did not have any meaning prior to their use. But remember that there are millions of businesses and even something you make up may already be in use. Do a search anyway.

ASSUMED NAMES

In Michigan, as in most states, unless you do business in your own name you must register the name you are using. (Mich. Comp. Laws Ann., beginning with Sec. 445.1.) Such a business name is called an *assumed name* in Michigan. Some other states call this a *fictitious name*.

The assumed name must be registered with the county clerk in each county where you own, conduct, or transact business. There is a filing fee of $6.00, although this may be higher in counties with a population of more than 2,000,000.

The law also says you should register in every county where you "intend" to conduct business. However, unless you know with a fair degree of certainty that you will soon be doing business in a particular county, there seems little point in registering until you are about to conduct business there. There is a special exception to the requirement of registering in a county if all you do is sell goods there through a travelling salesperson, by sample, or through the mail.

An assumed name registration is good for five years. It can be renewed for additional five year periods for a $4.00 renewal fee. The county clerk is required to mail you a renewal form prior to the expiration.

It is a misdemeanor to fail to register an assumed name, with a possible penalty of a $25 to $100 fine, and 30-days in jail; and each day of failing to register is considered a separate offense. Also, you may not sue anyone in your business name unless you are registered.

Example: John Doe operates a masonry business. He may operate his business as "John Doe, Mason" without registering it. But he would need to register if he used other names, such as:

Doe Masonry	Doe Masonry Company
Doe Company	Michigan Masonry

CORPORATIONS AND ASSUMED NAMES

Do not confuse an assumed name with the name of a corporation. Corporations are registered with the Michigan Department of Consumer and Industry Services, not the county clerk. You cannot use the words "corporation," "incorporated," "corp.," or "inc.," unless you have legally formed a corporation. If a corporation is doing business only under its official corporate name (i.e., the name that appears on its articles of incorporation filed with the Department of Consumer and Industry Services), it is not required to register that name as an assumed name with the county clerk. However, if the corporation is doing business under a name that is different from its registered corporate name, it would have to register that assumed name with the county clerk.

Example: Doe Masonry, Inc., would not need to register an assumed name if it conducted business under that name, because that is its registered corporate name. However, if Doe Masonry, Inc., decided to conduct business in Wayne County under the name "Wayne County Masonry," it would need to register "Wayne County Masonry" as an assumed name with the county clerk in Wayne County.

When you use an assumed name you are "doing business as" ("d/b/a") the assumed name you are using. To use our previous examples, John Doe, as a sole proprietor, would be "John Doe d/b/a Doe Masonry." As a corporation, Doe Masonry, Inc., would be "Doe Masonry, Inc., d/b/a Wayne County Masonry."

The registration of an assumed name only gives some protection to the name in the county of registration. The clerk may reject a name that is "likely to mislead the public, or any assumed name already filed in the county or so nearly similar thereto as to lead to confusion or deception."

Some types of businesses or professions have special requirements for the use of an assumed name. See Chapter 6 for a list of some of the state regulated professions, with references to the laws that apply to them.

CORPORATE NAMES

As stated above, a corporation does not have to register its name as an assumed name because it already has a legal name. The name of a corporation must contain one of the following words or abbreviations (Mich. Comp. Laws Ann., Sec. 450.1211.):

Corporation	Incorporated
Corp.	Inc.
Company	Limited
Co.	Ltd.

There are also other restrictions on corporate names. (Mich. Comp. Laws Ann., Sec. 450.1212.) It is not advisable to use only the word "Company" or "Co.," because unincorporated businesses also use these words and a person dealing with you might not realize you are incorporated. If this happens you might end up with personal liability for corporate debts. You can use a combination of two of the words, such as "ABC Co., Inc."

If the name of the corporation does not contain one of the above words or abbreviations it will be rejected by the Department of Consumer and Industry Services. It will also be rejected if:

- the name is already taken;

- it is similar to the name of another corporation or partnership;

- it "indicates or implies that the corporation is formed for a purpose other than [one] or more of the purposes permitted by its articles of incorporation;" or,

● it violates any other statutes restricting the use of a corporate name.

To check on a name, you may contact the Department of Consumer and Industry Services at:

> 517-241-6470
> 517-334-8239 (fax)
> Website: http://cis.state.mi.us/bcs_corp/sr_corp.asp

If a name you want is taken by another company, you may be able to change it slightly and have it accepted.

Example: You intend to operate a furniture upholstery business in Saginaw County, and want to register your corporation as Tri-City Upholstery, Inc. Your request for this name is rejected because there is already a Tri-City Upholstery, Inc., registered, but you find out it operates in Oakland County. You may be allowed to use Tri-City Upholstery of Saginaw County, Inc. However, even if this is approved by the Department of Consumer and Industry Services, you might get sued by the other company if your business is close to theirs or there is a likelihood of confusion.

Warning: Do not have anything printed until your corporate papers are returned to you. Sometimes a name is approved over the phone and rejected when sent in.

Once you have chosen a corporate name and know it is available, you should immediately register your corporation. A name can be "reserved" for ninety days for $20, but it is easier just to register the corporation than to waste time on the name reservation.

If a corporation wants to do business under a name other than its corporate name, it can register an assumed name such as "Doe Corporation d/b/a Doe Industries." But if the assumed name leads people to believe that the business is not a corporation, the right to limited liability may be lost. If such a name is used it should always be accompanied by the corporate name. You do not want anyone to be in doubt that they are dealing with a corporation.

PROFESSIONAL SERVICE CORPORATIONS

Professional service corporations are corporations formed by professionals such as attorneys, doctors, dentists, and architects. Under Michigan law, a professional corporation cannot use the usual corporate designations (e.g., Inc., Corp., or Co.), but *must* use the words "Professional Corporation" or the abbreviation, "P.C."

THE WORD "LIMITED"

Although legally permitted for a corporation, the word "Limited," or the abbreviation "Ltd.," at the end of a name should only be used for a limited partnership.

The term *limited liability company* is a relatively new form of doing business that was authorized in Michigan less than ten years ago, and those words should only be used with such an entity. If you form a limited liability company, your company name *must* include either "Limited Liability Company—L.L.C.," or "L.C." If you form a professional limited liability company, the name *must* include "Professional Limited Liability Company—P.L.L.C.," or "P.L.C."

TRADEMARKS, SERVICE MARKS, AND TRADE NAMES

As your business builds goodwill, its name will become more valuable and you will want to protect it from others who may wish to copy it. You can protect your company name by registering it as a *trade name* with the Michigan Department of Consumer and Industry Services. Another way to protect your company name in Michigan is to incorporate, since a particular corporate name can only be registered once in Michigan.

To protect a name used to describe your goods or services you can register it as a *trademark* (for goods) or a *service mark* (for services), with either the Michigan Department of Consumer and Industry Services, or with the United States Patent and Trademark Office.

You cannot obtain federal registration for the name of your business, but you can trademark a name you use on your goods and services. In most cases you will use your company name on your goods as your trademark, so it, in effect, protects your company name.

State registration would be useful if you expect to use the name or mark only within the state of Michigan. Federal registration would protect your mark anywhere in the country. The registration of a mark gives you exclusive use of the mark for the types of goods for which you register it. The only exception is persons who have already been using the mark. You cannot stop people who have been using the mark prior to your registration.

FEDERAL REGISTRATION

There are two types of applications for federal trademark and trade name registration. One depends upon whether you have already made actual use of the mark, and the other on whether you merely have an intention to use the mark in the future.

For a trademark that has been in use, you must file an application form along with specimens showing actual use and a drawing of the mark that complies with all of the rules of the United States Patent and Trademark Office.

For an *intent to use* application you must file two separate forms, one when you make the initial application and the other after you have made actual use of the mark as well as the specimens and drawing. Before a mark can be entitled to federal registration the use of the mark must be in *interstate commerce* or in commerce with another country. The fee for registration is $245, but if you file an "intent to use" application there is a second fee of $100 for the filing after actual use.

STATE
REGISTRATION

The procedure for state registration of a trade name, trademark, or service mark is simple and the cost is $50. First, you should contact the Michigan Department of Consumer and Industry Services at the address, phone number, or website on the bottom of this page, and ask them to search your desired name and tell you if it is available.

Before a trademark or service mark can be registered, it must be used in Michigan. For goods, this means it must be used on the goods themselves, or on containers, tags, or labels. For services, it must be used or displayed in the sale or advertising of the services. The use must be in connection with sales in the state of Michigan.

The $50 fee will register the mark in only one *class of goods*. If the mark is used on more than one class of goods, a separate registration must be filed.

The registration is good for ten years. It must be renewed six months prior to expiration, and the Department of Consumer and Industry Services is required to send you a renewal notice before the required renewal date. The renewal fee is $25 for each class of goods.

A sample filled-in APPLICATION FOR REGISTRATION OF TRADEMARK/SERVICEMARK form may be found in Appendix B as form 8. A blank form is included in Appendix C. (see form 8, p.231.)

Forms and more information may also be obtained from:

Department of Consumer & Industry Services
Bureau of Commercial Services
Corporation Division
P.O. Box 30054
Lansing, MI 48909-7554
517-241-6470
email: bcsinfo@cis.state.mi.us
Website: http://www.cis.state.mi.us/bcs/corp/home.htm

DOMAIN NAMES

With the Internet being so new and changing so rapidly, all of the rules for Internet names have not yet been worked out. Originally, the first person to reserve a name owned it, and enterprising souls bought up the names of most of the fortune 500 corporations and held them for ransom. Then a few of the corporations went to court and the rule was developed that if a company had a trademark for a name that company could stop someone else from using it as a domain name if the other person did not have a trademark.

You cannot yet get a trademark merely for using a domain name. Trademarks are granted for the use of a name in commerce. Once you have a valid trademark you will be safe in using it for your domain name.

In the next few years there will probably be several changes to the domain name system to make it more flexible and useful throughout the world. One proposed change is the addition of more *top level domains* (*TLDs*) which are the last parts of the names, like "com" and "gov." Some of the suggested additions are "firm," "store," "web," "arts," "rec," "nom," and "info." This should free up a lot of names since corporations like McDonald's are not in the arts business and would probably not be able to keep the names from legitimate users.

If you wish to protect your domain name the best thing to do at this point is to get a trademark for it. To do this you would have to use it on your goods or services. The following section gives some basic information about trademarks. See Chapter 9 for more information on domain names and the Internet.

FINANCING YOUR BUSINESS 4

The way to finance your business is determined by how fast you want your business to grow and how much risk of failure you are able to handle. Letting the business grow with its own income is the slowest but safest way to grow. Taking out a personal loan against your house to expand quickly is the fastest but riskiest way to grow.

GROWING WITH PROFITS

Many successful businesses have started out with little money and used the profits to grow bigger and bigger. If you have another source of income to live on (such as from a job or a spouse), you can plow all the income of your fledgling business into growth.

Some businesses start as hobbies or part-time ventures on the weekends and evenings, while the entrepreneur holds down a full time job. Many types of businesses can start this way. Even some multimillion-dollar corporations, such as Apple Computer started out this way.

This way you have no risk. If you find you are not good at running that type of business or the time or location was not right for your idea, all you are out is the time you spent and your start-up capital.

However, most businesses can only grow so big from their own income. As a business grows, in many cases, it gets to a point where the orders are so big that money must be borrowed to produce the product to fill the order. With this situation there is the risk that if your customer can't pay or goes bankrupt, your business will also go under. At such a point, a business owner should investigate the credit worthiness of the customer and weigh the risks. Some businesses have grown rapidly, some have gone under, and others have decided not to take the risk and stayed small. You can worry about that down the road.

USING YOUR SAVINGS

If you have savings you can tap to get your business started, that is the best source. You will not have to pay high interest rates and you will not have to worry about paying someone back (such as relatives).

USING YOUR
HOME EQUITY

If you have owned your home for several years, it is possible that the equity has grown substantially and you can get a second mortgage to finance your business. Some lenders will even make second mortgages that exceed the equity if you have been in the home for many years and have a good record of paying your bills. Just remember, if your business does not succeed, you can lose your home.

RETIREMENT
ACCOUNTS

Be careful about borrowing from your retirement savings. There are tax penalties for borrowing from or against certain types of retirement accounts, and again, if your business does not succeed, you will have lost your retirement nest egg.

HAVING TOO
MUCH MONEY

It probably does not seem possible to have too much money with which to start a business, but many businesses have failed for that reason. With plenty of start-up capital available, a business owner does not need to watch expenses and can become wasteful. Employees get used to lavish spending. Once the money runs out and the business must run on its own earnings, it fails.

Starting with the bare minimum forces a business to watch its expenses and be frugal. It necessitates finding the least expensive solutions to problems that crop up, and creative ways to be productive.

BORROWING MONEY

It is extremely tempting to look to others to get the money to start a business. The risk of failure is less worrisome and the pressure is lower than using your own money, but that is a problem with borrowing. If it is others' money, you do not have quite the same incentive to succeed as if everything you own is on the line.

Actually, you should be even more concerned when using the money of others. Your reputation should be more valuable than the money itself, which can always be replaced. Yet that is not always the case. How many people borrow again and again from their parents for failed business ventures? (Home equity loans were discussed in the previous section, so they will not be discussed again here.)

The Small Business Administration can help you with financing through its One Stop Capital Shop. If you cannot find a local office with this service, contact:

> One Stop Capital Shop
> 2051 Rosa Parks Blvd., Suite 1B
> Detroit, MI 48216
> 313-965-1100
> 313-964-1101 [fax]
> Website: http://www.sbaonline.sba.gov/onestop/oscs_detroit.html

FAMILY Depending on how much money your family can spare it may be the most comfortable or most uncomfortable source of funds for you. If you have been assured a large inheritance and your parents have more funds than they need to live on, you may be able to borrow against your inheritance without worry. It will be your money anyway and you need it much more now than you will ten or twenty or more years from now. If you lose it all it is your own loss anyway.

If, however, you are borrowing your widowed mother's source of income, asking her to cash in a CD she lives on to finance your business, you should have second thoughts about it. Stop and consider all the real reasons your business might not take off and what your mother would do without the income.

FRIENDS

Borrowing from friends is like borrowing from family members. If you know they have the funds available and could survive a loss, you may want to risk it, but if they would be loaning you their only resources, do not chance it.

Financial problems can be the worst thing for a relationship, whether it is a casual friendship or a long term romantic involvement. Before you borrow from a friend, try to imagine what would happen if you could not pay it back and how you would feel if it caused the end of your relationship.

The ideal situation is if your friend were a co-venturer in your business and the burden would not be totally on you to see how the funds were spent. Still, realize that such a venture will put extra strain on the relationship.

BANKS

In a way a bank can be a more comfortable party to borrow from because you do not have a personal relationship with them as you do with a friend or family member, and if you fail they will write your loan off rather than disown you. But a bank can be the least comfortable party to borrow from because it will demand realistic projections and be on top of you to perform. If you do not meet the bank's expectations it may call your loan just when you need it most.

The best thing about a bank loan is that they will require you to do your homework. You will have to have plans that make sense to a banker. If they approve your loan, you know that your plans are at least reasonable.

Bank loans are not cheap or easy. You will be paying a good interest rate, and you will have to put up collateral. If your business does not have equipment or receivables, they may require you to put up your house and other personal property to guarantee the loan.

Banks are a little easier to deal with when you get a Small Business Administration (SBA) loan. That is because the SBA guarantees that it will pay the bank if you default on the loan.

SBA loans are obtained through local bank branches. They have the paperwork to get your loan approved.

CREDIT CARDS Borrowing against personal credit cards can be the most expensive source of capital. The rates can go higher than twenty percent. But many cards offer lower rates, and some people are able to get numerous cards. Some successful businesses have used personal credit cards to get off the ground or to weather through a cash crunch, but if the business does not begin to generate the cash to make the payments you could soon end up in bankruptcy. A good strategy is only to use credit cards for a long term asset like a computer, or for something that will quickly generate cash, like buying inventory to fill an order. Do not use credit cards to pay salaries or expenses that are not generating revenue.

GETTING A RICH PARTNER

One of the best business combinations is a young entrepreneur with ideas and ambition, and a retired investor with business experience and money. Together they can supply everything the business needs.

How do you find such a partner? Be creative. You should have investigated the business you are starting and know others who have been in such businesses. Have any of them had partners retire over the last few years? Are any of them planning to phase out of the business?

SELLING SHARES OF YOUR BUSINESS

Silent investors are the best source of capital for your business. You retain full control of the business and if it happens to fail you have no obligation to them. Unfortunately, few silent investors are interested in a new business. It is only after you have proved your concept to be successful, and built up a rather large enterprise that you will be able to attract such investors.

The most common way to obtain money from investors is to issue stock to them. For this the best type of business entity is the corporation. It gives you almost unlimited flexibility in the number and kinds of shares of stock you can issue.

USING THE INTERNET TO FIND CAPITAL

In 1995, the owners of Wit Beer made headlines in all the business magazines by raising $1.6 million for their business on the Internet. It seemed so easy that every business wanted to try. What was not made clear in most of the stories was that the owner was a corporate securities lawyer and that he did all of the necessary legal work to prepare a prospectus and properly register the stock—something which would have cost anyone else over $100,000 in legal fees. Also, most of the interest in the stock came from the magazine articles, not from the internet promotion. Today a similar effort would probably not be nearly as successful.

Before attempting to market your company's shares on the Internet, be sure to get an opinion from a securities lawyer or do some serious research into securities laws. The lawyer who marketed Wit Beer's shares on the internet has started a business to advise businesses on raising capital.

> Wit SoundView Corporation
> 826 Broadway, 7th Floor
> New York, NY 10003.
> http://www.witcapital.com/home/index.jsp

The Internet does have some sources of capital listed. The following sites may be helpful.

America's Business Funding Directory:

> http://www.businessfinance.com

Angel Capital Electronic Network (SBA):

> http://www.sba.gov

Inc. Magazine:

> http://mothra.inc.com/finance

NVST:

> http://www.nvst.com

The Capital Network:

> http://www.thecapitalnetwork.com

SBA One Stop Capital Shop:

> http://www.sbaonline.sba.gov/onestop/oscs_detroit.html

LOCATING YOUR BUSINESS 5

The right location for your business will be determined by what type of business it is, and how fast you expect to grow. For some types of businesses the location will not be important to your success or failure in others it will be crucial.

WORKING OUT OF YOUR HOME

Many small businesses get started out of the home. Some eventually move out of the home, but many people prefer working at home and keep their businesses there. Chapter 6 discusses the legalities of home businesses. This section discusses the practicalities.

Starting a business out of your home can save you the rent, electricity, insurance, and other costs of setting up at another location. For some people this is ideal and they can combine their home and work duties easily and efficiently. But for other people it is a disaster. A spouse, children, neighbors, television, and household chores can be so distracting that no other work gets done.

Many people use their residential telephone line to conduct business, or add a second residential line, since residential rates are usually lower than business lines. However, if you wish to be listed in the yellow pages, then you will need to have a business line in your home. If you are running two or more types of businesses, you can probably add their names as additional listings on the original number and avoid paying for another business line.

You also need to consider whether operating out of your home will be compatible with the type of business you will operate. For example, if you run a consulting business where you are usually driving to a client's workplace to do most of your work, or conduct most of your business by telephone, you can probably operate comfortably out of your home. But if your business requires stocking inventory, having several - employees, or having many customers come to your office, your home may not be a convenient place from which to conduct business.

CHOOSING A RETAIL SITE

For most types of retail stores, the location is of prime importance. Such things to consider are how close it is to your potential customers, how visible it is to the public, and how easily accessible it is to both autos and pedestrians. The attractiveness and safety of the building and the general area should also be considered.

Location is less important for a business which is the only one of its kind in the area (for example, the only moped parts dealer or Armenian restaurant in a metropolitan area), since people would have to come to wherever you are if they want your products or services. However, even with such businesses, keep in mind that there is competition. People who want moped parts can order them by mail, and restaurant customers can choose another type of cuisine.

You should look up all the businesses like the one you plan in the phone book and mark them on a map. For some businesses, like a dry cleaners, you would want to be far from the others so that you are the most convenient location for people in your area. But for other businesses, like antique stores, you would want to be near the others. Antique stores usually do not carry the same things, so they don't directly compete, and people like to go to an "antique district" and visit all the shops.

Choosing Office, Manufacturing, or Warehouse Space

If your business will be the type where customers will not come to you, then locating it near customers is not as much of a concern, and you can probably save money by locating away from the high traffic central business districts. However, you should consider the convenience for employees and not locate in an area which would be unattractive to them or too far from where they would likely live (such as locating far out in the country instead of near town).

Leasing a Site

A lease of space can be one of the biggest expenses of a small business so you should do a lot of homework before signing one. There are a lot of terms in a commercial lease which can make or break your business. These are the most critical:

ZONING
Before signing a lease you should be sure that everything that your business will need to do is allowed by the zoning of the property.

RESTRICTIONS
In some shopping centers existing tenants have guarantees that other tenants do not compete with them. For example if you plan to open a restaurant and bakery you may be forbidden to sell carry out baked goods if the supermarket has a bakery and a noncompete clause.

SIGNS
Business signs are regulated by zoning laws, sign laws and property restrictions. If you rent a hidden location with no possibility for adequate signage your business will have a lot smaller chance of success than otherwise.

ADA COMPLIANCE
The Americans with Disabilities Act (ADA) requires that reasonable accommodations be made to make businesses accessible to the handicapped. When a business is remodeled many more changes are required

than if no remodeling is done. When renting space you should be sure that it complies with the law, or the landlord will be responsible for compliance, or you are aware of the full costs you will bear.

EXPANSION

As your business grows you may need to expand your space. The time to find out about your options is before you sign the lease. Perhaps you can take over adjoining units when those leases expire.

RENEWAL

For some businesses the location is a key to success. If you spend five years building up a clientele you don't want someone to take over when your lease is up. Therefore you should have a renewal clause on your lease. Usually this allows an increase in rent based on inflation.

GUARANTY

Most landlords of commercial space will not rent to a small corporation without a personal guaranty from the leasee. This is a very risky thing for a new business owner to do. The lifetime rent on a long term commercial lease can be hundreds of thousands of dollars and if your business fails the last thing you want to do is be personally responsible for five years of rent.

Where space is scarce or a location is hot, a landlord can get the guarantees he demands and there is nothing you can do about it (except perhaps set up an asset protection plan ahead of time). But where several units are vacant or the commercial rental market is soft, often you can negotiate out of the personal guaranty, or at least limit it. For example, if the lease is five years, maybe you can get away with a guaranty of just the first year. Give it a try.

DUTY TO OPEN

Some shopping centers have rules requiring all shops to be open certain hours. If you can't afford to staff it the whole time required, or if your business is seasonal, or if you have religious or other reasons which make this a problem, you should negotiate it out of the lease or find another location.

SUBLEASE

At some point you may decide to sell your business as a going concern and in many cases the location is the most valuable aspect of the business. For this reason you should be sure that you have the right to either assign your lease or to sublease the property. If this is impossible one way around a prohibition is to incorporate your business before signing the lease and then when you sell the business, sell the stock. But some lease clauses prohibit transfer of "any interest" in the business so read the lease carefully.

BUYING A SITE

If you are experienced with owning rental property you will probably be more inclined to buy a site for your business. If you have no experience with real estate you should probably rent and not take on the extra cost and responsibility of buying. One reason to buy your site is that you can build up equity.

EXPANSION   You should consider the growth potential of your business. If it grows quickly will you be able to expand at the site you are considering buying or will you have to move. If the site is a good investment, whether or not you have your business, then by all means buy it. But if its main use is for your business, think twice.

ZONING   Some of the concerns when buying a site are the same as when renting. You will want to make sure that the zoning permits the type of business you wish to start, or that you can get a variance without a large expense or delay. Be aware that just because a business is now using the site does not mean that you can expand or remodel the business at that site. Some zoning laws allow businesses to be grandfathered in but not to expand. Check with the zoning department and find out exactly what is allowed.

SIGNS   Signs are another concern. Some cities have regulated signs and do not allow new ones or require them to be smaller. Some businesses have used these laws to get publicity. A car dealer who was told to take down a large number of American flags on his lot filed a federal lawsuit and ralleyed the community behind him. It could not have hurt business except for a few over-controlling public officials.

ADA
COMPLIANCE

Compliance with the ADA is another concern when buying a commercial building. Find out from the building department if the building is in compliance or what needs to be done to put it in compliance. If you remodel the requirements may be more strict.

NOTE*: When dealing with public officials always keep in mind that they do not always know what the law is or do not accurately explain it. They often try to intimidate people into doing things that are not required by law. Read the requirements yourself and question them if they seem to be interpreting it wrong. Seek legal advice if they refuse to budge from a clearly erroneous position.*

NOTE*: Also consider that keeping them happy may be worth the price. If you are already doing something they have overlooked, do not make a big deal over a little thing they want changed, or they may subject you to a full inspection or audit.*

OWNERSHIP OF
THE BUSINESS
SITE

One risk in buying a business site is that if the business gets into financial trouble the creditors may go after the building as well. For this reason most people who buy a site for their business keep the ownership out of the business. For example, the business will be a corporation, and the real estate will be owned personally by the owner, by a different corporation, or by a trust unrelated to the business.

CHECKING GOVERNMENTAL REGULATIONS

When looking for a site for your business, you should investigate the different governmental regulations in your area. For example, a location just outside the city or county limits might have a lower licensing fee, a lower sales tax rate, and less strict sign requirements.

Licensing Your Business 6

Depending upon the type of business you intend to conduct, and where you intend to open your business, there may be various licensing requirements.

Business Licenses and Zoning

Before opening your business you may need to obtain a business license from your local city, county, or township. Each city, county, or township decides which types of businesses require a license. Businesses that do work in several areas, such as builders, may need to obtain a license from each city, county, or township in which they do work. This does not have to be done until you actually begin a job in a particular area.

All cities or counties have *zoning laws*, which divide property into various types of allowed uses. Some property may only be used for residential purposes. Other property may be used for retail business, but not for heavy industry. In rural areas, much of the property is limited to agricultural use. Be sure to find out if the zoning laws will allow your type of business before buying or leasing property. The licensing authority may check the zoning before issuing your license.

If you will be preparing or serving food, you will need to check with the local health department to be sure that the premises are in compliance with their requirements.

HOME
BUSINESSES

Problems occasionally arise when people attempt to start a business in their home. Small, new businesses often cannot afford to pay rent for commercial space, and cities often try to forbid businesses from operating in residential areas. Getting a business license or registering an assumed name often gives notice to the local government that a business is being conducted in a residential area.

Some people avoid the problem by starting their businesses without business licenses, figuring that the penalties are less expensive than the cost of office space. Others get the license and ignore the zoning rules. If you have commercial trucks and equipment all over your property, or even daily pick-ups and deliveries by UPS, there will probably be complaints from neighbors and the city will probably take legal action. But if your business consists merely of making phone calls out of your home and keeping supplies there, the problem may never come up.

If a problem does arise regarding a home business that does not disturb the neighbors, a good argument can be made that the zoning law that prohibits the business is unconstitutional. When zoning laws were first instituted they were not meant to stop people from doing things in a residence that had historically been part of life in a residence.

Example: Consider an artist. Should a zoning law prohibit a person from sitting in his home and painting pictures? If he sells them for a living is there a difference? Can the government force him to rent commercial space just because he decides to sell the paintings he paints?

Similar arguments can be made for many home businesses. For hundreds of years people performed income-producing activities in their homes. But court battles with a city are expensive and probably not worth the effort for a small business. The best course of action is to keep a low profile. Using a post office box can sometime help divert attention away from the residence.

STATE-REGULATED PROFESSIONS AND BUSINESSES

Many professionals, and types of businesses, require special licenses. Even if your business or profession does not required licensing, some of your business activities may be subject to licensing, certification, or permitting. A good source of information about such regulations is the State of Michigan website:

http://www.Michigan.gov

On the left side of the home page, under the heading "Topics," click on "Licensing, Certification and Permits." This will bring up a page which also has a heading of "Topics" on the left side, and here you can click on the type of licensing you want to review. Another excellent source of licensing information is:

Bureau of Commercial Services
Licensing Division
P.O. Box 30018
Lansing, MI 48909
517-241-9223
517-241-9280 [fax]
Website: http://www.cis.state.mi.us/bcs/licdiv.htm

The Licensing Division's website will also enable you to get information on specific licensing boards.

Many, but not all, occupations and businesses subject to regulation are included in Michigan Compiled Laws Annotated, Chapter 339. The best way to find out about laws affecting your business is to contact the appropriate state agency or licensing authority that regulates your type of business, contact any professional association for your type of business, and conduct your own research in the index to the *Michigan Compiled Laws Annotated*.

PARTIAL LIST OF
REGULATED
PROFESSIONS
AND BUSINESSES
IN MICHIGAN

The following is a list of some of the statutes relating to various professions, businesses, and business matters. It is by no means a comprehensive list. Even if you do not think you are subject to regulation, read through the list below and check with the Licensing Bureau anyway. Some licensing requirements may surprise you. Governments seem to endlessly pass laws adding to the professions and businesses regulated, so do not rely exclusively on the list below. Citations are given to the *Michigan Compiled Laws Annotated*.

PROFESSION/ACTIVITY	STATUTE SECTION
Accountants	339.720
Adoption agencies (child placing agencies)	710.22
Adult foster care facilities	400.701
Agricultural products	(See index to MCLA)
Aircraft & airports	259.1
Alarm system contractors	338.1051
Alcoholic beverages	436.1101
Ambulance services	333.20920
Amusement rides	408.660
Animal shelters	287.331
Appraisers, real estate	339.2601
Architects	339.2001
Asbestos contractors	338.3101
Athletic services providers	333.26301
Attorneys	600.901
Auctioneers	446.51
Barbers	339.1101 & 338.2217
Beverage containers	445.571
Bingo	432.101
Boarding & lodging houses	427.1
Boat liveries	324.44515
Boat races	324.80164
Boiler safety	408.751
Boxing	339.801
Carnivals	408.660
Casinos	432.203
Cemeteries	456.1
Chiropractors	333.16401
Coal mines	324.63514
Collection agencies	339.901
Commercial feed	287.521
Community planners	339.2301
Condominiums	559.101
Construction code	125.1501
Construction contractors	(See specific type of contractor)

Cosmetology	339.1201
Counseling services	333.16341 & 333.18101
Credit cards	750.157m
Credit insurance	550.601
Dentist and dental assistants & hygienists	333.16601
Detectives	338.821
Driver training schools	256.601
Druggists (pharmacists)	333.17741
Dry cleaners & launderers	333.13301
Electrical contractors & electricians	338.881
Electrologists	339.1208
Electronic fund transfers	488.1
Elevators, dumb waiters & escalators	408.801
Employment agencies	339.1001
Engineers	339.2001
Estheticians	339.1210
Explosives	29.41 & 750.200
Family day-care homes	125.216g
Fertilizer manufacture or distribution	324.8504
Fireworks	750.243a
Fitness centers	333.26301
Food	289.1101
Foresters	339.2101
Franchises	445.1501
Frozen desserts	288.321
Funeral directors & embalmers	339.1801
Grain dealers	285.67a
Guns	28.421 & 750.22
Gymnasiums	333.26301
Hawkers & peddlers	445.371
Hazardous materials	29.471
Hazardous substances labeling	286.451
Hazardous waste management	324.11101
Health spas	333.26301
Hearing aid dealers	339.1301
Home improvement financing	445.1101
Horse & mule dealers & brokers	287.112 & 287.121
Horse racing	431.301 & 750.330
Hotels	427.1
Insurance	500.100
Insurance adjusters, agents & counselers	500.240 & 500.1201
Junk dealers	445.401
Junk yards	445.451

Laboratories	333.20501
Land sales	565.801
Landscape architects	339.2201
Liquidation sales	442.211
Manicurists	339.1209
Meats	287.571 & 289.1101
Mechanical contractors	338.971
Messenger companies	484.1 & 750.539
Mobile homes & mobile home parks	125.991
Mortgage brokers, lenders & servicers	445.1651
Mortgage lending	445.1601
Motor carriers	475.1 & 476.1
Motor vehicle manufacturers, distributors & dealers	445.1561
Motor vehicle sales financing	492.101
Motor vehicles	257.1
Natural hair cultivation	339.1210a
Notaries public	55.107
Nurseries	286.209
Nurses	333.17201
Nursing homes	339.1901
Ocularists	339.2701
Optometry	333.17401
Osteopathy	333.17501
Outdoor advertising	252.301
Pawnbrokers	445.471 & 446.201
Pest control	286.201
Pet shops	287.331
Pharmacists	333.17741
Physical therapy	333.17801
Physicians	333.17001
Physicians assistants	333.17011
Plumbers	338.901
Podiatry	333.18001
Polygraph examiners	338.1701
Poultry	445.301
Precious metal & gem dealers	445.481
Private schools	388.551
Private trade schools	395.101
Psychiatric facilities & programs	330.1134
Psychologists	333.18201
Real estate appraisers	339.2601
Real estate brokerage	339.2501
Rental-purchase agreements	445.951
Residential builders and maintenance & alteration contractors	339.2403

Restaurants	289.1101 & 691.1521
Retail installment sales	445.851
Second hand & junk dealers	445.401
Securities transactions	451.501
Security agencies & guards	338.1051
Septic tanks	333.12751
Ski areas	408.329
Snowmobile dealers	324.82101
Storage, cleaning, or repair services (for clothing, curtains, draperies, carpets, or household furnishings)	445.1751
Summer resorts & parks	455.101
Surveyors	339.2001
Taverns & saloons	436.1525
Telegraph & telephone companies	484.1 & 750.539
Timber	324.50101; 324.52501; 426.151; 426.174; & 752.701
Transient merchants	445.371
Used car lots	445.501
Veterinary medicine	333.18811
Warehouses & warehousement	444.1
Watches, second hand dealers	445.551

FEDERAL LICENSES

So far there are few businesses that require federal licensing or registration. If you are in any of the types of businesses listed below, you should check with the federal agency listed below it.

Radio or television stations or manufacturers of equipment emitting radio waves:

> Federal Communications Commission
> 1919 M Street, NW
> Washington, DC 20550
> http://www.fcc.gov

Manufacturers of alcohol, tobacco, or firearms:

> Bureau of Alcohol, Tobacco, and Firearms
> U.S. Department of the Treasury
> 1200 Pennsylvania Ave., NW
> Washington, DC 20226
> http://www.atf.treas.gov

Securities brokers and providers of investment advice:

> Securities and Exchange Commission
> 450 5th Street, NW
> Washington, DC 20549
> http://www.sec.gov

Manufacturers of drugs and processors of meat:

> Food and Drug Administration
> 5600 Fishers Lane
> Rockville, MD 28057
> http://www.fda.gov

Interstate carriers:

> Interstate Commerce Commission
> 12th Street & Constitution Ave.
> Washington, DC 20423
> http://www.stb.dot.gov

Exporting:

> Bureau of Export Administration
> U.S. Department of Commerce
> 14th Street & Constitution Ave.
> Washington, DC 20220
> http://www.bxa.doc.gov

IMPORTANT ADDRESSES

The following list will provide you with a quick reference to the main offices of various agencies. If you call any of the numbers listed below, you may be transferred to a specific subdivision or be given a separate number to call. Portions of this book may have information on where to contact subdivisions of these agencies for specific types of information.

Office of the Attorney General
525 W. Ottawa Street
P.O. Box 30212
Lansing, MI 48909
517-373-1110 [general number]
517-373-3042 [fax]
517-373-1140 [Consumer Protection]
email: miag@ag.state.mi.us
Website: http://www.ag.state.mi.us

Michigan Department of Treasury
Lansing, MI 48922
517-373-3200
Forms: 800-367-6263
Website: http://www.treas.state.mi.us

Michigan Department of Environmental
Quality
Environmental Assistance Division
P.O. Box 30457
Lansing, MI 48909-7957
800-662-9278
Website: http://www.deq.state.mi.us

Michigan Department of Community
Health
Lewis Cass Building, Sixth Floor
320 South Walnut Street
Lansing, MI 48913
517-373-3500
Website: http://www.mdch.state.mi.us

Bureau of Commercial Services
Licensing Division
P.O. Box 30018
Lansing, MI 48909
517-241-9223
517-241-9280 [fax]
Website:
http://www.cis.state.mi.us/bcs/licdiv.htm

Michigan Department of Civil Rights
Manpower Building, Suite 101
741 N. Cedar Street
Lansing, MI 48906
517-334-9335
517-334-9350 [fax]
Website: http://www.mdcr.state.mi.us

Michigan Department of Consumer and
Industry Services
525 W. Ottawa Street
P.O. Box 30004
Lansing, MI 48909
517-373-1820
Website: http://www.cis.state.mi.us
[Note: This agency has many divisions,
including unemployment compensation,
worker's compensation, and employment relations.]

One Stop Capital Shop
2051 Rosa Parks Blvd., Suite 1B
Detroit, MI 48216
313-965-1100
313-964-1101 [fax]
http://www.sbaonline.sba.gov/onestop/o
scs_detroit.html

Small Business Administration
477 Michigan Avenue
Suite 515, McNamara Building
Detroit, MI 48226
313-226-6075
313-226-4769 [fax]
email: michigan@sba.gov
Website: http:/www.sba.gov/mi/

Small Business Development Center
Grand Valley State University
Seidman School of Business
510 W. Fulton Street
Grand Rapids, MI 49504
616-336-7480
616-336-7485 [fax]
http://www.mi-sbdc.org/

Equal Employment Opportunity
Commission
2401 E Street, NW
Washington, DC 20506
800-669-4000
Forms: 800-669-3362
Website: http://www.eeoc.gov

East Central Region
Federal Trade Commission
1111 Superior Avenue, Suite 200
Cleveland, OH 44114-2507
Website: http://www.ftc.gov

U.S. Internal Revenue Service
McNamara Building, Room 2040
477 Michigan Avenue
Detroit, MI 48226-2597
877-777-4778
313-628-3670
313-628-3669 [fax]
Website: http://www.irs.gov

U.S. Department of Labor
Occupational Safety and Health
Administration
801 South Waverly Road, Suite 306
Lansing, MI 48917
517-327-0904
517-327-1973
Website: http://www.osha-slc.gov

U.S. Department of Labor
200 Constitution Avenue, NW
Washington, DC 20210
Website: http://www.dol.gov

U.S. Department of Justice
Immigration and Naturalization Service
333 Mt. Elliot
Detroit, MI 48207
Office of Business Liaison: 800-357-2099
Forms: 800-830-3676
Website: http://www.ins.gov

U.S. Department of Labor
ESA Wage & Hour Division
211 W. Fort Street, Room 1317
Detroit, MI 48226-3237
313-226-7447
313-226-3072 [fax]
Website:
http://www.dol.gov/dol/esa/public/whd_org.htm

Contract Law 7

As a business owner you will need to know the basics of forming a simple contract for your transactions with both customers and vendors. There is a lot of misunderstanding and erroneous information, and relying on it can cost you money. This chapter will give you a quick overview of the principles that apply to your transactions, and pitfalls to avoid. If you face more complicated contract questions you should consult a law library or an attorney familiar with small business law.

Traditional Contract Law

One of the first things taught in law school is that a contract is not legal unless three elements are present: *offer*, *acceptance*, and *consideration*. Very basically, these terms may be defined as follows:

- An *offer* is a proposal to make a contract, made by one party to a second party.

  Example*:* "I promise to pay you $20 if you will promise to shovel the snow off my driveway before noon today."

- An *acceptance* is the second party's agreement to form a contract as proposed by the party who made the offer. The second party must accept the proposal exactly as made, without adding or changing anything, otherwise it is not an acceptance.

Example: You may accept the offer stated above by saying something as simple as "I accept."

- The *consideration* is what induces a party to enter into a contract, which is usually exchanging something of value, or exchanging promises.

Example: The consideration in the example above would be my promise to pay you $20 and your promise to shovel the snow by noon.

A basic course on contracts will spend the entire semester dissecting exactly what may be a valid offer, acceptance, and consideration. For your purposes, the important things to remember are as follows:

- If you make an offer to someone, it may result in a binding contract, even if you change your mind or find out it was a bad deal for you.

- Unless an offer is accepted (that is, with both parties agreeing to the same contract terms), there is no contract.

- A contract does not always have to be in writing. Some laws require certain contracts to be in writing, but as a general rule an oral contract is legal.

- Without consideration (the exchange of something of value or mutual promises) there is not a valid contract.

As mentioned above, an entire semester of a course in contracts is spent analyzing each of the three elements of a contract. The most important rules for the business owner are:

- An advertisement is not an offer.

Example: Suppose you intended to put an ad in the newspaper offering "New IBM computers only $1995!" but there is a typo in the ad and it says "$19.95." Can people come in and say "I accept, here's my $19.95," creating a legal contract? Fortunately, no.

Courts have ruled that the ad is not an offer that a person can accept. It is an invitation to come in and make offers, which the business can accept or reject.

- When a person makes an offer, several things may happen. It may be accepted, creating a legal contract. It may be rejected. It may expire before it has been accepted. Or, it may be withdrawn before acceptance. A contract may expire either by a date made in the offer ("This offer remains open until noon on January 29, 2003") or after a reasonable amount of time.

  What is reasonable is a legal question that a court must decide. If someone makes you an offer to sell goods, clearly you cannot come back 5 years later and accept. Can you accept a week later or a month later and create a legal contract? That depends on the type of goods and the circumstances.

- A person accepting an offer cannot add any terms to it.

  Example: If you offer to sell a car for $1,000, and the other party says they accept as long as you put new tires on it, there is not contract.

  An acceptance with changed terms is considered a rejection and a counteroffer.

- When someone rejects your offer and makes a counteroffer, a contract can be created if you accept the counteroffer.

These rules can affect your business on a daily basis. Suppose you offer to sell something to one customer over the phone and five minutes later another customer walks in and offers you more for it. To protect yourself you should call the first customer and withdraw your offer before accepting the offer of the second customer. If the first customer accepts before you have withdrawn your offer, you may be sued if you have sold the item to the second customer.

There are a few exceptions to the basic rules of contracts of which you should be aware.

- Consent to a contract must be voluntary. If it is made under a threat, the contract is not valid.

- Contracts to do illegal acts, or acts "against public policy," are not enforceable.

- If either party to an offer dies, the offer expires and cannot be accepted by the heirs.

- Contracts made under misrepresentation are not enforceable.

    Example: If someone tells you a car has 35,000 miles on it and you later discover it has 135,000 miles, you may be able to *rescind* (cancel) the contract due to fraud and misrepresentation.

- If there was a mutual mistake, a contract may be rescinded.

    Example: If both you and the seller thought the car had 35,000 miles on it and you both relied on that assumption, the contract could be rescinded. However, if the seller knew the car has 135,000 miles on it, but you assumed it only had 35,000 but did not ask, you probably could not rescind the contract.

STATUTORY CONTRACT LAW

The previous section discussed the basics of contract law. These are not stated in the statutes, but are the principles decided by judges over several hundred years. But in recent times the legislatures have made numerous exceptions to these principles. In most cases, these laws have been passed when the legislature felt that traditional law was not fair.

STATUTES OF
FRAUD

Statute of fraud laws state what types of contracts must be in writing to be valid. In Michigan, some of the contracts that must be in writing are as follows:

- sales or assignment of any interest in real estate, including leases for more than one year (Mich. Comp. Laws Ann., Sec. 566.106);

- agreements to modify or discharge a contract obligation without consideration (Mich. Comp. Laws Ann., Secs. 440.2209 & 566.1);

- representations concerning the character, business or credit of another (Mich. Comp. Laws Ann., Sec. 566.135);

- guarantees of debts of another person (Mich. Comp. Laws Ann., Sec. 566.132);

- antenuptial contracts (Mich. Comp. Laws Ann., Sec. 566.132);

- promises of a personal representative to answer damages personally (Mich. Comp. Laws Ann., Sec. 566.132);

- promises to pay a commission on the sale of an interest in real estate (Mich. Comp. Laws Ann., Sec. 566.132);

- warranties of cure relating to medical care (Mich. Comp. Laws Ann., Sec. 566.132);

- sales of goods of over $500 (Mich. Comp. Laws Ann., Sec. 440.2201);

- sales of personal property of over $5,000 (Mich. Comp. Laws Ann., Sec. 440.1206);

- agreements that take over one year to complete (Mich. Comp. Laws Ann., Sec. 566.132); or,

- sales of securities (Mich. Comp. Laws Ann., Secs. 440.1206).

If you choose to conduct business electronically, Michigan law provides that electronic records and signatures satisfy any legal requirements for a written statement and a signature. See the Uniform Electronic Transaction Act. (Mich. Comp. Laws Ann., Secs. 450.833 through 450.849.)

UNIFORM COMMERCIAL CODE   The Uniform Commercial Code is an important law that relates to sales of most goods. It is particularly applicable to dealings between merchants, such as between manufacturers and wholesalers, and between wholesalers and retailers. This law is covered more in Chapter 13.

OTHER LAWS   There are numerous other laws governing contracts in many area of business, especially where financing contracts are involved (i.e., where money is being loaned). Some of these laws are covered in later chapters of this book, but it would be impossible to include every law relating to every kind of business.

There is also a law regarding unsolicited merchandise, which provides that any merchandise sent to a consumer without a request or order by the consumer is deemed to be a gift. In other words, if you send merchandise to a consumer without an order by the consumer, the consumer may keep the merchandise and not pay for it.

INSURANCE 8

There are few laws *requiring* you to have insurance, but if you do not have insurance you may face lawsuit liability that may ruin your business (and your personal finances if you did not incorporate or form another type of business entity to protect you from personal liability). You should be aware of the types of insurance available and weigh the risks of a loss against the cost of a policy.

Be aware that there can be a wide range of prices and coverages in insurance policies. You should get at least three quotes from different insurance agents and ask each one to explain the benefits of his or her policy.

WORKERS' COMPENSATION

You are required by Michigan law to carry workers' compensation insurance if:

1. you regularly employ three or more part-time employees at one time or

2. you employ one or more employee(s) for at least thirty-five hours per week, for at least thirteen weeks during the preceding fifty-two weeks.

In Michigan, this type of insurance is governed by the "Workers' Disability Compensation Act of 1969." (Mich. Comp. Laws. Ann., beginning with Sec. 418.101.) The term *employee* is specifically defined. (Mich. Comp. Laws. Ann., Sec. 418.161.) You should read this law carefully if you think you need to comply with it. Part time employees, students, aliens or illegal workers count as employees. However, under certain conditions, volunteers, real estate agents, and independent contractors are not considered employees. There are also different requirements for agricultural employees.

Even if you are not required to have workers' compensation insurance, you may still wish to carry it because it can protect you from litigation.

This insurance can be obtained from most insurance companies and in many cases is not expensive. If you have such coverage, you are protected against suits by employees or their heirs in case of accident, and against potentially ruinous claims.

For high-risk occupations, such as roofing, it can be expensive, sometimes thirty to fifty cents for each dollar of payroll. For this reason, construction companies try all types of ways to become exempt, such as hiring independent contractors or only having a few employees who are also officers of the business. However, the requirements for exemptions are strict. If you so intend to obtain an exemption, check with an attorney specializing in workers' compensation law to be sure you do it right.

Failure to provide worker's compensation insurance when required is considered serious, as you are then personally responsible for paying any claims. Failure to pay a claim is a misdemeanor, which can result in a fine of $1,000 per day, up to six months in jail, personal liability for officers and directors of the corporation, plus any damages suffered by the employee.

There are other requirements of the workers' compensation law, such as maintaining records of injuries causing death or disability, and reporting to the Worker's Disability Compensation Division of the Michigan Department of Consumer and Industry Services.

For more information, contact the Division of Workers' Disability Compensation at:

Division of Workers' Disability Compensation
525 W. Ottawa Street
P.O. Box 30004
Lansing, MI 48909
517-373-1820
email: bwdcinfo@cis.state.mi.us
Website: http://www.cis.state.mi.us/wkrcomp/bwdc/home.htm
Publications: http://www.cis.state.mi.us/wkrcomp/pub.htm

LIABILITY INSURANCE

In most cases you are not required to carry liability insurance. However, be sure to check the requirements for your particular profession or business, because some may require liability insurance.

Liability insurance can be divided into two main areas:

1. coverage for injuries on your premises or by your employees and

2. coverage for injuries caused by your products.

Coverage for the first type of injury is usually very reasonably priced. Injuries in your place of business or by your employees (such as in an auto accident) are covered by standard premises or auto policies. But coverage for injuries by products may be harder to find and more expensive. Juries have awarded ridiculously high judgments for accidents involving products that had little if any impact on the accident. The situation has become so bad that some entire industries have gone out of business or moved overseas.

ASSET
PROTECTION

Hopefully, laws will soon be passed to protect businesses from these unfair awards. For now, if insurance is unavailable or unaffordable, you can go without and use a corporation and other asset protection devices to protect yourself from liability.

The best way to find out if insurance is available for your type of business is to check with other businesses of the same type as yours. If there is a trade organization for your type of industry, their newsletter or magazine may contain ads for insurers.

UMBRELLA
POLICY

As a business owner you will be a more visible target for lawsuits, even if there is little or no merit to them. Some people who know they cannot win in court will file suit anyway, counting on the fact that it will be cheaper for you to pay them something than to pay your lawyer to defend you. Lawyers know that such *nuisance suits* are often settled for thousands of dollars. Because of your greater exposure, you should consider getting a personal *umbrella* insurance policy. This is a policy that covers you for large claims, typically up to one-million dollars or more, which are not covered by other insurance. Umbrella policies are very reasonably priced.

HAZARD INSURANCE

One of the worst things that can happen to your business is a fire, flood, or other disaster. With lost customer lists, inventory and equipment, many businesses have been forced to close after such a disaster.

The premium for such insurance is usually reasonable and could protect you from loss of your business. You can even get *business interruption* insurance, which pays for fixed business expenses, such as utilities, rent, taxes, etc., during the period of time you are unable to operate your business due to damages from fire, flood, storms, etc.

HOME BUSINESSES AND INSURANCE

There is a special insurance problem for home businesses. Most homeowner and tenant insurance policies do not cover business activities. In fact, under some policies you may be denied coverage if you used your home for a business.

If you merely use your home to make business phone calls and send letters you will probably not have a problem and not need extra coverage. But if you own equipment or have dedicated a portion of your home exclusively to the business you could have a problem. Check with your insurance agent for the options that are available to you.

If your business is a sole proprietorship, and you have, say, a computer that you use both personally and for your business, it would probably be covered under your homeowners policy. But if you incorporate your business and bought the computer in the name of the corporation, coverage might be denied. If a computer is your main business asset you could get a special insurance policy in the company name covering just the computer. One company that offers such a policy is Safeware, which may be reached at 800-800-1492.

OTHER TYPES OF INSURANCE

The following are some other types of insurance that are available, and which you may want to consider and discuss with your insurance agent. However, for many small business some may be cost-prohibitive.

EMPLOYEE THEFT

If you fear employees may be able to steal from your business, you may want to have them *bonded*. This means that you pay an insurance company a premium to guarantee employees' honesty and if they cheat you the insurance company pays you damages. This can cover all existing and new employees.

KEY MAN

Key man insurance provides for the situation where an owner or employee is so important to your business that the business will be unable to operate for a period of time if that "key" owner or employee becomes incapacitated or dies.

OFFICER AND DIRECTOR

Officer and director insurance covers the officer or director for any actions that result in personal liability. While this type of insurance does not protect your business, it can be useful to:

1. protect you as an officer or director; or

2. provide an incentive to someone you would like to hire as an officer or have serve as a director.

AUTOMOBILE

Automobile coverage can be obtained for business use of your personal vehicle, for business-owned vehicles, and for business-leased vehicles.

HEALTH

While new businesses can rarely afford health insurance for their employees, the sooner they can obtain it, the better chance they will have to find and keep good employees. Those starting a business usually need insurance for themselves (unless they have a working spouse who can cover the family), and they can sometimes get a better rate if they get a small business package. Health insurance can be fully paid by the employee (with the employee benefit being lower premiums than if the employee obtained insurance independently), partially paid by the employee and partially by the employer, or fully paid by the employer.

Most employers that pay some or all of the employee's premiums, do not pay for their spouses and children. Still, the employee gets the advantage of paying lower rates for his or her family. Some large companies, especially those subject to labor unions, as well as many government agencies, pay the full premiums for both the employee and his or her dependents.

LIFE AND DISABILITY

Life insurance for employees is another fringe benefit, but it is not usually perceived by employees as being nearly as important as health insurance. Disability insurance is typically even less regarded, although disability is more likely than death among people in the age-range of most employees. The cost of such insurance coverages is much less than health insurance, so it can serve as an additional incentive for employees to stay with you.

Your Business and the Internet

9

The Internet has opened up a world of opportunities for businesses. A few years ago getting national visibility cost a fortune. Today a business can set up a Web page for a few hundred dollars and, with some clever publicity and a little luck, millions of people around the world will see it.

But this new world has new legal issues and new liabilities. Not all of them have been addressed by laws or by the courts. Before you begin doing business on the Internet, you should know the existing rules and the areas where legal issues exist.

Domain Names

A *domain name* is the address of your website. For example, www.apple.com is the domain name of Apple Computer Company. The last part of the domain name, the ".com" (or "dot com") is the *top level domain*, or TLD. Dot com is the most popular, but others are currently available in the United States, including .net and .org. (Originally .net was only available to network service providers and .org only to nonprofit organizations, but regulations have eliminated those requirements.)

It may seem like most words have been taken as a dot-com name, but if you combine two or three short words or abbreviations, a nearly unlimited number of possibilities are available. For example, if you have a business dealing with automobiles, most likely someone has already registered automobile.com and auto.com. But you can come up with all kinds of variations, using adjectives or your name, depending on your type of business:

autos4u.com	joesauto.com	autobob.com
myauto.com	yourauto.com	onlyautos.com
greatauto.com	autosfirst.com	usautos.com
greatautos.com	firstautoworld.com	4autos.com

When the Internet first began, some individuals realized that major corporations would soon want to register their names. Since the registration was easy and cheap, people registered names they thought would ultimately be used by someone else.

At first, some companies paid high fees to buy their names from the registrants. But one company, Intermatic, filed a lawsuit instead of paying. The owner of the mark they wanted had registered numerous trademarks, such as britishairways.com and ussteel.com. The court ruled that since Intermatic owned a trademark on the name, the registration of their name by someone else violated that trademark and that Intermatic was entitled to it.

Since then people have registered names that are not trademarks, such as CalRipkin.com, and have attempted to charge the individuals with those names to buy their domain. In 1998, Congress stepped in and passed the Anti-Cybersquatting Consumer Protection Act. This law makes it illegal to register a domain with no legitimate need to use it.

This law helped a lot of companies protect their names, but then some companies started abusing it and tried to stop legitimate users of similar names. This is especially likely against small companies. Two organizations have been set up to help small companies protect their domains: the Domain Defense Advocate and the Domain Name Rights Coalition. Their websites are:

http://www.ajax.org/dda

http://www.domain-name.org

Registering a domain name for your own business is a simple process. There are many companies that offer registration services. For a list of those companies, visit the site of the Internet Corporation for Assigned Names and Numbers (ICANN) at **http://www.icann.org**. You can link directly to any member's site and compare the costs and registration procedures required for the different top-level domains.

WEB PAGES

There are many new companies eager to help you set up a website. Some offer turnkey sites for a low flat rate. Custom sites can cost tens of thousands of dollars. If you have plenty of capital you may want to have your site handled by one of these professionals. However, setting up a website is a fairly simple process, and once you learn the basics you can handle most of it in-house.

If you are new to the Web, you may want to look at the following sites, which will familiarize you with the Internet jargon and give you a basic introduction to the Web:

http://www.learnthenet.com   http://www.webopedia.com

SITE SETUP There are seven steps to setting up a website: site purpose, design, content, structure, programming, testing, and publicity. Whether you do it yourself, hire a professional site designer, or use a college student, the steps toward creating an effective site are the same.

Before beginning your own site you should look at other sites, including those of major corporations and of small businesses. Look at the sites of all the companies that compete with you. Look at hundreds of sites and click through them to see how they work (or don't work!)

Site purpose. To know what to include on your site you must decide what its purpose will be. Do you want to take orders for your products or services, attract new employees, give away samples, or show off your company headquarters? You might want to do several of these things.

Site design. After looking at other sites you can see that there are numerous ways to design a site. It can be crowded, or open and airy; it can have several windows (frames) open at once or just one, and it can allow long scrolling or just click-throughs.

You will have to decide whether the site will have text only; text plus photographs and graphics; or text plus photos, graphics, and other design elements such as animation or Java script. Additionally, you will begin to make decisions about colors, fonts, and the basic graphic appearance of the site.

Site content. You must create the content for your site. For this, you can use your existing promotional materials, you can write new material just for the Web site, or you can use a combination of the two. Whatever you choose, remember that the written material should be concise, free of errors, and easy for your target audience to read. Any graphics, including photographs, and written materials not created by you require permission. You should obtain such permission from the lawful copyright holder in order to use any copyrighted material. Once you know your site's purpose, look, and content, you can begin to piece the site together.

Site structure. You must decide how the content (text plus photographs, graphics, animation, etc.) will be structured–what content will be on which page, and how a user will link from one part of the site to another. For example, your first page may have the business name and then choices to click on, such as "about us," "opportunities," "product catalog," etc. Have those choices connect to another page containing the detailed information so that a user will see the catalog when they click on "product catalog." Or your site could have a choice to click on a link to another website related to yours.

Site programming and setup. When you know nothing about setting up a website, it can seem like a daunting task that will require an expert. However, "programming" here means merely putting a site together. There are inexpensive computer programs available that make it very simple.

Commercial programs such as Microsoft FrontPage, Dreamweaver, Pagemaker, Photoshop, MS Publisher, and PageMill allow you to set up

Web pages as easily as laying out a print publication. These programs will convert the text and graphics you create into HTML, the programming language of the Web. Before you choose Web design software and design your site, you should determine which Web hosting service you will use. Make sure that the design software you use is compatible with the host server's system. The Web host will be the provider who will give you space on their server and who may provide other services to you, such as secure order processing and analysis of your site to see who is visiting and linking to it.

If you have an America Online account, you can download design software and a tutorial for free. AOL has recently collaborated with a Web hosting service at **http://www.verioprimehost.com** and offers a number of different hosting packages for the consumer and e-business. You do not have to use AOL's design software in order to use this service. You are eligible to use this site whether you design your own pages, have someone else do the design work for you, or use AOL's templates. This service allows you to use your own domain name and choose the package that is appropriate for your business.

If you have used a page layout program, you can usually get a simple Web page up and running within a day or two. If you don't have much experience with a computer, you might consider hiring a college student to set up a Web page for you.

Site testing. Some of the website setup programs allow you to thoroughly check your new site to see if all the pictures are included and all the links are proper. There are also websites you can go to that will check out your site. Some even allow you to improve your site, such as by reducing the size of your graphics so they download faster. Use a major search engine listed on page 82 to look for companies that can test your site before you launch it on the Web.

Site publicity. Once you set up your website, you will want to get people to look at it. *Publicity* means getting your site noticed as much as possible by drawing people to it.

The first thing to do to get noticed is to be sure your site is registered with as many *search engines* as possible. These are pages that people use to find things on the Internet, such as Yahoo and Excite. They do not automatically know about you just because you created a website. You must tell them about your site, and they must examine and catalog it.

For a fee, there are services that will register your site with numerous search engines. If you are starting out on a shoestring, you can easily do it yourself. While there are hundreds of search engines, most people use a dozen or so of the bigger ones. If your site is in a niche area, such as geneology services, then you would want to be listed on any specific geneology search engines. Most businesses should be mainly concerned with getting on the biggest ones. The biggest search engines at this time are:

www.altavista.com	www.lycos.com
www.dejanews.com	www.magellan.com
www.excite.com	www.netcrawler.com
www.fastsearch	www.northernlight.com
www.goto.com	www.webcrawler.com
www.hotbot.com	www.yahoo.com
www.infoseek.com	

Most of these sites have a place to click to "add your site" to their system. There are sites that rate the search engines, help you list on the search engines, or check to see if you are listed. One site is:

http://www.searchiq.com

A *meta tag* is an invisible subject word added to your site that can be found by a search engine. For example, if you are a pest control company, you may want to list all of the scientific names of the pests you control and all of the treatments you have available; but you may not need them to be part of the visual design of your site. List these words as meta tags when you set up your page so people searching for those words will find your site.

Some companies thought that a clever way to get viewers would be to use commonly searched names, or names of major competitors, as meta tags to attract people looking for those big companies. For example, a small delivery service that has nothing to do with UPS or Federal Express might use those company names as meta tags so people looking for them would find the smaller company. While it may sound like a good idea, it has been declared illegal trademark infringement. Today many companies have computer programs scanning the Internet for improper use of their trademarks.

Once you have made sure that your site is passively listed in all the search engines, you may want to actively promote your site. However, self-promotion is seen as a bad thing on the Internet, especially if its purpose is to make money.

Newsgroups are places on the Internet where people interested in a specific topic can exchange information. For example, expectant mothers have a group where they can trade advice and experiences. If you have a product that would be great for expectant mothers, that would be a good place for it to be discussed. However, if you log into the group and merely announce your product, suggesting people order it from your Web site, you will probably be *flamed* (sent a lot of hate mail).

If you join the group, however, and become a regular, and in answer to someone's problem, mention that you "saw this product that might help," your information will be better received. It may seem unethical to plug your product without disclosing your interest, but this is a procedure used by many large companies. They hire people to plug their product (or rock star) all over the Internet. So, perhaps it has become an acceptable marketing method and consumers know to take plugs with a grain of salt. Let your conscience be your guide.

Keep in mind that Internet publicity works both ways. If you have a great product and people love it, you will get a lot of business. If you sell a shoddy product, give poor service, and don't keep your customers happy, bad publicity on the Internet can kill your business. Besides being an equalizer between large and small companies, the Internet can be a filtering mechanism between good and bad products.

There is no worse breach of Internet etiquette ("netiquette") than to send advertising by e-mail to strangers. It is called *spamming*, and doing it can have serious consequences. There is anti-spamming legislation currently pending at the federal level. Many states, including California, Colorado, Connecticut, Delaware, Idaho, Illinois, Iowa, Louisiana, Missouri, Nevada, North Carolina, Oklahoma, Pennsylvania, Rhode Island, Tennessee, Virginia, Washington, and West Virginia, have enacted anti-spamming legislation. This legislation sets specific requirements for unsolicited bulk e-mail and makes certain practices illegal. You should check with an attorney to see if your business practices fall within the legal limits of these laws. Additionally, many Internet Service Providers (ISPs) have restrictions on unsolicited bulk e-mail (spam); you should check with your ISP to make sure you do not violate its policies.

ADVERTISING

Banner ads are the small rectangular ads on many Web pages which usually blink or move. Although most computer users seem to have become immune to them, there is still a big market in the sale and exchange of them.

If your site gets enough viewers, people may pay you to place their ads there. Another possibility is to trade ads with another site. In fact there are companies that broker ad trades among Web sites. Such trades used to be taxable transactions, but after January 5, 2000, such trades are no longer taxable under IRS Notice 2000-6.

LEGAL ISSUES

Before you set up a Web page, you should consider the legal issues described below.

JURISDICTION

Jurisdiction is the power of a court in a particular location to decide a particular case. Usually you have to have been physically present in a jurisdiction or have done business there before you can be sued there. Since the Internet extends your business's ability to reach people in far-away places, there may be instances when you could be subject to legal jurisdiction far from your own state (or country). There are a number of cases that have been decided in this country regarding the Internet and jurisdiction, but very few cases have been decided on this issue outside of the United States.

In most instances, U.S. courts use the pre-Internet test–whether you have been present in another jurisdiction or have had enough contact with someone in the other jurisdiction. The fact that the Internet itself is not a "place" will not shield you from being sued in another state when you have shipped you company's product there, have entered into a contract with a resident of that state, or have defamed a foreign resident with content on your website.

According to the Court, there is a spectrum of contact required between you, your website, and consumers, or audiences. (*Zippo Manufacturing Co. v. Zippo Dot Com, Inc.*, 952 F. Supp. 1119 (W.D. Pa 1997)) It is *clear* that the one end of the spectrum includes the shipping, contracting, and defamation mentioned above as sufficient to establish jurisdiction. The more interactive your site is with consumers, the more you target an audience for your goods in a particular location, and the farther you reach to send your goods out into the world, the more it becomes possible for someone to sue you outside of your own jurisdiction–possibly even in another country.

The law is not even remotely final on these issues. The American Bar Association, among other groups, is studying this topic in detail. At present, no final, global solution or agreement about jurisdictional issues exists.

One way to protect yourself from the possibility of being sued in a faraway jurisdiction would be to have a statement on your website stating that those using the site or doing business with you agree that "jurisdiction for any actions regarding this site" or your company will be in your home county.

For extra protection you can have a preliminary page that must be clicked before entering your website. However, this may be overkill for a small business with little risk of lawsuits. If you are in any business for which you could have serious liability, you should review some competitors' sites and see how they handle the liability issue. They often have a place to click for "legal notice" or "disclaimer" on their first page.

You may want to consult with an attorney to discuss the specific disclaimer you will use on your website, where it should appear, and whether you will have users of your site actively "agree" to this disclaimer or just "passively" read it. However, these disclaimers are not enforceable everywhere in the world. Until there is global agreement on jurisdictional issues, this may remain an area of uncertainty for some time to come.

LIBEL

Libel is any publication that injures the reputation of another. This can occur in print, writing, pictures, or signs. All that is required for *publication* is that you transmit the material to at least one other person. When putting together your website you must keep in mind that it is visible to millions of people all over the planet and that if you libel a person or company you may have to pay damages. Many countries do not have the freedom of speech that we do and a statement that is not libel in the United States may be libelous elsewhere.

COPYRIGHT
INFRINGEMENT

It is so easy to copy and "borrow" information on the Internet that it is easy to infringe copyrights without even knowing it. A *copyright* exists for a work as soon as the creator creates it. There is no need to register the copyright or to put a copyright notice on it. So, practically everything on the Internet belongs to someone. Some people freely give their works away. For example, many people have created web artwork (*gifs* and *animated gifs*) that they freely allow people to copy. There are numerous sites that provide hundreds or thousands of free gifs that you can add to your Web pages. Some require you to acknowledge the source; some don't.

You should always be sure that the works are free for the taking before using them.

LINKING AND
FRAMING

One way to violate copyright laws is to improperly link other sites to yours either directly or with framing. *Linking* is when you provide a place on your site to click, which takes someone to another site. *Framing* occurs when you set up your site so that when you link to another site, your site is still viewable as a frame around the linked-to site.

While many sites are glad to be linked to others, some, especially providers of valuable information, object. Courts have ruled that linking and framing can be a copyright violation. One rule that has developed is that it is usually okay to link to the first page of a site, but not to link to some valuable information deeper within the site. The rationale for this is that the owner of the site wants visitors to go through the various levels of their site (viewing all the ads) before getting the information. By linking to the information you are giving away their product without the ads.

The problem with linking to the first page of a site is that it may be a tedious or difficult task to find the needed page from there. Many sites are poorly designed and make it nearly impossible to find anything.

The best solution, if you wish to link to another page, is to ask permission. Email the Webmaster or other person in charge of the site, if one is given, and explain what you want to do. If they grant permission, be sure to print out a copy of their e-mail for your records.

PRIVACY   Since the Internet is such an easy way to share information, there are many concerns that it will cause a loss of individual privacy. The two main concerns arise when you post information that others consider private, and when you gather information from customers and use it in a way that violates their privacy.

While public actions of politicians and celebrities are fair game, details about their private lives are sometimes protected by law, and details about persons who are not public figures are often protected. The laws in each state are different, and what might be allowable in one state could be illegal in another. If your site will provide any personal information about individuals, you should discuss the possibility of liability with an attorney.

Several well-known companies have been in the news lately for violations of their customers' privacy. They either shared what the customer was buying or downloading, or looked for additional information on the customer's computer. To let customers know that you do not violate certain standards of privacy, you can subscribe to one of the privacy codes that have been promulgated for the Internet. These allow you to put a symbol on your site guaranteeing to your customers that you follow the code.

The websites of three of the organizations that offer this service, and their fees at the time of this publication, are:

www.privacybot.com	$30
www.bbbonline.com	$150 to $3,000
www.trustee.com	$299 to $4,999

PROTECTING YOURSELF
The easiest way to protect yourself personally from the various possible types of liability is to set up a corporation or limited liability company to own the website. This is not foolproof protection since, in some cases, you could be sued personally as well, but it is one level of protection.

COPPA
If your website is aimed at children under the age of thirteen, or if it attracts children of that age, then you are covered by the federal Children Online Privacy Protection Act of 1998 (COPPA). This law requires such Web sites to:

- give notice on the site of what information is being collected;

- obtain verifiable parental consent to collect the information;

- allow the parent to review the information collected;

- allow the parent to delete the child's information or to refuse to allow the use of the information;

- limit the information collected to only that necessary to participate on the site; and,

- protect the security and confidentiality of the information.

FINANCIAL TRANSACTIONS

In the future, there will be easy ways to exchange money on the Internet. Some companies have already been started that promote their own kinds of electronic money. Whether any of these become universal is yet to be seen.

For now, the easiest way to exchange money on the Internet is through traditional credit cards. Because of concerns that email can be abducted in transit and read by others, most companies use a "secure" site in which customers are guaranteed that their card data is encrypted before being sent.

When setting up your website, you should ask the provider if you can be set up with a secure site for transmitting credit card data. If they cannot provide it, you will need to contract with another software provider. Use a major search engine listed on page 82 to look for companies that provide credit card services to businesses on the web.

As a practical matter, there is very little to worry about when sending credit card data by email. If you do not have a secure site, another option is to allow purchasers to fax or phone in their credit card data. However, keep in mind that this extra step will lose some business unless your products are unique and your buyers are very motivated.

The least effective option is to provide an order form on the site, which can be printed out and mailed in with a check. Again, your customers must be really motivated or they will lose interest after finding out this extra work is involved.

FTC RULES

Because the Internet is an instrument of interstate commerce, it is a legitimate subject for federal regulation. The Federal Trade Commission (FTC) first said that all of its consumer protection rules applied to the

Internet, but lately it has been adding specific rules and issuing publications. The following publications are available from the FTC website at **http://www.ftc.gov/bcp/menu-internet.htm** or by mail from Consumer Response Center, Federal Trade Commission, 600 Pennsylvania, NW, Room H-130, Washington, DC 20580-0001.

- *Advertising and Marketing on the Internet: The Rules of the Road*

- *BBB-Online: Code of Online Business Practices*

- *Electronic Commerce: Selling Internationally. A Guide for Business Alert*

- *How to Comply With The Children's Online Privacy Protection Rule*

- *Internet Auctions: A Guide for Buyer and Sellers*

- *Selling on the Internet: Prompt Delivery Rules Alert*

- *Website Woes: Avoiding Web Service Scams Alert*

FRAUD

Because the Internet is somewhat anonymous, it is a tempting place for those with fraudulent schemes to look for victims. As a business consumer, you should exercise caution when dealing with unknown or anonymous parties on the Internet.

Recently, the U.S. Department of Justice, the FBI, and the National White Collar Crime Center launched the Internet Fraud Complaint Center (IFCC). If you suspect that you are the victim of fraud online, whether as a consumer or a business, you can report incidents to the IFCC on their website, **http://www.ifccfbi.gov**. The IFCC is currently staffed by FBI agents and representatives of the National White Collar Crime Center and will work with state and local law enforcement officials to prevent, investigate, and prosecute high-tech and economic crime online.

HEALTH AND SAFETY LAWS 10

If you plan to have at least one employee, or if your business will involve certain products or services, you will need to be concerned with health and safety laws.

FEDERAL LAWS

OSHA   Federal health and safety laws include the rules of the Occupational Safety and Health Administration, various laws concerning hazardous materials, and consumer safety regulations.

The Occupational Safety and Health Administration (OSHA) is a good example of government regulation so severe it strangles businesses out of existence. Robert D. Moran, a chairman of the committee that hears appeals from OSHA rulings once said that "there isn't a person on earth who can be certain he is in full compliance with the requirements of this standard at any point in time." The point of the law is to place the duty on the employer to see that the workplace is free from recognized hazards that are likely to cause death or serious bodily injury, but OSHA tends to go overboard.

For example, OSHA decided to take a look at *repetitive-strain injuries*, or "RSI," (such as carpal tunnel syndrome). The Bureau of Labor Statistics estimates that 7% of workplace illnesses are RSI, and the National Safety Council estimates it at 4%. OSHA, however, determined that 60% is a more accurate figure and came out with a 600 page list of proposed regulations, guidelines, and suggestions. These regulations would have affected over one-half of the businesses in America, costing billions of dollars.

Fortunately, these regulations were rejected by Congress in June 1995, after an outcry from the business community. But shortly thereafter OSHA officials promised they would launch a new effort.

Fortunately for small businesses, the regulations are not as cumbersome as for larger enterprises. If you have ten or fewer employees or if you are in certain types of businesses, you do not have to keep a record of illnesses, injuries, and exposure to hazardous substances of employees. If you have eleven or more employees, you do have to keep this record, which is called *Log 200*. All employers are required to display a poster that you can get from OSHA.

Within forty-eight hours of the on-the-job death of an employee, or injury of five or more employees on the job, the area director of OSHA must be contacted.

For more information you should write or call the OSHA office:

OSHA Regional Office
230 South Dearborn Street, Room 3244
Chicago, IL 60604
312-353-2220
312-353-7774 (fax)
Lansing: 517-327-0904

or visit their general website: **http://www.osha.gov** and obtain copies of their publications, *OSHA Handbook for Small Business* (OSHA 2209) and *OSHA Publications and Audiovisual Programs Catalog* (OSHA 2019). They also have a poster that is required to be posted in the workplace. Find it at:

http://www.osha.gov/oshpubs/poster.html

HAZARD COMMUNICATION STANDARD

The hazard communication standard requires that employees be made aware of the hazards in the workplace. (Code of Federal Regulations (C.F.R.), Title 29, Section (Sec.) 1910.1200.) It is especially applicable to those working with chemicals but this can include even offices which use copy machines. Businesses using hazardous chemicals must have a comprehensive program for informing employees of the hazards and for protecting them from contamination.

For more information you can contact OSHA at the previously mentioned address, phone numbers, or website. They can supply a copy of the regulation and a booklet called *OSHA 3084*, that explains the law.

PESTICIDES

A revision of the worker protection standard for agricultural pesticides was phased in during 1994. It concerns businesses that deal with agricultural pesticides and requires safety training, decontamination sites and, of course, posters. The Environmental Protection Agency will provide information on compliance with this law. They can be reached at 800-490-9198 or at:

http://www.epa.gov

PURE FOOD AND DRUG ACT

The Pure Food and Drug Act of 1906 prohibits the misbranding or adulteration of food and drugs. It also created the Food and Drug Administration (FDA), which has promulgated tons of regulations and which must give permission before a new drug can be introduced into the market. If you will be dealing with any food or drugs you should keep abreast of their policies. Their website is: **http://www.fda.gov**, their small business site is: **http://www.fda.gov/ora/fed_state/small_business/ sb_guide/default.htm** and their local small business representative is:

FDA, Southeast Region
Small Business Representative, Barbara Ward-Groves
60 Eight St. NE
Atlanta, GA 30309
Phone 404-347-4001 Ext 5256
Fax 404-347-4349

HAZARDOUS
MATERIALS
TRANSPORTATION

There are regulations that control the shipping and packing of hazardous materials. For more information contact:

> Office of Hazardous Materials Transportation
> 400 Seventh St.
> S.W., Washington, DC 20590
> 202-366-8553.
> http://hazmat.dot.gov

CPSC

The Consumer Product Safety Commission has a set of rules that cover the safety of products. The commission feels that because its rules cover products, rather than people or companies, they apply to everyone producing such products. However, federal laws do not apply to small businesses that do not affect interstate commerce. Whether a small business would fall under a CPSC rule would depend on the size and nature of your business.

The CPSC rules are contained in the Code of Federal Regulations, Title 16 in the following parts. These can be found at most law libraries, some public libraries, and on the Internet at: **http://www.access.gpo.gov/nara/cfr/cfr-table-search.html**. The CPSC's site is: **http://cpsc.gov/index.html**.

PRODUCT	PART
Antennas (CB and TV)	1402
Architectural Glazing Material	1201
Articles Hazardous to Children Under 3	1501
Baby Cribs-Full Size	1508
Baby Cribs-Non-Full Size	1509
Bicycle Helmets	1203
Bicycles	1512
Carpets and Rugs	1630 and 1631
Cellulose Insulation	1209 and 1404
Cigarette Lighters	1210
Citizens Band Base Station Antennas	1204
Coal and Wood Burning Appliances	1406
Consumer Products Containing Chlorofluorocarbons	1401
Electrically Operated Toys	1505
Emberizing Materials Containing Asbestos (banned)	1305
Extremely Flammable Contact Adhesives (banned)	1302
Fireworks	1507
Garage Door Openers	1211
Hazardous Lawn Darts (banned)	1306
Hazardous Substances	1500

Human Subjects	1028
Lawn Mowers, Walk-Behind	1205
Lead-containing Paint (banned)	1303
Matchbooks	1202
Mattresses	1632
Pacifiers	1511
Patching Compounds Containing Asbestos (banned)	1304
Poisons	1700
Rattles	1510
Self-Pressurized Consumer Products	1401
Sleepwear-Children's	1615 and 1616
Swimming Pool Slides	1207
Toys, Electrical	1505
Unstable Refuse Bins (banned)	1301

ADDITIONAL REGULATIONS

Every day there are proposals for new laws and regulations. It would be impossible to include every conceivable one in this book. To be up to date on the laws that affect your type of business, you should belong to a trade association for your industry and subscribe to newsletters that cover your industry. Attending industry conventions is a good way to learn more and to discover new ways to increase your profits.

MICHIGAN LAWS

MICHIGAN OCCUPATIONAL SAFETY AND HEALTH ACT

The Michigan Occupational Safety and Health Act, is Michigan's OSHA. (Mich. Comp. Laws Ann., Sec. 408.1001) It applies to any business with one or more employees. Except for laws about labeling hazardous chemicals in the workplace, the Act itself does not contain specific health and safety rules, but adopts the OSHA standards and allows additional rules to be made by the Michigan Department of Consumer and Industry Services and the Michigan Department of Community Health.

The Act also creates several commissions to make rules or "standards." These are the General Industry Safety Standards Commission, the Construction Safety Standards Commission, and the Occupational Health Standards Commission.

The Act gives the Michigan Department of Consumer and Industry Services and the Michigan Department of Community Health the right to conduct unannounced inspections and obtain warrants for inspections. A representative of the employer and a representative of the employees may accompany an inspector during his or her inspection of the premises.

A violation of any of the standards subjects the employer to a fine of up to $7,000 per violation. Failure to correct the violation within the timeframe allowed subjects the employer to an additional fine of up to $7,000 per day, up to a total of $70,000. If death results from a wilful or repeated violation, it is a felony with a fine up to $10,000 and up to one year in jail. A second conviction carries a penalty of a fine up to $20,000 and up to three years in jail.

For more information, or to obtain the standards that apply to your business, contact the following state agencies:

Michigan Department of
Consumer and Industry Services
525 W. Ottawa Street
P.O. Box 30004
Lansing, MI 48909
517-373-1820
Website: http://www.cis.state.mi.us

Michigan Department of
Community Health
Lewis Cass Building, Sixth Floor
320 South Walnut Street
Lansing, MI 48913
517-373-3500
Website: http://www.mdch.state.mi.us

Environmental Laws

The Michigan Department of Natural Resources was granted broad powers to promulgate regulations to protect the natural resources and the environment of the state under Michigan's Natural Resources and Environmental Protection Act. (Mich. Comp. Laws Ann., beginning with Section 324.101.) This act replaced numerous previous acts, in an attempt to consolidate responsibility in one state agency.

For most business owners, these regulations will never have an impact on their business. However, it is good to be aware that such regulations exist. Even the owner of a toy store may find that he or she has a leaking underground storage tank beneath the building. If you wish to learn more about these regulations, contact the Michigan Department of Natural Resources.

Smoking   The Michigan Clean Indoor Air Act contains the following rules regarding smoking in "public places" and at "public meetings." (Mich. Comp. Laws Ann., Sec. 333.12601.)

- "Public places" are defined as the following areas:

    1. "an enclosed, indoor area owned or operated by a state or local governmental agency and used by the general public or serving as a place of work for public employees or a meeting place for a public body, including an office, educational facility, home for the aged, nursing home, county medical care facility, hospice, hospital long-term care unit, auditorium, arena, meeting room, or public conveyance, and

    2. an enclosed, indoor area which is not owned or operated by a state or local governmental agency, is used by the general public, and is one of the following: an educational facility, home for the aged, nursing home, county medical care facility, hospice, or hospital long-term care unit, auditorium, arena, theater, museum, concert hall, or any other facility during the period of its use for a performance or exhibit of the arts."

A public place does not include a private, enclosed room or office occupied exclusively by a smoker, even if it may be visited by a nonsmoker.

- Meetings of public bodies are all meetings of any state or local governing body (e.g., boards, commissions, etc.).

- No person may smoke in a public place or at a public meeting except in a designated smoking area, except that this prohibition does not apply to:

    1. a room, hall, or building used exclusively for a private function where seating is controlled by the function sponsor and not by the state or local government agency or the person who owns or operates the room, hall, or building;

    2. food service establishments or alcohol-licensed premises; or,

    3. a private educational facility after regularly scheduled school hours.

- If a smoking area is designated, the following rules apply:

  1. existing physical barriers and ventilation systems must be used to minimize the toxic effect of smoke in smoking and adjacent nonsmoking areas;

  2. a written policy must be created for the separation of smokers and nonsmokers, which must provide at a minimum that nonsmokers be located closest to the source of fresh air, that special consideration be given to persons with a hypersensitivity to tobacco smoke, and that a procedure be established to receive, investigate, and take action on complaints; and,

  3. anyone who operates a single room is considered to be in compliance if one-half of the room is reserved and posted as a no smoking area.

- Smoking is not permitted at all in the common or treatment areas of a private practice office of a person who is licensed in a health occupation. (Mich. Comp. Laws Ann., Sec. 333.)

- Smoking is not permitted in a health facility unless prohibition of smoking would be detrimental to the patient's treatment (in which case the patient must be placed in a separate room from nonsmokers), or unless the health facility permits smoking (in which case smoking may only be allowed in designated areas that are enclosed, ventilated, or constructed to ensure a smoke free environment in patient care areas and common areas.

- Owners and operators of public places have the following duties:

  1. to post signs stating that smoking is prohibited, except in designated smoking areas;

  2. to arrange seating to provide a smoke-free area; and,

  3. to implement and enforce the policy for the separation of smokers and nonsmokers.

- Violations of this Act subject the owner or operator to penalties of a fine of up to $100 for the first violation, and up to $500 for a second or subsequent violation.

Employment and Labor Laws 11

If you intend to hire anyone to do work for you, you will need to become familiar with numerous state and federal legal issues.

Hiring and Firing Laws

For small businesses there are not many rules regarding whom you may hire or fire. Fortunately, the ancient law that an employee can be fired at any time (or may quit at any time) still prevails for small businesses. But in certain situations, and as you grow, you will come under a number of laws that affect your hiring and firing practices.

One of the most important things to consider when hiring someone is that if you fire them they may be entitled to unemployment compensation. If so, your unemployment compensation taxes will go up and it can cost you a lot of money. Therefore, ideally you should only hire people you are confident you will keep and you should avoid situations where your former employees can collect compensation.

This can be done by hiring only part-time or temporary employees. The drawback to this is that you may not be able to attract the best - employees. When hiring dishwashers or busboys this may not be an issue, but when hiring someone to develop a software product, you do not want them to leave halfway through the development.

A better solution is to screen applicants to begin with and only hire those whom you feel confident will work out. Of course, this is easier said than done. Some people interview well, but then turn out to be incompetent or bad employees.

In the authors' experience, the intelligence of an employee is more important than his or her experience. An employee with years of typing experience may be fast, but unable to figure out how to use your new computer. Whereas an intelligent employee can learn the equipment quickly and eventually gain speed. Of course, common sense is important in all situations.

The bottom line is that you cannot know if an employee will be able to fill your needs from a resumé and interview. Once you have found someone whom you think will work out, offer them a job with a ninety-day probationary period. If you are not completely satisfied with them after the ninety days, you can always offer to extend the probationary period for an additional thirty, sixty, or ninety days rather than end the relationship immediately. Of course, all of this should be in writing.

CHECKING
REFERENCES

Checking references is important, but beware that a former boss may be a current boyfriend, or even a relative. It has always been considered acceptable to exaggerate on resumés, but in today's tight job market, some applicants are completely fabricating sections of their education and experience.

POLYGRAPH
TESTS

Under the federal Employee Polygraph Protection Act, you cannot require an employee or prospective employee to take a polygraph test, unless you are in the armored car, guard, or pharmaceutical business.

DRUG TESTS

Under the Americans with Disabilities Act (ADA), drug testing can only be required of applicants who have been offered jobs conditioned upon passing a drug test.

NEW HIRE
REPORTING

The Personal Responsibility and Work Opportunity Reconciliation Act of 1996 (PRWORA) requires employers to report new hires to the state in order for child support enforcement agencies to track down deadbeat parents. However, the law leaves the reporting requirements up to each state.

FIRING   In most cases, unless you have a contract with an employee for a set time period, or are subject to an agreement with a labor union, you can fire an employee at any time. This seems fair since the employee can quit at any time. The exceptions to this are if you fire someone based on some illegal discrimination, for filing some sort of health or safety complaint, for engaging in union activities, or for refusing your sexual advances. All of these matters are discussed in other parts of this book.

EMPLOYMENT AGREEMENTS

To avoid misunderstanding with employees you may want to use an employment agreement or an employee handbook. These can spell out in detail the policies of the company and the rights of the employee. They can protect your trade secrets and should spell out clearly that employment can be terminated at any time by either party.

In any agreement, policy statement, or handbook, you need to be careful to include a provision that the employment is *at will* and that the employee may be discharged at any time, with or without any reason being given. If you do not include such a provision, a court could determine that your agreement, employee handbook, or policy statement created a binding contract that limits your ability to fire the employee. Even oral statements can create such a contract if they are determined by a court to create in the employee a legitimate expectation of continued employment based upon the employer's conduct and practices.

While it may be difficult or awkward to ask an existing employee to sign an agreement, an applicant hoping you will hire them will usually sign whatever is necessary to obtain the job. However, because of the unequal bargaining position, you should not use an agreement that would make you look bad if the matter ever went to court.

If having an employee sign an agreement is awkward, you can obtain the same rights by putting the company policies in an employee handbook. Each existing and new employee should be given a copy along with a letter stating that the rules apply to all employees and that by accepting employment at your company they agree to abide by the rules. Having an employee sign a receipt for the letter and handbook is proof that they received it.

INDEPENDENT CONTRACTORS

One way to avoid problems with employees and taxes at the same time is to have all of your work done through independent contractors. This can relieve you of most of the burdens of employment laws and the obligation to pay social security and medicare taxes for the workers.

An independent contractor is, in effect, a separate business that you pay to do a job. You pay them just as you pay any company that you have do work for you. At the end of the year, instead of issuing a W-2 form, you issue a 1099, if the amount is over $600.

This may seem too good to be true; and in some situations it is. The IRS does not like independent contractor arrangements because it is too easy for the independent contractors to cheat on their taxes. To limit the use of independent contractors the IRS has strict regulations on who may and may not be classified an independent contractor. They also audit companies that do not appear to pay enough in wages for the type of business they are in.

Especially risky are jobs that are not traditionally done by independent contractors. For example, you could not get away with hiring a secretary as an independent contractor. One of the most important factors considered in determining if a worker can be an independent contractor, is the amount of control the company has over his or her work.

Example 1: If you need someone to paint your building and you agree to pay them a certain price to do it according to their own methods and schedule, you can pay them as an independent contractor. But if you tell them when to work and how to do the job, and provide them with the tools and materials, they will be classified as an employee.

Example 2: If you just need some typing done and you take it to a typing service and pick it up when it is ready, you will be safe in treating them as independent contractors. But if you need someone to come into your office to type, on your machine, at your schedule, you will probably be required to treat that person as an employee for tax purposes.

The IRS has a form you can use in determining if a person is an employee or an independent contractor. It is the DETERMINATION OF EMPLOYEE WORK STATUS (IRS FORM SS-8). (see form 9, p.235.)

INDEPENDENT CONTRACTORS VERSUS EMPLOYEES

In deciding whether to make use of independent contractors of employees, you should weigh the following advantages and disadvantages:

Advantages.

- Lower taxes. You do not have to pay social security, medicare, unemployment, or other employee taxes.

- Less paperwork. You do not have to handle federal withholding deposits or the monthly employer returns to the state or federal government.

- Less insurance. You do not have to pay workers' compensation insurance and since the workers are not your employees you do not have to insure against their possible liabilities.

- More flexibility. You can use independent contractors when you need them and not pay them when business is slow.

Disadvantages.

- The IRS and state tax offices are strict about when workers can qualify as independent contractors and they will audit companies whose use of them does not appear to be legitimate.

- If your use of independent contractors is found to be improper you may have to pay back taxes and penalties and have problems with your pension plan.

- While employees usually cannot sue you for their injuries (if you have covered them with workers' compensation) independent contractors can sue you if their injuries were your fault.

- If you are paying someone to produce a creative work (writing, photography, artwork, etc.), you receive less rights to the work of an independent contractor.

- You have less control over the work of an independent contractor, and less flexibility in terminating them if you are not satisfied that the job is being done the way you require.

- You have less loyalty from an independent contractor, who works sporadically for you and possibly others than from your own full-time employees.

For some businesses the advantages outweigh the disadvantages, but for others they do not. Consider your business plans and the consequences from each type of arrangement. Keep in mind that it will be easier to start with independent contractors and switch to employees than to hire employees and have to fire them to hire independent contractors.

DISCRIMINATION LAWS

One of the more common types of employee complaints and lawsuits involve alleged violation of state or federal discrimination laws.

FEDERAL LAW   There are numerous federal laws forbidding discrimination based upon race, sex, pregnancy, color, religion, national origin, age, or disability. The laws apply to both hiring and firing, and to employment practices such as salaries, promotions, and benefits. Most of these laws only apply to an employer who has fifteen or more employees for twenty weeks of a calendar year, or an employer who has federal contracts or subcontracts. Therefore, you most likely will not be required to comply with the law immediately upon opening your business.

One exception is the Equal Pay Act which applies to employers with two or more employees, and requires that women be paid the same as men in the same type of job.

Employers with fifteen or more employees are required to display a poster regarding discrimination, available from both of the following:

U.S. Equal Employment
Opportunity Commission
2401 E. Street, N.W.
Washington, DC 20506

Michigan Dept. of Civil Rights
Manpower Building, Suite 101
741 N. Cedar Street
Lansing, MI 48906
517-334-9335
517-334-9350 (fax)

Employers with 100 or more employees are required to file an annual report with the Equal Employment Opportunity Commission (EEOC). Federal forms may be obtained from the EEOC at 800-669-3362 or through its websites:

http://www.eeoc.gov

http://www.mdcr.state.mi.us

When hiring employees, some questions are illegal or inadvisable to ask. The following questions should not be included on your employment application, or in your interviews, unless the information is somehow directly tied to the duties of the job:

- Do not ask about an applicant's citizenship or place of birth. But after hiring an employee you must ask about his or her right to work in this country.

- Do not ask a female applicant her maiden name. You can ask if she has been known by any other name in order to do a background check.

- Do not ask if applicants have children, plan to have them, or have child care. You can ask if an applicant will be able to work the required hours.

- Do not ask if the applicant has religious objections for working Saturday or Sunday. You can mention if the job requires such hours and ask whether the applicant can meet this job requirement.

- Do not ask an applicant's age. You can ask if an applicant is eighteen or over, or for a liquor-related job if they are twenty-one or over.

- Do not ask an applicant's weight.

- Do not ask if an applicant has AIDS or is HIV positive.

- Do not ask about the applicant's previous health problems.

- Do not ask if the applicant has filed a workers' compensation claim.

- Do not ask if the applicant is married or whether their spouse would object to the job, hours, or duties.

- Do not ask if the applicant owns a home, furniture, or car, as it is considered racially discriminatory.

- Do not ask if the applicant has ever been arrested. You can ask if the applicant was ever *convicted* of a crime.

The most recent, and perhaps most onerous, law is the Americans with Disabilities Act of 1990 (ADA). Under this law employers who do not make "reasonable accommodations for disabled employees" will face fines of up to $100,000, as well as other civil penalties and civil damage awards.

While the goal of creating more opportunities for people with disabilities is a good one, the result of this law is to place all of the costs of achieving this goal on businesses that are faced with disabled applicants. For example, it has been suggested that the requirement of "reasonable accommodation" will require some companies to hire blind applicants for jobs that require reading and then to hire second employees to read to the blind employees. We will only know the extent to which this law can be applied after some unlucky employers have been taken to court.

The ADA currently applies to employers with fifteen or more employees. Employers who need more than fifteen employees might want to consider contracting with independent contractors to avoid problems with this law, particularly if the number of employees is only slightly larger than fifteen.

To find out how the ADA affects your business, you might want to order the government's *ADA Technical Assistance Manual* (for $25) from The Superintendent of Documents, P. O. Box 371954, Pittsburgh, PA 15250-7954, or fax your credit card order to 202-512-2233.

In any case, all employers should keep detailed records showing reasons for hiring or not hiring applicants and for firing employees.

Tax benefits. There are three types of tax credits to help small business with the burden of these laws.

- Businesses can deduct up to $15,000 a year for making their premises accessible to the disabled and can depreciate the rest. (Internal Revenue Code (IRC), Section 190.)

- Small businesses (under $1,000,000 in revenue and under thirty employees) can get a tax credit each year for 50% of the cost of making their premises accessible to the disabled, but this only applies to the amount between $250 and $10,500.

- Small businesses can get a credit of up to 40% of the first $6,000 of wages paid to certain new employees who qualify through the PRE-SCREENING NOTICE AND CERTIFICATION REQUEST (IRS FORM 8850). The form and instructions are in Appendix C. (see form 10, p.241.)

Records. To protect against potential claims of discrimination, all employers should keep detailed records showing reasons for hiring or not hiring applicants and for firing employees.

MICHIGAN LAWS

Elliot-Larsen Civil Rights Act. This is Michigan's law prohibiting discrimination in employment (as well as in other areas) on the basis of "religion, race, color, national origin, age, sex, height, weight, familial status, or marital status." This law also covers sexual harassment. (Mich. Comp. Laws Ann., Sec. 37.2101.)

Discriminatory Job Advertisements and Applications. Michigan law prohibits an employer from publishing any notice or advertisement "which indicates a preference, limitation, specification, or discrimination, based on religion, race, color, national origin, age, sex, height, weight, or marital status." It also prohibits any use of a written or oral inquiry or form of application that elicits information about a prospective employee's status with respect to any of these matters. An exemption may be granted if you can convince the Civil Rights Commission that such discrimination is a "bona fide occupational qualification reasonably necessary to the normal operation of the business or enterprise." (Mich. Comp. Laws Ann., Sec. 37.2206.)

Equal Pay. Michigan has a counterpart to the federal law providing for equal pay for the same job to both sexes. This state statute is meant to fill the gap of workers not covered by federal law and, therefore, does not apply to workers who are under the Fair Labor Standards Act. (Mich. Comp. Laws Ann., Sec. 408.397.)

Persons with Disabilities Civil Rights Act. This Act applies to any employer with four or more employees, and prohibits discrimination in employment against anyone because of the person's mental or physical handicap, but only if the handicap is "unrelated to the individual's ability to perform the duties of a particular job or position." Even if the handicap does relate to the job, the employer must use any available adaptive aids or devices which would allow the handicapped person to perform the job, unless the employer can show it would create an "undue hardship."

NOTE: *Persons with AIDS and who are HIV positive are covered.*

The Act also prohibits the use of any physical or mental examinations which do not relate to the job duties. It also prohibits the use of advertisements, applications, or inquiries which indicate or tend to discriminate against persons with handicaps, and prohibits the employer from keeping records of employees' handicaps. (Mich. Comp. Laws Ann., beginning with Sec. 37.1101.)

Sexual Harassment

In today's employment climate, any employer must pay attention to state and federal laws regarding sexual harassment in the workplace.

FEDERAL LAW   What began as protection for employees who were fired or not promoted for failing to succumb to sexual advances of their superiors has been expanded to outlaw nearly any sexual comments or references in the workplace. As an example of how far this has gone, one university was forced to take down a painting by Goya depicting a nude because a teacher felt sexually harassed by its presence.

In the 1980s, the Equal Employment Opportunity Commission interpreted the Title VII of the Civil Rights Act of 1964 to forbid sexual harassment. After that, the courts took over and reviewed all types of conduct in the workplace. The numerous lawsuits that followed revealed a definite trend toward expanding the definition of sexual harassment and favoring employees.

The EEOC has held the following in sexual harassment cases:

- The victim as well as the harasser may be a woman or a man.

- The victim does not have to be of the opposite sex.

- The harasser can be the victim's supervisor, an agent of the employer, a supervisor in another area, a co-worker, or a non-employee.

- The victim does not have to be the person harassed but could be anyone affected by the offensive conduct.

- Unlawful sexual harassment may occur without economic injury to or discharge of the victim.

- The harasser's conduct must be unwelcome.

Some of the actions that have been considered harassment are:

- displaying sexually explicit posters in the workplace;

- requiring female employees to wear revealing uniforms;

- rating of sexual attractiveness of female employees as they passed male employees' desks;

- continued sexual jokes and innuendos.;

- demands for sexual favors from subordinates;

- unwelcomed sexual propositions or flirtation;

- unwelcomed physical contact; and,

- whistling or leering at members of the opposite sex.

In 1993, the United States Supreme Court ruled that an employee can make a claim for sexual harassment even without proof of a specific injury. However, lower federal courts in more recent cases (such as the Paula Jones case against President Clinton) have dismissed cases where no specific injury was shown (although these decisions may be overruled once they reach a higher court). These new cases may indicate that the pendulum has stopped swinging in the direction of continual expansion of the law in favor of the employee.

On the other hand, another recent case determined that an employer can be held liable for sexual harassment of an employee by a supervisor, even if the employer was unaware of the supervisor's conduct. The law of sexual harassment area is still developing, so it is difficult to make clear rules of conduct.

Some things a business can do to protect against claims of sexual harassment are:

- Distribute a written policy against all kinds of sexual harassment to all employees.

- Encourage employees to report all incidents of sexual harassment.

- Insure there is no retaliation against those who complain.

- Make clear that your policy is "zero tolerance."

- Explain that sexual harassment includes both requests for sexual favors and a work environment that some employees may consider hostile.

- Allow employees to report harassment to someone other than their immediate supervisor in case that person is involved in the harassment.

- Promise as much confidentiality as possible to complainants.

MICHIGAN LAW The Elliot-Larsen Civil Rights Act (see page 90) has been determined to give individuals the right to sue their employer for sexual harassment. Suits under this law are not as broad as under federal law. Under this Michigan law, the employee must have been sexually harassed by a supervisor and there must have been a decision that affected their employment. Or, there must have been sexual conduct, communication which was intended to, or did, substantially interfere with the employee's employment, or communication that created an intimidating, hostile, or offensive work environment.

WAGE AND HOUR LAWS

There are state and federal laws governing wages paid to workers and the hours employees work. Some of these laws apply to all employers, while some only apply to certain employers.

FEDERAL LAW

Businesses covered. The Federal Fair Labor Standards Act (FLSA) applies to all employers who are engaged in *interstate commerce* or in the production of goods for interstate commerce (anything that will cross a state line), and to all employees of hospitals, schools, residential facilities for the disabled or aged, or public agencies. It also applies to all employees of enterprises that gross $500,000 or more per year.

While many small businesses might not think they are engaged in interstate commerce, the laws have been interpreted broadly so that nearly any use of the mails, interstate telephone service, or other interstate services, however minor, is enough to bring a business under the law. The writers of our Constitution clearly intended for most rights to be reserved to the states, but the *commerce clause* has been used to expand federal control to many unintended areas.

Minimum wage. The federal wage and hour laws are contained in the Federal Fair Labor Standards Act (FLSA). In 1996, legislation was passed by Congress and signed by President Clinton which raised the federal minimum wage to $5.15 per hour.

In certain circumstances a wage of $3.62 may be paid to employees under twenty years of age for a ninety-day training period.

For employees who regularly receive more than $30 a month in tips, the minimum wage is $2.13 per hour. But if the employee's tips do not bring him or her up to the full $5.15 minimum wage, then the employer must make up the difference.

Overtime. Workers who work over forty hours in a week must be paid time-and-a-half for the time worked over forty hours.

Exempt employees. While nearly all businesses are covered, certain employees are exempt from the FLSA. Exempt employees include employees that are considered executives, administrative and managerial, professionals, computer professionals, and outside sales people.

Whether one of these exceptions applies to a particular employee is a complicated legal question. Thousands of court cases have been decided on this issue but they have given no clear answers. In one case a person could be determined to be exempt because of his duties, but in another, a person with the same duties could be found not exempt.

One thing that is clear is that the determination is made on the employee's function, and not just the job title. You cannot make a secretary exempt by calling her a manager if most of her duties are clerical. For more information contact:

> Wage and Hour Division
> U. S. Department of Labor
> 200 Constitution Ave., N.W. Room S-3325
> Washington, DC 20210
> http://www.dol.gov/dol/esa/public/whd_org.htm

Or call a local office:

> Michigan Department of Consumer and Industry Services
> 525 W. Ottawa Street
> P.O. Box 30004
> Lansing, MI 48909
> 517-373-1820
> Website: http://www.cis.state.mi.us

You can obtain information on the Department of Labor's Small Business Handbook at:

> http://www.dol.gov/asp/public/programs/handbook/main.htm

MICHIGAN LAWS

Minimum Wage Law of 1964. This law currently provides for a minimum wage of $3.35 per hour. The law also requires the payment of overtime at the rate of one and one-half times the non-overtime hourly rate. Overtime is considered work in excess of forty hours per week, or in excess of 216 hours in twenty-eight consecutive days. Violation of the law gives the employee a cause of action for the difference between actual pay and the amount required by law, plus the same amount as additional liquidated damages, plus attorney's fees and court costs. (Mich. Comp. Laws Ann., beginning with Sec. 408.382.)

The law does not apply to a temporary employee, defined as one who is employed for less than ten weeks. However, a consistent pattern of discharging employees within the first ten weeks of employment will be deemed to show an intent to violate the law, which is a misdemeanor punishable by a fine of from $5.00 to $50.00 per offense.

The law also tells when employees must be paid. Unless there is a properly established schedule, employees must be paid on or before the first day of the month for wages earned during the first 15 days of the preceding month, and on or before the 15th day of the month for wages earned during the second half of the preceding month. (For persons employed in the hand harvesting of crops, wages for a particular week must be paid on or before the second day after the end of the work week, unless another method is agreed to in a written contract.)

A regularly scheduled weekly or biweekly payday is acceptable if wages are paid on the established payday and the payday occurs on or before the 14th day after the end of the pay period. A monthly payday is acceptable if wages for a calendar month are paid on or before the first day of following calendar month.

In the event of either voluntary or involuntary termination of employment, wages due must be paid "as soon as the amount can, with due diligence, be determined." In the case of a person employed in the hand harvesting of crops, this may not be later than three days after the date of termination.

Other restrictions on wages include:

- Wages must be paid in United States currency, or by check or other draft payable in United States currency.

- No direct deposit may be made without the free and written consent of the employee.

- No deductions can be made from wages without the written consent of the employee (except for deductions required by law or a collective bargaining agreement).

PENSION AND BENEFIT LAWS

There are no laws requiring small businesses to provide any types of special benefits to employees. Such benefits are given to attract and keep good employees. With pension plans the main concern is if you do start one it must comply with federal tax laws.

HOLIDAYS

There are no federal or Michigan laws requiring that employees be given holidays off. You can require them to work Thanksgiving and Christmas, and dock their pay or fire them for failing to show up. Of course you will not have much luck keeping employees.

Most companies give full time employees a certain number of paid holidays, such as New Year's Day (January 1), Memorial Day (last Monday in May), Fourth of July, Labor Day (first Monday in September), Thanksgiving (fourth Thursday in November) and Christmas (December 25). Some, but not many, employers include other holidays such as Martin Luther King, Jr. Day (third Monday in January), Lincoln's birthday (February 12), Washington's birthday (third Monday in February), Columbus Day (second Monday in October), and Veterans' Day (November 11). If one of the holidays falls on a Saturday or Sunday, some employers give the preceding Friday or following Monday off.

Michigan law says that statewide legal holidays include all of those in the previous paragraph as well as Mrs. Rosa L. Parks Day (first Monday after February 4).

However, the fact that these are designated state holidays does not mean anything. In fact the state government is not even closed on all of these days.

SICK LEAVE

There is no federal or Michigan law mandating that an employee be paid for time that he or she is home sick. The situation seems to be that the larger the company, the more paid sick leave is allowed. Part time workers rarely get sick leave and small business sick leave is usually limited for the simple reason that they cannot afford to pay for time that employees do not work.

Some small companies have an official policy of no paid sick leave, but when an important employee misses a day because he or she is clearly sick, it is paid.

LUNCH AND COFFEE BREAKS There are no federal or Michigan laws requiring coffee breaks or lunch breaks. However, it is common sense that employees will be more productive if they have reasonable breaks for nourishment or to use the toilet facilities.

PENSION PLANS AND RETIREMENTS ACCOUNTS Few small new businesses can afford to provide pension plans for their employees. The first concern of a small business is usually how the owner can shelter income in a pension plan without having to set up a pension plan for an employee. Under most pension plans this is not allowed.

IRA. Anyone with $2,000 of earnings can put up to that amount in an Individual Retirement Account. Unless the person or his or her spouse are covered by a company pension plan and have income over a certain amount, the amount put into the account is tax deductible.

SEP/IRA. With a SEP/IRA a person can put a much greater amount into a retirement plan and deduct it. Employees must also be covered by such a plan, but certain employees are exempt so it is sometimes possible to use these for the owners alone. The best source for more information is a mutual fund company (such as Vanguard, Fidelity, Dreyfus, etc.) or a local bank, which can set up the plan and provide you with all of the rules. These have an advantage over qualified plans (discussed below) since they do not have the high annual fees.

Qualified Retirement Plans. Qualified retirement plans are 401(k) plans, Keough plans and corporate retirement plans. These are covered by ERISA, the Employee Retirement Income Security Act which is a complicated law meant to protect employee pension plans. Congress did not want employees who contributed to pension plans all their lives ending up with nothing when the plan goes bankrupt.

The law is so complicated and the penalties so severe that some companies are cancelling their pension plans, and applications for new plans are a fraction of what they were previously. However, many banks and mutual funds have created *canned plans* which can be used instead of drafting one from scratch. Still the fees for administering them are steep. Check with a bank or mutual fund for details.

FAMILY AND MEDICAL LEAVE LAW

To assist business owners in deciding what type of leave to offer their employees, Congress passed the Family and Medical Leave Act of 1993 (FMLA). This law requires an employee to be given up to twelve weeks of unpaid leave when:

- the employee or employee's spouse has a child;

- the employee adopts a child or takes in a foster child;

- the employee needs to care for an ill spouse, child or parent; or,

- the employee becomes seriously ill.

Fortunately, the law only applies to employers with fifty or more employees. Also, the top ten percent of an employer's salaried - employees can be denied this leave because of the disruption in business their loss could cause.

NOTE: *There is no Michigan law requiring family or medical leave.*

CHILD LABOR LAWS

If you intend to employ any children, you will need to pay close attention to the federal and state child labor laws.

FEDERAL LAWS   The Federal Fair Labor Standards Act also contains rules regarding the hiring of children. The basic rules are that children under sixteen years old may not be hired at all except in a few jobs such as acting and newspaper delivery, and those under eighteen may not be hired for dangerous jobs. Children may not work more than three hours a day/eighteen hours a week in a school week or more than eight hours a day/forty hours a week in a non-school week. If you plan to hire children you should check the Federal Fair Labor Standards Act which is in the United States Code (U.S.C.), Title 29 and also the related regulations, which are in Chapter 29 of the Code of Federal Regulations (C.F.R.).

MICHIGAN   ***Michigan Youth Employment Standards Act***. This law has numerous
LAWS   rules governing the employment of children. (Mich. Comp. Laws Ann., Sec. 409.101.) It applies to all employees under the age of eighteen. The following is a summary of the main provisions of this act:

- No child under the age of fourteen may work, except children age eleven and older may work as golf caddies, and children age thirteen and up may work in farming operations.

- No child may be employed in a hazardous or injurious occupation.

- In order to work, a minor must obtain a work permit from the school district, by submitting an application along with a statement from the prospective employer indicating the intent to employ the child and stating the nature of the job.

- If the child is under the age of sixteen, work is limited as follows:
  - no more than six days per week;
  - no more than a weekly average of eight hours per day;
  - no more than forty-eight hours per week total;
  - no more than ten hours in any single day;
  - no work between the hours of 9:00 p.m. and 7:00 a.m; and,

- if the child is a student, the number of hours in work and school combined may not exceed forty-eight hours per week while school is in session. (In other words, this limitation does not apply during summer, Christmas, and other vacations from school.)

● If the child is at least sixteen, the following restrictions apply:

  - the same restrictions as 1-4, and 6 above; and

  - no work between the hours of 10:30 p.m. and 6:00 a.m. while school is in session; 11:30 p.m. and 6:00 a.m. during school vacations.

● The child must be given at least a thirty-minute rest and lunch period after no more than five hours of work.

● If the child is working in cash transactions at a fixed location (such as a convenience store), he or she may not work after sunset or 8:00 p.m., whichever is earlier, unless there is an adult present.

● No child may be employed in a business that deals in alcoholic beverages unless the sale of food and other goods is at least fifty percent of the gross receipts. Except:

  - fourteen and fifteen-year-olds may work in the non-alcohol-related part of the business if the sale of food and other goods in the alcohol-related part is at least fifty percent of gross receipts;

  - sixteen-year-olds may work if they have completed the requirements for high school graduation (in which case the employer must obtain and keep on file a certificate from the school);

  - seventeen-year-olds who have passed the GED may work (the employer must obtain proof of passing); and,

  - any legally emancipated minor may work (the employer must obtain proof of emancipation).

- There are several exceptions to this Act for such jobs as domestic work in a private residence, selling newspapers, shining shoes, and family businesses.

Poster. Anyone employing a minor must display a poster explaining the child labor laws. This poster is available from:

Michigan Department of Consumer and Industry Services
525 W. Ottawa Street
P.O. Box 30004
Lansing, MI 48909
517-373-1820
Website: http://www.cis.state.mi.us

IMMIGRATION LAWS

If you intend to hire even one employee, you need to be aware of certain immigration laws. At least some of these laws will apply to you even if you will only be hiring U.S. citizens.

FEDERAL LAW

Under Federal law, you must verify both the identity and the employment eligibility of anyone you hire by using the EMPLOYMENT ELIGIBILITY (IRS FORM I-9). (see form 4, p.217.) Both you and the employee must fill out the form and you must check an employee's identification cards or papers.

Fines for hiring illegal aliens range from $250 to $2,000 for the first offense and up to $10,000 for the third offense. Failure to maintain the proper paperwork may result in a fine of up to $1,000. The law does not apply to independent contractors with whom you may contract, and it does not penalize you if the employee used fake identification.

There are also penalties that apply to employers of four or more persons for discriminating against eligible applicants because they appear foreign or because of their national origin or citizenship status.

In Appendix B there is a sample filled-in **IRS FORM I-9**. A blank form, along with instructions and a list of acceptable documentation, may be found in Appendix C. (see form 4, p.217.) For more information, call the Immigration and Naturalization Service (in Michigan at 313-259-8560, or in Washington, DC at 202-514-2000) and ask for the *Handbook for Employers and Instructions for Completing Form I-9*, check the INS website at **http://www.ins.usdoj.gov** or write to the following address:

> U. S. Department of Justice
> Immigration and Naturalization Service
> 425 I Street, NW
> Washington, DC 20536

The Illegal Immigration Reform and Immigrant Responsibility Act of 1996 (IIRIRA) required changes in the rules but as of early 1999 the INS had not yet promulgated final versions of the rules. The interim rule made the following changes to the requirements:

- remove documents 2, 3, 8, and 9 from column A;

- allow document 4 only for aliens authorized to work for a specific employer; and,

- new rules for employees who do not have their original documents.

However, no new forms or instructions have been made available and employers are not yet being prosecuted for violations of these changes. Employers can receive updates to these laws by fax. To receive them, send your name address and fax number to 202-305-2523.

Foreign employees. If you wish to hire employees who are foreign citizens and are not able to provide the documentation explained above, they must first obtain a work visa from the Immigration and Naturalization Service (INS) of the United States Department of Justice.

Work visas for foreigners are not easy to get. Millions of people around the globe would like to come to the U.S. to work and the laws are designed to keep most of them out to protect the jobs of American citizens.

Whether or not a person can get a work visa depends on whether there is a shortage of U.S. workers available to fill the job. For jobs requiring few or no skills, it is practically impossible to get a visa. For highly skilled jobs, such as nurses, physical therapists, and for those of exceptional ability, such as Nobel Prize winners and Olympic medalists, obtaining a visa is fairly easy.

There are several types of visas and different rules for different countries. For example, NAFTA has made it easier for some types of workers to enter the U.S. from Canada and Mexico. For some positions the shortage of workers is assumed by the INS. For others, a business must first advertise a position available in the U.S. Only after no qualified persons apply, can it hire someone from another country.

The visa system is complicated and subject to regular change. (In late 2000 a new law expanded the number of certain worker visas from 115,000 to 195,000.) If you wish to hire a foreign worker you should consult with an immigration specialist or a book on the subject.

MICHIGAN LAWS   There are no Michigan laws relating to the hiring of aliens, other than allowing licensing of aliens legally permitted to work in the United States.

HIRING "OFF THE BOOKS"

Because of the taxes, insurance, and red tape involved with hiring employees, some new businesses hire people "off the books." They pay them in cash and never admit they are employees. While the cash paid in wages would not be tax-deductible, they consider this a smaller cost than compliance. Some even use off the books receipts to cover it.

Except when your spouse or child is giving you some temporary help, this is a terrible idea. Hiring people off the books can result in civil fines, loss of insurance coverage, and even criminal penalties. When engaged in dangerous work, such as roofing or anything using power tools, you are risking millions of dollars in potential damages if a worker is killed or seriously injured.

It may be more costly and time consuming to comply with the employment laws, but if you are concerned with long term growth with less risk, it's the wiser way to go.

FEDERAL CONTRACTS

Companies that do work for the federal government are subject to several laws. In the event you plan to bid on government contracts, you will need to be aware of these laws, which include the following:

The *Davis-Bacon Act* requires contractors engaged in U. S. government construction projects to pay wages and benefits which are equal to or better than the prevailing wages in the area.

The *McNamara-O'Hara Service Contract Act* sets wages and other labor standards for contractors furnishing services to agencies of the U.S. government.

The *Walsh-Healey Public Contracts Act* requires the Department of labor to settle disputes regarding manufacturers supplying products to the U. S. government.

MISCELLANEOUS LAWS

It is nearly impossible to list every single state and federal law that may apply in some way to every business. However, this section will discuss a few of the more common laws that do not fit into any of the specific categories already mentioned.

FEDERAL LAWS   ***Affirmative action.*** In most cases, the federal government does not yet tell employers who they must hire. This would be especially true for small new businesses. The only situation where a small business would need to comply with affirmative action requirements would be if it accepted federal contracts or subcontracts. These requirements could include the hiring of minorities or of Vietnam veterans.

Layoffs. Companies with 100 or more full-time employees at one location are subject to the Worker Adjustment and Retraining Notification Act. This law requires a sixty-day notification prior to certain layoffs and has other strict provisions.

Unions. The National Labor Relations Act of 1935 gives employees the right to organize a union or to join one. (U.S.C., Title 29, Sec. 151.) There are things employers can do to protect themselves, but you should consult a labor attorney or a book on the subject before taking action which might be illegal and result in fines.

Pension/benefit laws. ERISA, the Employee Retirement Income Security Act is a law that is meant to protect employee pension plans. Congress did not want employees who contributed to pension plans all their lives ending up with nothing when the plan goes bankrupt. Unfortunately, the law is so complicated and the penalties so severe that companies are cancelling their pension plans. Applications for new plans are a fraction of what they once were. If you wish to set up a pension plan, consult an accountant or attorney experienced in them.

Poster laws. Yes, there are laws regarding what posters you may or may not display in the workplace. A previous edition of this book stated that nothing forbids Playboy or Playgirl posters, but a "politically correct" federal judge in 1991, ruled that Playboy posters in a workplace were sexual harassment.

There are other poster laws which require certain posters to be displayed to inform employees of their rights.

All employers must display the wage and hour poster, and the employee polygraph protection notice poster, both of which are available from:

> U.S. Department of Labor
> 200 Constitution Ave., NW
> Washington, DC 20210

All employers must display the OSHA poster available from:

> OSHA Regional Office
> 230 South Dearborn Street, Room 3244
> Chicago, IL 60604
> 312-353-2220
> 312-353-7774 (fax)
> Lansing: 517-327-0904

Employers with fifteen or more employees for twenty weeks of the year must display the sex, race, religion, and ethnic discrimination poster and the age discrimination poster available from:

> EEOC
> 2401 E Street NW
> Washington, DC 20506

Employers with federal contracts or subcontracts of $10,000 or more must display the sex, race, etc. discrimination poster mentioned above plus a poster regarding Vietnam Era Veterans available from the local federal contracting office.

Employers with government contracts subject to the Service Contract Act or the Public Contracts Act must display a notice to employees working on government contracts available from:

> Employment Standards Division
> U. S. Department of Labor
> 200 Constitution Ave., NW
> Washington, DC 20210

MICHIGAN LAWS

Bullard-Plawecki Employee Right to Know Act. This law relates to an employee's rights with respect to his or her personnel file kept by an employer. It applies to all businesses with four or more employees. Basically, it gives the employee the right to review his or her personnel record at least two times per year. If the employee disagrees with anything, he or she can submit a written statement, which must be disclosed to any third party seeking information about the employee if any other information is given. If the employer intends to disclose information in any disciplinary reports, letters of reprimand, etc., the employer must notify the employee in writing on or before the date of disclosure. Disciplinary reports, letters of reprimand, etc., must be deleted after four years. (Mich. Comp. Laws Ann., beginning with Sec. 423.501.)

Polygraph Protection Act of 1981. This Act applies to anyone employing one or more people, and prohibits an employer from requiring a polygraph examination of an employee or applicant for employment. It does permit an examination at the request of the employee or applicant, but still puts limitations and requirements on the employer. Violation of the Act allows the employee or applicant to sue for an injunction and damages (including double wages lost if the person was discharged), and is also a misdemeanor subjecting the employer to a fine of up to $1,000 and up to ninety days in jail. (Mich. Comp. Laws Ann., Sec. 37.201.)

Whistleblowers' Protection Act. This Act prohibits an employer from taking any retaliatory action against an employee for reporting a violation of a law or regulation. It applies to any employer with one or more employees. Violation subjects the employer to a fine of up to $500. It also allows the employee to sue the employer for an injunction, damages (including attorney's fees), and reinstatement with full back pay. The Act also requires the employer to "post notices and use other appropriate means to keep his or her employees informed of their protections and obligations under this act." (Mich. Comp. Laws Ann., Sec. 15.361.)

Prohibited requirements of employment. It is a misdemeanor to require an employee or prospective employee to do any of the following things as a condition of hiring, continued employment, promotion, etc.:

1. make a contribution to a charity;

2. purchase, or contribute toward the purchase, of a life or accident insurance policy;

3. pay for all or part of a medical examination, polygraph examination or fingerprinting; or,

4. pay any money to anyone in consideration of employment, except to an employment agency. (Mich. Comp. Laws Ann., Secs. 750.351 to 750.354a.)

Molesting or disturbing employees. It is a misdemeanor to use threats, intimidation, or otherwise "interfere with, or in any way molest, or attempt to interfere with, or in any way molest or disturb" any person "in the quiet and peaceable pursuit of his lawful occupation, vocation or avocation, or on the way to and from such occupation, vocation or avocation..." (Mich. Comp. Laws Ann., Sec. 750.352.)

Migrant and farm labor. If you plan to hire or house migrant or farm labor, read the sections in the statutes on wages and child labor, and contact the Michigan Commission on Agricultural Employment for more information. (Mich. Comp. Laws Ann., Sec. 333.12401.)

Poster laws. Michigan has its own poster requirements and the following should be obtained:

- Federal Minimum Wage poster:

    U.S. Department of Labor
    Employment Standards Administration
    Wage & Hour Division
    Washington, D.C. 20210

- Equal Employment Opportunity poster:

    Office of Federal Contract Compliance Programs
    U.S. Department of Labor
    Employment Standards Administration
    200 Constitution Avenue, N.W.
    Washington, D.C. 20210

- Employee Polygraph Protection Notice:

    U.S. Department of Labor
    Employment Standards Administration
    Wage & Hour Division
    Washington, D.C. 20210

- OSHA poster:

    U.S. Department of Labor
    Occupational Safety & Health Administration
    801 S. Waverly Road, Suite 306
    Lansing, MI 48917

- Unemployment Agency poster:

    Unemployment Agency
    7310 Woodward Avenue
    Detroit, MI 48202

- MIOSHA poster:

    Michigan Department of Public Health
    Division of Occupational Health
    3500 N. Logan
    Lansing, MI 48909

- ADA (Americans with Disabilities Act) poster:

    U.S. Equal Employment Opportunity Commission
    P.O. Box 12549
    Cincinnati, OH 45212-0549

Advertising and Promotion Laws 12

Almost every business engages in some forms of advertising and promotion. There are many laws you should consider before you begin any advertising or promotional campaigns.

Advertising Laws and Rules

This section will discuss various federal and Michigan laws and regulations relating to advertising.

FEDERAL LAWS   The federal government regulates advertising through the Federal Trade Commission (FTC). The rules are contained in the Code of Federal Regulations (C.F.R.). You can find these rules in most law libraries and many public libraries. If you plan any advertising which you think may be questionable, you might want to check the rules. As you read the rules below you will probably think of many violations you see every day.

Federal rules do not apply to every business; and small businesses that operate only within the state and do not use the postal service may be exempt. However, many of the federal rules have been adopted into law by the state of Michigan. Therefore, a violation could be prosecuted by the state rather than the federal government. Some of the important rules are summarized below. If you wish, you should obtain copies from your library.

Deceptive pricing. When prices are being compared, it is required that actual and not inflated prices are used.

Example: If an object would usually be sold for $7, one should not first offer it for $10 and then start offering it at 30% off.

It is considered misleading to suggest that a discount from list price is a bargain if the item is seldom actually sold at list price. If most surrounding stores sell an item for $7 it is considered misleading to say it has a "retail value of $10" even if there are some stores elsewhere selling it at that price. (C.F.R., Title 16, Ch. I, Part 233.)

Bait advertising. Bait advertising is placing an ad when you don't really want the respondents to buy the product offered but to switch to another item. (C.F.R., Title 16, Ch. I, Part 238.)

Use of "free," "half-off" and similar words. Use of words such as "free," "1¢ sale" and the like must not be misleading. This means that the "regular price" must not include a mark-up to cover the "free" item. The seller must expect to sell the product without the free item at some time in the future. (C.F.R., Title 16, Ch. I, Part 251.)

Substantiation of claims. The FTC requires that advertisers be able to substantiate their claims. (C.F.R., Title 16, Sec. 3.40; F.R., Volume (Vol.) 48, Page 10471, March 11, 1983.) Some information on this policy is contained on the Internet at:

http://www.ftc.gov/bcp/guides/ad3subst.htm

Endorsements. This rule forbids endorsements which are misleading. An example is a quote from a film review which is used in such a way as to change the substance of the review. It is not necessary to use the exact words of the person endorsing the product as long as the opinion is not distorted. If a product is changed, an endorsement which does not apply to the new version cannot be used. For some items, such as drugs, claims cannot be used without scientific proof. Endorsements by organizations cannot be used unless one is sure that the membership holds the same opinion. (C.F.R., Title 16, Ch. I, Part 255.)

Unfairness. Any advertising practices which can be deemed to be "unfair" are forbidden by the FTC. (U.S.C., Title 15, Sec. 45.) An explanation of this policy is located on the Internet at:

http://www.ftc.gov/bcp/policy stmt/ad-unfair.htm

Negative option plans. When a seller uses a sales system in which the buyer must notify the seller if he does not want the goods, the seller must provide the buyer with a form to decline the sale and at least ten days in which to decline. Bonus merchandise must be shipped promptly and the seller must promptly terminate any who so request after completion of the contract. (C.F.R., Title 16, Ch. I, Part 425.)

Laser eye surgery. Under the laws governing deceptive advertising the FTC and the FDA are regulating the advertising of laser eye surgery. Anyone involved in this area should obtain a copy of these rules. (U.S.C., Title 15, Secs. 45, 52-57.) They are located on the Internet at:

http://www.ftc.gov/bcp/guides/eyecare2.htm

Food and dietary supplements. Under the Nutritional Labeling Education Act of 1990 the FTC and the FDA regulate the packaging and advertising of food and dietary products. Anyone involved in this area should obtain a copy of these rules. (U.S.C., Title 21, Secs. 343.) They are located on the Internet at:

http://www.ftc.gov/bcp/guides/ad4diet.htm

and

http://www.ftc.gov/bcp/guides/ad-food.htm

Jewelry and precious metals. The FTC has numerous rules governing the sale and advertising of jewelry and precious metals. Anyone in this business should obtain a copy of these rules. (F.R., Vol. 61, page 27212.) They are located on the Internet at:

http://www.ftc.gov/bcp/guides/jewel-gd.htm

MICHIGAN
LAWS

Most of Michigan's advertising laws are in the criminal statutes (Michigan Penal Code). (Mich. Comp. Laws Ann., Secs. 750.33 through 750.42b.) The following discussion summarizes these laws.

False advertising. It is a misdemeanor to issue any advertising which is "untrue, deceptive or misleading, or calculated to subject any person to disadvantage or injury..." This includes untrue statements as to the motive or purpose of the sale, and inaccurate illustrations. Violation is punishable by a fine of up to $500 and up to one year in jail. (Mich. Comp. Laws Ann., Sec. 750.33.)

Misrepresentation of character or extent of business. "Any person who states, in an advertisement of his goods, that he is a producer, manufacturer, processor, wholesaler or importer, or that he owns or controls a factory or other source of supply of goods, when such is not the fact, or in any other manner knowingly misrepresents the character, extent, volume or type of his business, is guilty of a misdemeanor." (Mich. Comp. Laws Ann., Sec. 750.33a.)

Advertising of consumer goods. These laws only apply to consumer items for sale at retail. Consumer items are those "used or consumed, or bought for use or consumption, primarily for personal, family, or household purposes." For sale at retail means "the transfer of an interest in a consumer item by a person regularly and principally engaged in the business of selling consumer items to a buyer for use or consumption and not for resale." (Mich. Comp. Laws Ann., beginning with Sec. 445.351.)

It is illegal to knowingly advertise a consumer item for sale at retail at a sale, special, or reduced price, unless the advertisement includes the dates the item is available, or the quantity available together with a statement that the item is available at that price only as long as the advertised quantity lasts. Any limitation in availability must be clearly disclosed in the ad. (Mich. Comp. Laws Ann., Sec. 445.355.)

If a consumer item is advertised at a specific price, which is not indicated to be a special, sale, or reduced price, you must either:

- make the item available at the advertised price for at least five days after the last date of advertisement (unless it is made unavailable by government action, a plant closing, or an "act of God," and the reason is conspicuously posted);

- indicate in the ad the dates the item is available at that price; or

- indicate in the ad the quantity available and state that the item will only be available at that price for as long as the stated quantity lasts.

If the ad does not state the quantity available, and if the item cannot be sold at the advertised price throughout the advertised sales period, the customer must be given a written guarantee that the item will be delivered under the advertised conditions at a future date as agreed upon, or upon notification by the merchant (in not more than ninety days). If this is not possible, the merchant may provide a similar item of equal or greater value. After the merchant notifies the customer of the availability of the item, the merchant must hold the item for the customer for at least seven days (two days if it is a perishable item).

NOTE: *None of the above applies to baked goods, fresh fruit, or fresh vegetables.*

It is also illegal to have an advertisement that contains a statement or representation that is untrue, deceptive or misleading. According to Michigan Law, it is illegal to:

- have an advertisement that contains a statement or representation that is untrue, deceptive, or misleading;

- issue an ad with the intent not to sell at the price stated; or,

- issue an ad which fails to call attention to the fact that the items offered are "substantially defective and therefore not first class, or which consist of articles or units or parts known as seconds or blemished goods, merchandise, or commodities, which goods, merchandise, or commodities have been rejected by the manufacturer...as not being first class..." (Mich. Comp. Laws Ann., Sec. 445.356.)

Unsolicited facsimile (fax) advertising. Under this law, it is unlawful to send advertising by fax without the consent of the person (which includes business entities) to whom it is sent. The mere fact that the other person has a published fax number is not consent to receive unsolicited fax advertising. Violation of this law subjects the sender to a fine of up to $500 per violation, and a civil penalty to the receiver of actual damages or $250 whichever is greater. (Mich. Comp. Laws Ann., Secs. 445.1771 through 445.1776.)

If you receive unsolicited fax advertising, report it to the Michigan Attorney General's office or your local prosecuting attorney; and send the sender a letter stating that the sender did not have your consent to send the advertisement. Be sure to follow up your complaint to be sure the Attorney General takes action, as this is essential to your ability to file suit against the sender if you later receive more unsolicited fax advertising.

The Attorney General is to send the sender a *cease and desist order*. This is simply a letter telling the sender to immediately stop sending unsolicited fax advertising. The sender must then send the Attorney General a written *assurance of discontinuance*. This is simply a letter telling the Attorney General that the sender will not send anymore unsolicited fax advertising. If no such assurance is received, the Attorney General should take the sender to court and seek an injunction.

You may only file suit after the following events:

- the Attorney General receives an assurance of discontinuance or an injunction is granted;

- you have sent the sender a letter stating you did not consent to the advertising; and,

- the sender again sends unsolicited advertising after the first two things listed here have been done.

There are several other Michigan advertising laws, which may violate the Constitutional guarantee of free speech. Although these laws are of questionable constitutional validity, it would be very expensive and time-consuming for you to take a case all the way to the United States Supreme Court to try to declare the law unconstitutional and secure your right to continue your advertising. Therefore, you may want to consider this before you decide to try advertising that may violate one of these laws.

Immoral advertising. This set of laws prohibit advertising the cure or treatment of any maladies or problems relating to sexual organs, including miscarriage and abortion. (Mich. Comp. Laws Ann., Secs. 750.34 to 750.37.)

Advertisement displaying violence or the human form. This law makes it a misdemeanor to "post, place or display on any sign board, bill board, fence, building, sidewalk, or other object, or in any street, road, or other public place, any sign, picture, printing or other representation of murder, assassination, stabbing, fighting or any personal violence, or of the commission of any crime, or any representation of the human form in an attitude or dress which would be indecent in the case of a living person, if such person so appeared in any public street, square or highway." (Mich. Comp. Laws Ann., Sec. 750.38.)

Immoral or ambiguous language in advertisements for patent medicines, certain diseases, and contraceptive preventatives. The first law makes it a misdemeanor to use "language of immoral tendency or of ambiguous character" in advertisement of any medicine. The second makes it a misdemeanor to use "indecent or obscene language" in an advertisement for "the cure of chronic female complaints or private diseases," or recipes or prescriptions "to prevent contraception, or tending to produce miscarriage or abortion." (Mich. Comp. Laws Ann., Secs. 750.39 & 750.40.)

Tobacco products advertising. These laws place restrictions, and require certain warnings, on outdoor signs advertising smokeless tobacco products; and place restrictions on the distribution of tobacco products through the mail or other common carriers (such as UPS). (Mich. Comp. Laws Ann., Secs. 750.42a and 750.42b.)

INTERNET SALES LAWS

There are not yet specific laws governing Internet transactions that are different from laws governing other transactions. The FTC feels that its current rules regarding deceptive advertising, substantiation, disclaimers, refunds, and related matters must be followed by Internet businesses and that consumers are adequately protected by them. See the first three pages of this chapter and Chapter 9 for that information.

For some specific guidelines on Internet advertising, see the FTC's site at:

http://ftc.gov/bcp/conline/pubs/buspubs/ruleroad.htm

HOME SOLICITATION LAWS

There are specific state and federal rules governing personal or telephone solicitation of sales at people's homes.

FEDERAL LAWS   The Federal Trade Commission has rules governing door-to-door sales. In any such sale it is a deceptive trade practice to fail to furnish a receipt explaining the sale (in the language of the presentation) and giving notice that there is a three day right of recision. The notice must be supplied in duplicate, must be in at least 10-point type and must be captioned either "NOTICE OF RIGHT TO CANCEL" or "NOTICE OF CANCELLATION." The notice must be worded as follows:

```
┌─────────────────────────────────────────────────────────┐
│                 NOTICE OF CANCELLATION                   │
│                                   _____     │
│                                       Date               │
│                                                          │
│        YOU MAY CANCEL THIS TRANSACTION, WITHOUT ANY      │
│   PENALTY OR OBLIGATION, WITHIN THREE BUSINESS DAYS FROM  │
│   THE ABOVE DATE.                                        │
│        IF YOU CANCEL, ANY PROPERTY TRADED IN, ANY        │
│   PAYMENTS MADE BY YOU UNDER THE CONTRACT OR SALE, AND    │
│   ANY NEGOTIABLE INSTRUMENT EXECUTED BY YOU WILL BE       │
│   RETURNED TO YOU WITHIN 10 BUSINESS DAYS FOLLOWING       │
│   RECEIPT BY THE SELLER OF YOUR CANCELLATION NOTICE, AND  │
│   ANY SECURITY INTEREST ARISING OUT OF THE TRANSACTION    │
│   WILL BE CANCELLED.                                     │
│        IF YOU CANCEL, YOU MUST MAKE AVAILABLE TO THE      │
│   SELLER AT YOUR RESIDENCE, IN SUBSTANTIALLY AS GOOD      │
│   CONDITION AS WHEN RECEIVED, ANY GOODS DELIVERED TO      │
│   YOU UNDER THIS CONTRACT OR SALE; OR YOU MAY IF YOU      │
│   WISH, COMPLY WITH THE INSTRUCTIONS OF THE SELLER        │
│   REGARDING THE RETURN SHIPMENT OF THE GOODS AT THE       │
│   SELLER'S EXPENSE AND RISK.                             │
│        IF YOU DO MAKE THE GOODS AVAILABLE TO THE SELLER   │
│   AND THE SELLER DOES NOT PICK THEM UP WITHIN 20 DAYS OF  │
│   THE DATE OF YOUR NOTICE OF CANCELLATION, YOU MAY        │
│   RETAIN OR DISPOSE OF THE GOODS WITHOUT ANY FURTHER      │
│   OBLIGATION. IF YOU FAIL TO MAKE THE GOODS AVAILABLE TO  │
│   THE SELLER, OR IF YOU AGREE TO RETURN THE GOODS AND     │
│   FAIL TO DO SO, THEN YOU REMAIN LIABLE FOR PERFORMANCE   │
│   OF ALL OBLIGATIONS UNDER THE CONTRACT.                 │
│        TO CANCEL THIS TRANSACTION, MAIL OR DELIVER A      │
│   SIGNED AND DATED COPY OF THIS CANCELLATION NOTICE OR    │
│   ANY OTHER WRITTEN NOTICE, OR SEND A TELEGRAM, TO        │
│   [name of seller], AT [address of seller's place of     │
│   business] NOT LATER THAN MIDNIGHT OF _____ (date). │
│        I HEREBY CANCEL THIS TRANSACTION.                 │
│        (DATE) _____                        │
│                                                          │
│                          _____   │
│                                (Buyer's signature)       │
└─────────────────────────────────────────────────────────┘
```

The seller must complete the notice and orally inform the buyer of the right to cancel. He cannot misrepresent the right to cancel, assign the contract until the fifth business day, nor include a confession of judgment in the contract. For more specific details see the rules contained in the Code of Federal Regulations. (C.F.R., Title 16, Ch. I, Part 429.)

MICHIGAN
LAWS

Michigan Home Solicitation Sales Act. If you are going to engage in the type of sales governed by this act, get a copy and read it. Basically, the Act covers the sale of goods or services of more than $25.00, in which the seller engages in personal or telephone solicitation of the sale at the buyer's residence, when the buyer's agreement or offer to purchase occurs in the residence. Insurance agents and real estate sales people are covered by separate laws. (Mich. Comp. Laws Ann., beginning with Sec. 445.111.)

This act prohibits the use of recorded messages in a telephone sales offer, and gives the buyer certain cancellation rights. The act requires the following notice to appear on a written offer to purchase, "in immediate proximity to the space reserved in the agreement or offer to purchase for the signature of the buyer:"

> You, the buyer, may cancel this transaction at any time prior to midnight of the third business day after the date of this transaction. See the attached notice of cancellation form for an explanation of this right.

This notice may be attached to the offer or printed on the reverse side. It is the same as the Notice of Cancellation under Federal law.

TELEPHONE SOLICITATION LAWS

Both the federal and Michigan governments have passed laws regarding telephone solicitations, also known as telemarketing. If you will be engaging in telephone solicitations, you should keep alert for any new laws in this area. With the large number of people who find telemarketing calls extremely annoying, it is likely that they will be pressuring legislators for more laws restricting this form of solicitation.

FEDERAL LAWS   *Phone calls.* Telephone solicitations are governed by the Telephone Consumer Protection Act (U.S.C., Title 47, Page 227) and the Federal Communications Commission rules implementing the act. (C.F.R., Title 47, Sec. 64.1200.) Violators of the act can be sued for $500 damages by consumers and can be fined $10,000 by the FCC. Some of the requirements under the law follow.

- Calls can only be made between 8 a.m. and 9 p.m.

- Solicitors must keep a "do not call" list and honor requests to not call.

- There must be a written policy that the parties called are told the name of the caller, the caller's business name and phone number or address, that the call is a sales call and the nature of the goods or services.

- Personnel must be trained in the policies

- Recorded messages cannot be used to call residences.

Faxes. It is illegal under the act to send advertising faxes to anyone who has not consented to receiving such faxes or is an existing customer.

MICHIGAN LAWS

Michigan has three laws relating to telephone solicitations. First, it is a misdemeanor to make an unsolicited sales call that includes a recorded message. The use of an automatic dialing system with a recorded message is considered sufficient evidence for conviction, absent any proof to the contrary by the business. Violation is punishable by a fine of up to $1,000 and up to ten days in jail. (Mich. Comp. Laws Ann., Sec. 484.125.)

Second, it is also a misdemeanor (fine of up to $500 and up to six months in jail) to make an unsolicited sales call between the hours of 9:00 p.m. and 9:00 a.m. (Mich. Comp. Laws Ann., Sec. 750.540e.)

Third, it is illegal to send unsolicited facsimile (fax) advertisements. See above for more information on this law.

PRICING, WEIGHTS, AND LABELING

Depending upon the type of business you are in, you may need to be aware of the various federal and Michigan laws relating to pricing, weights, and labeling of products.

FEDERAL LAWS

Food products. Beginning in 1994, all food products were required to have labels with information on the product's nutritional values such as calories, fat, and protein. For most products, the label must be in the required format so that consumers can easily compare products.

However, if such a format will not fit on the product label, the information may be in another format which is easily readable.

Metric measures. In 1994, federal rules requiring metric measurement of products took effect. While some federal agencies, such as the federal highway department, indefinitely postponed implementation of the rules the Federal Trade Commission (FTC) and the Food and Drug Administration intend to enforce the rules against businesses.

Under these rules, metric measures do not have to be the first measurement on the container, but they must be included. Food items that are packaged as they are sold (such as delicatessen items) do not have to contain metric labels.

MICHIGAN
LAWS

Michigan Weights and Measures Act of 1964. This Act adopts federal weights and measures standards. It also created the office of the Director of Weights and Measures, which maintains the official standards for use in inspections of weights and measures used by businesses in Michigan. Inspection and enforcement powers lie with the Director of Weights and Measures, and with the Sealer of Weights and Measures in the various cities and counties. Basically, the Act requires accuracy in weights and measures used in the sale and labeling of goods. The Act also provides the requirements for commodities listed next. (Mich. Comp. Laws Ann., beginning with Sec. 290.601.)

Weights and measures. Liquid commodities must be sold only by liquid measure or by weight. Non-liquid must be sold only by weight, measure, or count. However, liquids may only be sold by weight and nonliquids may only be sold by count if the measurement used gives accurate information as to the quantity sold. These rules do not apply to commodities sold for immediate consumption on the premises where sold, vegetables sold by the head or bunch, commodities in containers standardized by state or federal law, or commodities packaged in a form generally used by consumers to show quantity in another manner. (Mich. Comp. Laws Ann., Sec. 290.623.)

Labeling. Any commodity in package form must bear on the outside of the packaging:

- the identity of the commodity unless it can easily be identified through the wrapper or container;

- the net quantity of the contents in terms of weight, measure, or count; and

- the name and place of business of the manufacturer, packer, or distributor if sold at any place other than where it was packed.

Terms that tend to qualify or exaggerate the quantity, such as "when packed," "jumbo," "giant," or "full," are prohibited. The Director of Weights and Measures may make more detailed regulations and exemptions. Some regulations may require the quantity to be stated in more than one unit of measure (e.g., ounces and liters). (Mich. Comp. Laws Ann., Sec. 290.624.)

Random weights and measures. If the package bears one selling price, and is one of a lot that contains random weights, measures or counts, it must be labeled as to the price per single unit. (Mich. Comp. Laws Ann., Sec. 290.626.)

Advertisements. Any advertisement for a packaged commodity must include the basic quantity of the package, except for agricultural and horticultural products where the custom is to state the number of objects or the amount of area which can be treated per package unit (e.g., pesticides and fertilizer). If a regulation requires the package itself to contain more than one unit of measurement, only the smallest unit need be stated in the ad. Also, the types of terms mentioned in the section above on "Labeling" may not be used in an ad either. (Mich. Comp. Laws Ann., Sec. 290.627.)

Meat, poultry and seafood. Except for items sold for immediate consumption on the premises where sold (e.g., restaurants), or as part of a ready-to-eat meal sold for consumption elsewhere (e.g., fast food restaurants), all meat, meat products, poultry, and seafood except shellfish, must be sold by weight. If it is included in a package with other foods (e.g., spaghetti sauce or frozen dinner), only the weight of the entire package need be indicated. (Mich. Comp. Laws Ann., Sec. 290.628a.)

Representation of price. "Whenever any commodity or service is sold...by weight, measure or count, the price shall not be misrepresented, nor shall the price be represented in any manner calculated or tending to mislead or deceive an actual or prospective purchaser. Whenever any advertised, posted or labeled price per unit of weight, measure or count included a fraction of a cent, all elements of the fraction shall be prominently displayed and the numeral or numerals expressing the fraction shall be immediately adjacent to, of the same general design and style as, and at least 1/2 the height and width of the numeral representing the whole cents." (Mich. Comp. Laws Ann., Sec. 290.628b.)

UNFAIR OR DECEPTIVE PRACTICES

Unfair and deceptive trade practices are set forth in Michigan Law and is part of the Michigan Consumer Protection Act. (Mich. Comp. Laws Ann., Sec. 445.903.) This section provides that unfair, unconscionable, or deceptive methods, acts or practices in the conduct of trade or commerce are unlawful and are defined as follows:

- causing a probability of confusion or misunderstanding as to the source, sponsorship, approval, or certification of goods or services;

- using deceptive representations or deceptive designations of geographic origin in connection with goods or services;

- representing that goods or services have sponsorship, approval, characteristics, ingredients, uses, benefits, or quantities which they do not have or that a person has sponsorship, approval, status, affiliation, or connection which he does not have;

- representing that goods are new if they are deteriorated, altered, reconditioned, used, or secondhand;

- representing that goods or services are of a particular standard, quality, or grade, or that goods are of a particular style or model, if they are of another;

- disparaging the goods, services, business, or reputation of another by false or misleading representation of fact;

- advertising goods or services with intent not to dispose of those goods or services as advertised or represented;

- advertising goods or services with intent not to supply reasonably expectable public demand, unless the advertisement discloses a limitation of quantity in immediate conjunction with the advertised goods or services;

- making false or misleading statements of fact concerning the reasons for, existence of, or amounts of, price reductions;

- representing that a part, replacement, or repair service is needed when it is not;

- representing to a party to whom goods or services are supplied that the goods or services are being supplied in response to a request made by or on behalf of the party, when they are not;

- misrepresenting that because of some defect in a consumer's home the health, safety, or lives of the consumer or his family are in danger if the product or services are not purchased, when in fact the defect does not exist or the product or services would not remove the danger;

- causing a probability of confusion or of misunderstanding with respect to the authority of a salesperson, representative, or agent to negotiate the final terms of a transaction;

- causing a probability of confusion or of misunderstanding as to the legal rights, obligations, or remedies of a party to a transaction;

- causing a probability of confusion or of misunderstanding as to the terms or conditions of credit if credit is extended in a transaction;

- disclaiming or limiting the implied warranty of merchantability and fitness for use, unless a disclaimer is clearly and conspicuously disclosed;

- representing or implying that the subject of a consumer transaction will be provided promptly, or at a specified time, or within a reasonable time, if the merchant knows or has reason to know it will not be so provided;

- representing that a consumer will receive goods or services "free," "without charge," or words of similar import without clearly and conspicuously disclosing with equal prominence in immediate conjunction with the use of those words the conditions, terms, or prerequisites to the use or retention of the goods or services advertised;

- failing to reveal a material fact, the omission of which tends to mislead or deceive the consumer, and which fact could not reasonably be known by the consumer;

- entering into a consumer transaction in which the consumer waives or purports to waive a right, benefit, or immunity provided by law, unless the waiver is clearly stated and the consumer has specifically consented to it;

- failing to promptly return a deposit, down payment, or other payment in a consumer transaction, when the purchaser has rescinded, canceled, or otherwise terminated the agreement as provided in the agreement, an advertisement, or by law;

- if a purchaser in a consumer transaction traded in property which is no longer available to return, failing to promptly pay an agreed upon value or fair market value of the property when the purchaser has rescinded, canceled, or otherwise terminated the agreement as provided in the agreement, an advertisement, or by law;

- where a security interest has been acquired in a consumer transaction, failing to cancel the security interest within a specified time or an otherwise reasonable time when the purchaser has rescinded, canceled, or otherwise terminated the agreement as provided in the agreement, an advertisement, or by law;

- taking or arranging for the consumer to sign an acknowledgement, certificate, or other writing affirming acceptance, delivery, compliance with a requirement of law, or other performance, if the merchant knows or has reason to know that the statement is not true;

- representing that a consumer will receive a rebate, discount, or other benefit as an inducement for entering into a transaction, if the benefit is contingent on an event to occur subsequent to the consummation of the transaction;

- taking advantage of the consumer's inability reasonably to protect his interests by reason of disability, illiteracy, or inability to understand the language of an agreement presented by the other party to the transaction who knows or reasonably should know of the consumer's inability;

- gross discrepancies between the oral representations of the seller and the written agreement covering the same transaction or failure of the other party to the transaction to provide the promised benefits;

- charging the consumer a price which is grossly in excess of the price at which similar property or services are sold;

- causing coercion and duress as the result of the time and nature of a sales presentation;

- making a representation of fact or statement of fact material to the transaction such that a person reasonably believes the represented or suggested state of affairs to be other than it actually is; and,

- failing to reveal facts that are material to the transaction in light of representations of fact made in a positive manner.

Additional rules are made by the attorney general.

PAYMENT AND COLLECTION 13

Depending on the business you are in, you may be paid by cash, checks, credit cards, or some sort of financing arrangement such as a promissory note and mortgage. Both state and federal laws affect the type of payments you collect, and failure to follow the laws can cost you considerably.

CASH

Cash is probably the easiest form of payment and it is subject to few restrictions. The most important one is that you keep an accurate accounting of your cash transactions and that you report all of your cash income on your tax return.

Recent efforts to stop the drug trade have resulted in some serious penalties for failing to report cash transactions and for money laundering. The laws are so sweeping that even if you deal in cash in an ordinary business you may violate the law and face huge fines and imprisonment.

The most important law to be concerned with is the one requiring the filing of REPORT OF CASH PAYMENTS OVER $10,000 (IRS FORM 8300) for cash transactions of $10,000 or more. (see form 11, p.243.) A transaction does not have to happen in one day. If a person brings you smaller amounts of cash which add up to $10,000 and the government can construe them as one transaction, the form must be filed. Under this law "cash" also includes travelers' checks and money orders, but does not include cashier's checks or bank checks. For more information, Look at IRS FORM 8300 and instructions in Appendix C. (see form 11, p.243.)

CHECKS

It is important to accept checks in your business. While there is a small percentage which will be bad, most checks will be good, and you will be able to accommodate more customers. To avoid having problems, follow the following rules.

ACCEPTING CHECKS

Most major credit card companies forbid a business to require a customer to provide their credit card number in order to pay by or cash a check.

BAD CHECKS

It is a crime in Michigan to give someone a bad check. If a bad check is given on an existing account, there are increasing penalties based upon the amount of the check and number of times the person has been convicted of the offense. Fines range from $100 to $500, and jail terms range from ninety-three days to thirteen months. If a check is written on a closed account, the penalties are a fine of up to $500 and up to two years in jail. (Mich. Comp. Laws Ann., Secs. 750.131 & 750.131a.)

Anyone giving you a bad check should be notified in writing that the check has been dishonored by the bank, and that he or she has five days in which to make payment (including any bank charges and other costs). To aid in prosecution, you should be able to identify the person who gave you the check. To do this you should require identification and write down the sources of identification on the face of the check.

Do not accept post-dated checks. If you are going to be accepting a lot of checks, you should check with the prosecuting attorneys office in your county for what you will need to do to obtain prosecution of those giving you bad checks.

REFUNDS AFTER ACCEPTING A CHECK

A popular scam is for a person to purchase something by using a check and then come back the next day demanding a cash refund. After making the refund, the business discovers the initial check bounced. Do not make refunds until checks clear.

CREDIT CARDS

In our buy-now, pay-later society, charge cards can add greatly to your sales potential, especially with large, discretionary purchases. For MasterCard, Visa and Discover, the fees are about 2%, and this amount is easily paid for by the extra purchases that the cards allow.

American Express charges 4% to 5% and you may decide this is not worth paying, since almost everyone who has an American Express card also has another card. You will find that affluent purchasers prefer to use American Express.

For businesses that have a retail outlet there is usually no problem getting merchant status. Most commercial banks can handle it. Discover can also set you up to accept their card as well as MasterCard and Visa, and they will wire the money into your bank account daily.

For mail order businesses, especially those operating out of the home, it is much harder to get merchant status. This is because of the number of scams in which large amounts are charged, no products are shipped and the company folds. At one point, even a business offering to post a large cash bond and let the bank hold the charges for six months was turned down.

Today things are a little better. Some companies are even soliciting merchants. But beware of those which charge exorbitant fees (such as $5 or $10 per order for "processing"). One good thing about American Express is that they will accept mail order companies operating out of the home. However, not as many people have their cards as others.

Some companies open a small storefront (or share one) to get merchant status, then process mostly mail orders. The processors usually do not want to accept you if you will do more than 50% mail order; but if you do not have many complaints, you may be allowed to process mostly mail orders. Whatever you do, keep your charge customers happy so that they do not complain.

You might be tempted to try to run your charges through another business. This may be okay if you actually sell your products through them, but if you run your business charges through their account the other business may lose its merchant status. People who bought a book by mail from you and then have a charge on their statement from a florist shop will probably call the credit card company saying that they never bought anything from the florist shop. Too many of these and the account will be closed.

Financing Laws

Some businesses can more easily make sales if they finance the purchases themselves. If the business has enough capital to do this it can earn extra profits on the financing terms. However, because of abuses, many consumer protection laws have been passed by both the federal and state governments.

Federal Law

Regulation Z. Two important federal laws regarding financing are called the Truth in Lending Act and the Fair Credit Billing Act. These are implemented by what is called *Regulation Z* (commonly known as *Reg. Z*), issued by the Board of Governors of the Federal Reserve System. It is contained in Volume 12 of the Code of Federal Regulations, page 226. This is a very complicated law and some have said that no business can be sure to be in compliance.

The regulation covers all transactions in which four conditions are met:

1. credit is offered;

2. the offering of credit is done regularly;

3. there is a finance charge for the credit or there is a written agreement with more than four payments; or,

4. the credit is for personal, family, or household purposes.

It also covers credit card transactions where only the first two conditions are met. It applies to leases if the consumer ends up paying the full value and keeping the item leased. It does not apply to the following transactions:

- transactions with businesses or agricultural purposes;

- transactions with organizations such as corporations or the government;

- transactions of over $25,000 which are not secured by the consumer's dwelling;

- credit involving public utilities;

- credit involving securities or commodities; or,

- home fuel budget plans.

The way for a small business to avoid Reg. Z violations is to avoid transactions which meet the conditions or to make sure all transactions fall under the exceptions. For many businesses this is easy. Instead of extending credit to customers, accept credit cards and let the credit card company extend the credit. However, if your customers usually do not have credit cards or if you are in a business, such as used car sales, which often extends credit, you should consult a lawyer knowledgeable about Reg. Z. Or, get a copy for yourself.

MICHIGAN LAWS

Michigan also has laws regarding financing arrangements. Anyone engaged in installment sales in Michigan should carefully review the latest versions of the following statutes:

- Retail Installment Sales Act (Mich. Comp. Laws Ann., Sec. 445.851.)

- Home Improvement Financing Act (Mich. Comp. Laws Ann., Sec. 445.1101.)

- Rental-purchase Agreement Act (Mich. Comp. Laws Ann., Sec. 445.951.)

USURY

Charging an illegally high rate of interest is *usury*. In Michigan, the maximum rate of interest you may charge is 7%. (Mich. Comp. Laws Ann., Sec. 438.31.) However, there are exceptions, such as for credit cards and mortgages. Also, if the borrower is a business, any rate may be charged if agreed to in writing. (Mich. Comp. Laws Ann., Sec. 438.61.)

The penalty for charging in excess of the legal rate is that the borrower does not have to pay any interest or other penalties such as late payment charges, and the lender has to pay the borrower's attorney's fees and court costs. (Mich. Comp. Laws Ann., Sec. 438.32.) Anyone charging or receiving interest at a rate of over 25% is guilty of a misdemeanor carrying a penalty of a fine up to $10,000 and up to five years in jail. Possession of usurious loan records carries a penalty of a fine up to $1,000 and up to one year in jail. (Mich. Comp. Laws Ann., Secs. 438.41 & 438.42.)

COLLECTIONS

When trying to collect money you are owed, you need to be careful not to violate any state or federal laws regarding collection practices.

FEDERAL LAWS The Fair Debt Collection Practices Act of 1977 bans the use of deception, harassment, and other unreasonable acts in the collection of debts.

The Federal Trade Commission has issued some rules which prohibit deceptive representations such as pretending to be in the motion picture industry, the government, or a credit bureau, and/or using questionnaires which do not say that they are for the purpose of collecting a debt. (C.F.R., Title 16, Ch I, Part 237.)

MICHIGAN LAW Debt collection practices are controlled by the provisions of Michigan law. (Mich. Comp. Laws Ann., beginning with Sec. 445.251.) This law forbids:

- communicating with a debtor in a misleading or deceptive manner, such as using the stationery of an attorney or credit bureau, unless the person is an attorney, or a credit bureau and discloses it is the collection department of the credit bureau;

- using forms or instruments which simulate the appearance of judicial process;

- using seals or printed forms of a government agency or instrumentality;

- using forms that may otherwise induce the belief that they have judicial or official sanction;

- making an inaccurate, misleading, untrue, or deceptive statement or claim in a communication to collect a debt or concealing or not revealing the purpose of a communication when it is made in connection with collecting a debt;

- misrepresenting in a communication with a debtor one or more of the following:
  - the legal status of a legal action being taken or threatened;
  - the legal rights of the creditor or debtor;
  - that the nonpayment of a debt will result in the debtor's arrest or imprisonment, or the seizure, garnishment, attachment, or sale of the debtor's property; or,
  - that accounts have been turned over to innocent purchaser for value.

- communicating with a debtor without accurately disclosing the caller's identity or cause expenses to the debtor for a long distance telephone call, telegram, or other charge;

- communicating with a debtor, except through billing procedure when the debtor is actively represented by an attorney, the attorney's name and address are known, and the attorney has been contacted in writing by the credit grantor or the credit grantor's representative or agent, unless the attorney representing the debtor fails to answer written communication or fails to discuss the claim on its merits within thirty days after receipt of the written communication;

- communicating information relating to a debtor's indebtedness to an employer or an employer's agent unless the communication is specifically authorized in writing by the debtor subsequent to the forwarding of the claim for collection, the communication is in response to an inquiry initiated by the debtor's employer or the employer's agent, or the communication is for the purpose of acquiring location information about the debtor;

- using or employing, in connection with collection of a claim, a person acting as a peace or law enforcement officer or any other officer authorized to serve legal papers;

- using or threatening to use physical violence in connection with collection of a claim;

- publishing, causing to be published, or threatening to publish lists of debtors, except for credit reporting purposes, when in response to a specific inquiry from a prospective credit grantor about a debtor;

- using a shame card, shame automobile, or otherwise bring to public notice that the consumer is a debtor, except with respect to a legal proceeding which is instituted;

- using a harassing, oppressive, or abusive method to collect a debt, including causing a telephone to ring or engaging a person in a telephone conversation repeatedly, continuously, or at unusual times or places which are known to be inconvenient to the debtor. All communications shall be made from 8 a.m. to 9 p.m. unless the debtor expressly agrees in writing to communications at another time. All telephone communications made from 9 p.m. to 8 a.m. shall be presumed to be made at an inconvenient time in the absence of facts to the contrary;

- using profane or obscene language;

- using a method contrary to a postal law or regulation to collect an account;

- failing to implement a procedure designed to prevent a violation by an employee;

- communicating with a consumer regarding a debt by postcard; and,

- employing a person required to be licensed under article 9 of Act No. 299 of the Public Acts of 1980, being section 339.901 to 339.916 of the Michigan Compiled Laws, to collect a claim unless that person is licensed under article 9 of Act No. 299 of the Public Acts of 1980.

The attorney general may issue a cease and desist order for violations. An administrative hearing may be requested within thirty days of the effective date of the cease and desist order. Failure to cease and desist can result in a circuit court action, filed by the attorney general, which may result in a fine of up to $500 for each violation. The attorney general may also ask the circuit court to issue an injunction (an order that the business stop the illegal activity).

BUSINESS RELATIONS LAW 14

In this chapter we will discuss the numerous federal and Michigan laws governing relations between businesses.

THE UNIFORM COMMERCIAL CODE

The *Uniform Commercial Code (UCC)* is a set of laws regulating numerous aspects of doing business. To avoid having a patchwork of different laws around the fifty states, a national group drafted this set of uniform laws.

Although some states modified some sections of the laws, the code is basically the same in most of the states. In Michigan the UCC is contained in the statutes. (Mich. Comp. Laws Ann., beginning with Sec. 440.1101.) The UCC is divided into chapters, each of which is concerned with a different aspect of commercial relations such as sales, warranties, bank deposits, commercial paper, and bulk transfers.

Businesses that wish to know their rights in all types of transactions should obtain a copy of the UCC and become familiar with it. It is especially useful in transactions between merchants. However, the meaning is not always clear from a reading of the statutes. In law school, students usually spend a full semester studying each chapter of this law.

UNLAWFUL BUSINESS PRACTICES

While competition between businesses is generally considered healthy and desirable for the economy, certain activities designed to get an advantage over your competition are illegal.

FEDERAL LAW

Robinson-Patman Act of 1936. This Act prohibits businesses from injuring competition by offering the same goods at different prices to different buyers. It also requires that promotional allowances must be made on proportionally the same terms to all buyers.

Sherman Antitrust Act of 1890. This is one of the earliest federal laws affecting business. The purpose of the law was to protect competition in the marketplace by prohibiting monopolies. For example, one large company might buy out all of its competitors and then raise prices to astronomical levels. (In recent years, this law was used to break up AT&T.)

Examples of some things that are prohibited are:

- agreements between competitors to sell at the same prices;

- agreements between competitors on how much will be sold or produced;

- agreements between competitors to divide up a market;

- refusing to sell one product without a second product; or,

- exchanging information among competitors which results in similarity of prices.

As a new business, you probably will not be in a position to violate the Sherman Antitrust Act, but you should be aware of it in case a larger competitor tries to put you out of business.

MICHIGAN LAW

Under Michigan law, it is unlawful to have any contract, combination or conspiracy to restrain trade or to monopolize trade or commerce in a relevant market controlling, fixing or maintaining prices. The penalty for violation is up to two years in jail, and a fine of up to $10,000 for an individual and up to $1,000,000 for other entities. However, no prosecution under this law will be allowed if there is already a prosecution under the Federal Sherman anti-trust act for the same transactions. (beginning with Mich. Comp. Laws Ann., beginning with Sec. 445.771.)

INTELLECTUAL PROPERTY PROTECTION

As a business owner you should know enough about intellectual property law to protect your own creations and to keep from violating the rights of others. *Intellectual property* is that which is the product of human creativity, such as writings, designs, inventions, melodies and processes. They are things that can be stolen without being physically taken. For example, if you write a book, someone can steal the words from your book without stealing a physical copy of it.

As the Internet grows, intellectual property is becoming more valuable. Business owners should take the action necessary to protect their company's intellectual property. Additionally, business owners should know intellectual property law to be sure that they do not violate the rights of others. Even an unknowing violation of the law can result in stiff fines and penalties.

The following are the types of intellectual property and the ways to protect them.

PATENT   A *patent* is protection given to new and useful inventions, discoveries and designs. To be entitled to a patent, a work must be completely new and "unobvious." A patent is granted to the first inventor who files for the patent. Once an invention is patented, no one else can make use of that invention, even if they discover it independently after a lifetime of research. A patent protects an invention for 17 years; for designs it is 3-1/2, 7 or 14 years. Patents cannot be renewed. The patent application must clearly explain how to make the invention so that when the patent expires, others will be able to freely make and use the invention. Patents are registered with the United States Patent and Trademark

Office (PTO). Examples of things that would be patentable would be mechanical devices or new drug formulas.

COPYRIGHT

A *copyright* is protection given to "original works of authorship," such as written works, musical works, visual works, performance works, or computer software programs. A copyright exists from the moment of creation, but one cannot register a copyright until it has been fixed in tangible form. Also, one cannot copyright titles, names, or slogans. A copyright currently gives the author and his heirs exclusive right to his work for the life of the author plus seventy years.

Copyrights first registered before 1978 last for 95 years. (This was previously 75 years but was extended 20 years to match the European system.) Copyrights are registered with the Register of Copyrights at the Library of Congress. Examples of works that would be copyrightable are books, paintings, songs, poems, plays, drawings, and films.

TRADEMARK

A *trademark* is protection given to a name or symbol which is used to distinguish one person's goods or services from those of others. It can consist of letters, numerals, packaging, labeling, musical notes, colors or a combination of these. If a trademark is used on services as opposed to goods, it is called a *service mark*.

A trademark lasts indefinitely if it is used continuously and renewed properly. Trademarks are registered with the United States Patent and Trademark Office and with individual states. (This is explained further in Chapter 3.) Examples of trademarks are the "Chrysler" name on automobiles, the red border on TIME magazine and the shape of the Coca-Cola bottle.

TRADE SECRETS

A *trade secret* is some information or process that provides a commercial advantage that is protected by keeping it a secret. Examples of trade secrets may be a list of successful distributors, the formula for Coca-Cola, or some unique source code in a computer program. Trade secrets are not registered anywhere, they are protected by the fact that they are not disclosed. They are protected only for as long as they are kept secret. If you independently discover the formula for Coca-Cola tomorrow, you can freely market it. (But you cannot use the trademark "Coca-Cola" on your product to market it.)

Non-protectable Creations

Some things are just not protectable. Such things as ideas, systems and discoveries are not allowed any protection under any law. If you have a great idea, such as selling packets of hangover medicine in bars, you cannot stop others from doing the same thing. If you invent a new medicine, you can patent it; if you pick a distinctive name for it, you can register it as a trademark; if you create a unique picture or instructions for the package, you can copyright them. But you cannot stop others from using your basic business idea of marketing hangover medicine in bars.

Notice the subtle differences between the protective systems available. If you invent something two days after someone else does, you cannot even use it yourself if the other person has patented it. But if you write the same poem as someone else and neither of you copied the other, both of you can copyright the poem. If you patent something, you can have the exclusive rights to it for the term of the patent, but you must disclose how others can make it after the patent expires. However, if you keep it a trade secret, you have exclusive rights as long as no one learns the secret.

We are in a time of transition of the law of intellectual property. Every year new changes are made in the laws and new forms of creativity win protection. For more information, you should consult a new edition of a book on these types of property. Some are listed at the end of this book.

ENDLESS LAWS 15

The state of Michigan and the federal government have numerous laws and rules that apply to every aspect of every type of business. There are laws governing even such things as fence posts, hosiery, rabbit raising, refund policies, frozen desserts and advertising. Every business is affected by one or another of these laws.

Some activities are covered by both state and federal laws. In such cases you must obey the stricter of the rules. In addition, more than one agency of the state or federal government may have rules governing your business. Each of these may have the power to investigate violations and impose fines or other penalties.

Penalties for violations of these laws can range from a warning to a criminal fine and even jail time. In some cases, employees can sue for damages. Recently, employees have been given awards of millions of dollars from employers who violated the law. Since "ignorance of the law is no excuse," it is your duty to learn which laws apply to your business, or to risk these penalties.

Very few people in business know the laws which apply to their businesses. If you take the time to learn them you can become an expert in your field, and avoid problems with regulators. You can also fight back if one of your competitors uses some illegal method to compete with you.

Some of the Federal laws and rules affecting various businesses are referenced in this chapter. Some of the state laws are found in the following section of this chapter.

No one could possibly know all the rules that affect business, much less comply with them all. The Interstate Commerce Commission alone has 40 trillion (that is 40 million million or 40,000,000,000,000) rates on its books telling the transportation industry what it should charge. But if you keep up with the important rules you will stay out of trouble and have more chance of success.

FEDERAL LAWS

The federal laws that are most likely to affect small businesses are rules of the Federal Trade Commission (FTC). The FTC has some rules which affect many businesses such as the rules about labeling, warranties, and mail order sales. Other rules affect only certain industries.

If you sell goods by mail you should send for their booklet, *A Business Guide to the Federal Trade Commission's Mail Order Rule*. If you are going to be involved in a certain industry such as those listed below, or using warranties or your own labeling, you should ask for their latest information on the subject. The address is:

> Federal Trade Commission
> Washington, DC 20580

The rules of the FTC are contained in the Code of Federal Regulations (CFR) in Chapter 16. Some of the industries covered are:

INDUSTRY	PART
Adhesive Compositions	235
Aerosol Products Used for Frosting Cocktail Glasses	417
Automobiles (New car fuel economy advertising)	259
Barber Equipment and Supplies	248
Binoculars	402
Business Opportunities and Franchises	436
Cigarettes	408

INDUSTRY	PART
Decorative Wall Paneling	243
Dog and Cat Food	241
Dry Cell Batteries	403
Extension Ladders	418
Fallout Shelters	229
Feather and Down Products	253
Fiber Glass Curtains	413
Food (Games of Chance)	419
Funerals	453
Gasoline (Octane posting)	306
Gasoline	419
Greeting Cards	244
Home Entertainment Amplifiers	432
Home Insulation	460
Hosiery	22
Household Furniture	250
Jewelry	23
Ladies' Handbags	247
Law Books	256
Light Bulbs	409
Luggage and Related Products	24
Mail Order Insurance	234
Mail Order Merchandise	435
Men's and Boys' Tailored Clothing	412
Metallic Watch Band	19
Mirrors	21
Nursery	18
Ophthalmic Practices	456
Photographic Film and Film Processing	242
Private Vocational and Home Study Schools	254
Radiation Monitoring Instruments	232
Retail Food Stores (Advertising)	424
Shell Homes	230
Shoes	231
Sleeping Bags	400
Tablecloths and Related Products	404
Television Sets	410
Textile Wearing Apparel	423
Textiles	236
Tires	228
Used Automobile Parts	20
Used Lubricating Oil	406
Used Motor Vehicles	455
Waist Belts	405
Watches	245
Wigs and Hairpieces	252

Some other federal laws that affect businesses are as follows:

- Alcohol Administration Act (U.S.C., Title 29, beginning with Section 201.)

- Child Protection and Toy Safety Act (1969)

- Clean Water Act (U.S.C., Title 33)

- Comprehensive Smokeless Tobacco Health Education Act (1986). See also C.F.R., Title 16, Ch. I, Part 307 for rules.

- Consumer Credit Protection Act (1968)

- Consumer Product Safety Act (1972)

- Energy Policy and Conservation Act. See also C.F.R., Title 16, Ch. I, Part 305 for rules about energy cost labeling.

- Environmental Pesticide Control Act of 1972

- Fair Credit Reporting Act (1970)

- Fair Packaging and Labeling Act (1966). See also C.F.R., Title 16, Ch. I, Parts 500-503 for rules.

- Flammable Fabrics Act (1953). See also C.F.R., Title 16, Ch. II, Parts 1602-1632 for rules.

- Food, Drug, and Cosmetic Act (U.S.C., Title 21, beginning with Sec. 301.)

- Fur Products Labeling Act (1951). See also C.F.R., Title 16, Ch. I, Part 301 for rules.

- Hazardous Substances Act (1960)

- Hobby Protection Act. See also C.F.R., Title 16, Ch. I, Part 304 for rules.

- Insecticide, Fungicide, and Rodenticide Act (U.S.C., Title 7, beginning with Sec. 136.)

- Magnuson-Moss Warranty Act. See also C.F.R., Title 16, Ch. I, Part 239 for rules.

- Poison Prevention Packaging Act of 1970. See also C.F.R., Title 16, Ch. II, Parts 1700-1702 for rules.

- Solid Waste Disposal Act (U.S.C., Title 42, beginning with Sec. 6901.)

- Textile Fiber Products Identification Act. See also C.F.R., Title 16, Ch. I, Part 303 for rules.

- Toxic Substance Control Act (U.S.C., Title 15.)

- Wool Products Labeling Act (1939). See also C.F.R., Title 16, Ch. I, Part 300 for rules.

- Nutrition Labeling and Education Act of 1990. See also C.F.R., Title 21, Ch. 1, Subchapter B

- Food Safety Enforcement Enhancement Act of 1997.

A law passed by Congress in late 1990 imposed new packaging and labeling requirements for food items. The rules under this law are contained in Title 21 of the CFR. And of course, we can't overlook the Americans with Disabilities Act (ADA), which mandates what businesses must do to accommodate persons with handicaps (for more information on the ADA, see Chapter 10). For more information on this law call 202-663-4900, and for copies of publications about the ADA, call 800-669-3392.

Michigan Laws

Michigan has numerous laws regulating specific types of professions, businesses, or certain activities of businesses, and many of these are listed in Chapter 6. Even if your profession or business is not regulated, as a part of your business operation you may engage in some kind of activity that is regulated or subject to some kind of legal restrictions. The three best sources of information to avoid problems are the trade organization for your type of business, the various state and local governmental agencies with whom you come in contact, and the index to the *Michigan Compiled Laws Annotated.*

Bookkeeping and Accounting 16

It is beyond the scope of this book to explain all the intricacies of setting up a business's bookkeeping and accounting systems. However, if you do not set up an understandable bookkeeping system your business will undoubtedly fail.

Without accurate records of where your income is coming from and where it is going you will be unable to increase your profits, lower your expenses, obtain needed financing or make the right decisions in all areas of your business. The time to decide how you will handle your bookkeeping is when you open your business, not a year later when it is tax time.

Initial Bookkeeping

If you do not understand business taxation you should pick up a good book on the subject as well as the IRS tax guide for your type of business (proprietorship, partnership, or corporation). A few good books on the subject are listed in the "For Further Reference" section of this book on page 179.

The IRS tax book for small businesses is Publication 334, *Tax Guide for Small Businesses*. There are also instruction booklets for each type of business's form, Schedule C for proprietorships, Form 1120 or 1120S for C corporations and S corporations, and 1165 for partnerships and businesses that are taxed like partnerships (LLCs, LLPs).

Keep in mind that the IRS does not give you the best advice for saving on taxes and does not give you the other side of contested issues. For that you need a private tax guide or advisor.

The most important thing to do is to set up your bookkeeping so that you can easily fill out your monthly, quarterly, and annual tax returns.

The best way to do this is to get copies of the returns, not the totals that you will need to supply and set up your bookkeeping system to group those totals.

For example, for a sole proprietorship you will use "Schedule C" to report business income and expenses to the IRS at the end of the year. Use the categories on that form to sort your expenses. To make your job especially easy, every time you pay a bill, put the category number on the check.

ACCOUNTANTS

Most likely your new business will not be able to afford hiring an accountant to handle your books, but that is good. Doing them yourself will force you to learn about business accounting and taxation. The worst way to run a business is to know nothing about the tax laws and turn everything over to an accountant at the end of the year to find out what is due.

You should know the basics of tax law before making basic decisions such as whether to buy or rent equipment or premises. You should understand accounting so you can time your financial affairs appropriately. If you were a boxer who only needed to win fights, you could turn everything over to an accountant. If your business needs to buy supplies, inventory, or equipment and provides goods or services throughout the year, you need to at least have a basic understanding of the system you are working within.

Once you can afford an accountant you should weigh the cost against your time and the risk you will make an error. Even if you think you know enough to do your own corporate tax return, you might take it to an accountant one year to see if you have been missing any deductions that you didn't know about. You might decide that the money saved is worth the cost of the accountant's services.

COMPUTER PROGRAMS

Today every business should keep its books by computer. There are inexpensive programs such as Quicken that can instantly provide you with reports of your income and expenses and the right figures to plug into your tax returns.

Most programs offer a tax program each year that will take all of your information and print it out on the current year's tax forms.

TAX TIPS

Here are a few tax tips that may help businesses save money:

- Usually when you buy equipment for a business you must amortize the cost over several years. That is, you don't deduct it all when you buy it, you take, say, 25% of the cost off your taxes each year for four years. (The time is determined by the theoretical usefulness of the item.) However, small businesses are allowed to write off the entire cost of a limited amount of items under Internal Revenue Code, Section 179. If you have income to shelter, use it.

- Owners of S corporations do not have to pay social security or medicare taxes on the part of their profits that is not considered salary. As long as you pay yourself a reasonable salary, other money you take out is not subject to these taxes.

- Do not neglect to deposit withholding taxes for your own salary or profits. Besides being a large sum to come up with at once in April, there are penalties which must be paid for failure to do so.

- Be sure to keep track of, and remit, your employees' withholding. You will be personally liable for them even if your business is a corporation.

- If you keep track of your use of your car for business you can deduct 31.5¢ per mile (this may go up or down each year). If you use your car for business a considerable amount of time you may be able to depreciate it.

- If your business is a corporation and if you designate the stock as "section 1244 stock" then if the business fails you are able to get a much better deduction for the loss.

- By setting up a retirement plan you can exempt up to 20% of your salary from income tax. But don't use money you might need later. There are penalties for taking it out of the retirement plan.

- When you buy things which will be resold or made into products which will be resold (i.e., you are buying from a wholesaler), you do not have to pay sales tax on those purchases.

PAYING FEDERAL TAXES 17

All businesses need to be concerned with one or more types of federal taxes. In this chapter we will discuss the federal income tax, withholding of taxes from employee paychecks, federal excise taxes, and federal unemployment compensation taxes.

FEDERAL INCOME TAX

The manner in which each type of business pays taxes is as follows:

PROPRIETORSHIP

An individual reports profits and expenses on Schedule C attached to the usual Form 1040 and pays tax on all of the net income of the business. Each quarter Form ES-1040 must be filed along with payment of one-quarter of the amount of income tax and social security taxes estimated to be due for the year.

PARTNERSHIP

A partnership files a return showing the income and expenses but pays no tax. Each partner is given a form showing his share of the profits or losses and reports these on Schedule E of Form 1040. Each quarter, Form ES-1040 must be filed by each partner along with payment of one-quarter of the amount of income tax and social security taxes estimated to be due for the year.

C CORPORATION

A regular corporation is a separate taxpayer, and pays tax on its profits after deducting all expenses, including officers' salaries. If dividends are distributed, they are paid out of after-tax dollars, and the shareholders pay tax a second time when they receive the dividends. If a corporation needs to accumulate money for investment, it may be able to do so at lower tax rates than the shareholders. But if all profits will be distributed to shareholders, the double-taxation may be excessive unless all income is paid as salaries. A C corporation files Form 1120.

S CORPORATION

A small corporation has the option of being taxed like a partnership. If Form 2553 is filed by the corporation and accepted by the Internal Revenue Service, the S corporation will only file an informational return listing profits and expenses. Then each shareholder will be taxed on a proportional share of the profits (or be able to deduct a proportional share of the losses). Unless a corporation will make a large profit which will not be distributed, S-status is usually best in the beginning.

An S corporation files Form 1120S and distributes Form K-1 to each shareholder. If any money is taken out by a shareholder which is not listed as wages subject to withholding, then the shareholder will usually have to file form ES-1040 each quarter along with payment of the estimated withholding on the withdrawals.

LIMITED LIABILITY COMPANY

Limited liability companies will, in most cases, be taxed as partnerships, passing on their income and losses to the owners. However, if the entity has too many corporate attributes, it may be taxed as a corporation.

TAX WORKSHOPS AND BOOKLETS

The IRS offers publications and recorded information, and conducts workshops to inform businesses about the tax laws. (Do not expect an in-depth study of the loopholes.) Recorded information can be obtained by calling 313-961-4282 in Detroit, and 800-829-4477 elsewhere. Publications may be obtained by calling 800-829-3676. Some of the publications you may want to obtain are:

PUBLICATION NUMBER	TITLE
334	Tax Guide for Small Business
505	Tax Withholding and Estimated Tax
533	Self-Employment Tax
541	Tax Information on Partnerships
542	Tax Information on Corporations
583	Taxpayers Starting a Business
589	Information on S Corporations
910	Guide to Free Tax Services
937	Employment Taxes and Information Returns

The IRS also conducts seminars under the Small Business Tax Education Program (S.T.E.P.). For information about S.T.E.P. contact your local IRS office or:

Taxpayer Education Coordinator
P.O. Box 330500, Room 1196
Detroit, MI 48232-6500
313-226-3674
Toll free: 800-829-1040

You may also visit, or write to, the following IRS offices (unless otherwise noted below, office hours are 8:00 a.m. to 4:30 p.m., Monday, Tuesday, Thursday, and Friday; and 8:30 a.m. to 4:30 p.m., Wednesday):

I.R.S. LOCAL OFFICES

Ann Arbor:
Eisenhower Corporate Park
2850 S. Industrial, Ste. 600
Ann Arbor, MI 48104

Detroit:
McNamara Bldg., Rm. 2040
477 Michigan Ave.
Detroit, MI 48226-2597

Flint:
815 South Saginaw
Flint, MI 48502

Grand Rapids:
678 Front Street NW, Suite 200
Grand Rapids, MI 49504

Kalamazoo:
Trestlebridge Center
5220 Lovers Lane, 2nd Floor
Kalamazoo, MI 49003

Lansing:
Southwind Office Park I
921 West Holmes
Lansing, MI 48910

Livonia:
37405 Ann Arbor Road
Livonia, MI 48150

Marquette:
1055 West Baraga
Marquette, MI 49855

Mt. Pleasant:
316 North Mission
Mt. Pleasant, MI 48858
Hours: Tu, 8am-4pm

Pontiac:
Pontiac Place Building 140
S. Saginaw, Room 101
Pontiac, MI 48342

Saginaw:
4901 Town Center, Room 100
Vanguard Building
Saginaw, MI 49604

Traverse City:
Logan Place West
3241 Racquet Club Drive
Traverse City, MI 49684
Tuesday only, 8am-4:30pm

FEDERAL WITHHOLDING, SOCIAL SECURITY, AND MEDICARE TAXES

If you need basic information on business tax returns, the IRS publishes a rather large booklet which answers most questions and is available for free. Call or write them and ask for Publication No. 334, *Tax Guide for Small Business.* You should be able to find an IRS toll-free number in the phone book under U. S. Government/Internal Revenue Service. If you want more creative answers and tax saving information, you should find a good local accountant or tax attorney. But to get started you will need the following:

EMPLOYER IDENTIFICATION NUMBER

If you are a sole proprietor with no employees, you can use your social security number for your business. If you have employees, or are a corporation or partnership, you must obtain an *employer identification number,* by filing APPLICATION FOR EMPLOYER IDENTIFICATION NUMBER **(IRS FORM SS-4)**. (see form 2, p.207.) In about three weeks you will get your number, which you will need to open bank accounts for the business. A sample filled-in form may be found in Appendix B. A blank form with instructions is in Appendix C.

If you need a number quickly, you may obtain one by telephone by calling 606-292-5467, Monday through Friday, between 9:30 a.m. and 5:15 p.m. You must have your **IRS FORM SS-4** filled out before you call, and you will still need to mail or fax the form with your number on it. You can fax it to 606-292-5760 between 10:00 a.m. and 5:30 p.m. If you mail it in, send it to:

Internal Revenue Service
Entity Control
Stop #422
Cincinnati, OH 45999

EMPLOYEE'S WITHHOLDING ALLOWANCE CERTIFICATE	You must have each employee fill out an EMPLOYEE'S WITHHOLDING ALLOWANCE CERTIFICATE **(IRS FORM W-4)** to calculate the amount of federal taxes to be deducted and to obtain their social security numbers. (The number of allowances on this form is used with IRS Circular E, Publication 15, to figure out the exact deductions.) A sample filled-in form may be found in Appendix B. A blank is in Appendix C. (see form 5, p.221.)
FEDERAL TAX DEPOSIT COUPON	After making withholdings from employees' wages, you must deposit them at a bank that is authorized to accept such funds. If, at the end of any month, you have over $1,000 in withheld taxes (including your contribution to FICA), you must make a deposit prior to the 15th of the following month. If, on the 3rd, 7th, 11th, 19th, 22nd, or 25th of any month, you have over $3,000 in withheld taxes, you must make a deposit within three banking days. The deposit is made using the coupons in the Form 8109 booklet. A sample coupon is in Appendix B.
ESTIMATED TAX PAYMENT VOUCHER	Sole proprietors and partners often take money from their businesses without the formality of withholding. However, they are still required to make deposits of income and FICA taxes each quarter. If more than $500 is due in April on a person's 1040 form, then not enough money was withheld each quarter and a penalty is assessed unless the person falls into an exception.

The quarterly withholding is submitted on Form 1040-ES on the 15th of April, June, September, and January of each year. If these days fall on a weekend, then the due date is the following Monday. The worksheet with Form 1040-ES can be used to determine the amount to pay.

NOTE: *One of the exceptions to the rule is that if you withhold the same amount as last year's tax bill, you do not have to pay a penalty. This is usually a lot easier than filling out the 1040-ES worksheet.*

A sample Form 1040-ES may be found in Appendix B, page 198.

EMPLOYER'S QUARTERLY TAX RETURN	Each quarter you must file Form 941, reporting your federal withholding and FICA taxes. If you owe more than $1,000 at the end of the quarter, you are required to make a deposit at the end of the month in which you have $1,000 in withholding. The deposits are made to the

159

Federal Reserve Bank or an authorized financial institution on Form 501. Most banks are authorized to accept deposits. If you owe more than $3,000 for any month, you must make a deposit at any point in the month in which you owe $3,000. After you file **IRS FORM SS-4**, the 941 forms will be sent to you automatically if you checked the box saying that you expect to have employees.

WAGE AND TAX STATEMENT

At the end of each year, you are required to issue a W-2 form to each employee. This form shows the amount of wages paid to the employee during the year, as well as the amounts withheld for taxes, social security, medicare, and other deductions. A sample W-2 form may be found in Appendix B, page 199.

MISCELLANEOUS INCOME

If you pay at least $600 to a person other than an employee (such as an independent contractor), you must file a Form 1099 for that person, along with Form 1096, which is a summary sheet.

Many people are not aware of this law and fail to file these forms, but they are required for such things as services, royalties, rents, awards and prizes that you pay to individuals (but not to corporations). The rules for this are quite complicated, so you should either obtain "Package 1099" from IRS, or consult your accountant. Sample 1099 and 1096 forms are in Appendix B, pages 200 and 201.

EARNED INCOME CREDIT

Persons who are not liable to pay income tax, may have the right to a check from the government because of the "Earned Income Credit." You are required to notify your employees of this. You can satisfy this requirement with one of the following:

- a W-2 Form with the notice on the back;

- a substitute for the W-2 with a notice on it;

- a copy of Notice 797; or,

- a written statement with the wording from Notice 797.

A Notice 797 can be obtained by calling 800-829-3676.

FEDERAL EXCISE TAXES

Excise taxes are taxes on certain activities or items. Most federal excise taxes have been eliminated since World War II, but a few remain. Some things that are subject to federal excise taxes are tobacco, alcohol, gasoline, tires and inner tubes, some trucks and trailers, firearms, ammunition, bows, arrows, fishing equipment, the use of highway vehicles over 55,000 pounds, aircraft, wagering, telephone and teletype services, coal, hazardous wastes, and vaccines. If you are involved in any of these, you should obtain the IRS publication #510, *Information on Excise Taxes*.

UNEMPLOYMENT COMPENSATION TAXES

You must pay federal unemployment taxes if you paid wages of $1,500 or more in any quarter, or if you had at least one employee for twenty calendar weeks. The federal tax amount is 0.8% of the first $7,000 of wages paid each employee. If more than $100 is due by the end of any quarter (if you paid $12,500 in wages for the quarter), then IRS Form 508 must be filed with an authorized financial institution or the Federal Reserve Bank in your area. You will receive IRS Form 508 when you obtain your employer identification number.

You must file Form 940 or Form 940EZ at the end of each year, as your annual report of federal unemployment taxes. IRS will send you the form. For more information, call the IRS at 800-829-1040.

NOTE: *There are also state unemployment compensation taxes, which are discussed in the next chapter.*

PAYING MICHIGAN TAXES 18

Depending upon the details of your particular business, you may need to be concerned with several types of Michigan taxes (i.e., sales, use, single business, motor fuel, and tobacco products taxes). You will need to complete a REGISTRATION FOR MICHIGAN TAXES form (Form C-3400) if any of these taxes apply to your business. (see form 7, p.225.) A copy of the registration form, completed for a fictional business, may be found in Appendix B on page 192, and a blank form with instructions is contained in Appendix C. (see form 7, p.225.)

Approximately four to six weeks after you file your registration form, you will receive your tax license and any necessary reporting forms. To obtain forms, or if you have general questions, you can call the Michigan Department of Treasury, Registration Section at 800-367-6263, or use the order form in Appendix C. (see form 6, p.223.)

If you have employees, you will also need to be concerned with the Michigan unemployment tax, and withholding state income tax from your employees' paychecks. This chapter will provide you with a summary of information about each of these taxes.

Finally, if you receive income that is not wages, you will need to file quarterly tax estimates of both Michigan and Federal income taxes.

SALES AND USE TAX

If you will be selling goods at retail, you must register and collect Michigan Sales Tax. This applies to tangible personal property sold to the end user from a location in Michigan. It does not apply to wholesalers. You will need to register for Michigan Use Tax if you:

- lease tangible personal property in Michigan;

- sell telecommunication services;

- provide transient hotel or motel room rentals; or,

- buy goods for your own use from an out-of-state unlicensed vendor.

A good source of information (with tax rules for specific types of businesses) is the booklet, *General and Specific Sales and Use Tax Rules*, which (along with answers to your questions about these taxes) and it may be obtained from the Michigan Department of Treasury, by calling 517-373-3190.

SINGLE BUSINESS TAX

You will need to register for the Michigan Single Business Tax if you have "apportioned gross receipts" plus "capital acquisition recapture" greater than $250,000. If you expect gross receipts to exceed $250,000, you definitely need an accountant. Your accountant can explain these terms and determine if you need to be concerned about this tax.

If you have any questions, call the Michigan Department of Treasury at 517-373-8030. Forms may be obtained by calling 800-367-6263. You should also obtain their two publications: *Michigan Single Business Tax Questions & Answers*, and *Single Business Tax Instructions for Individuals, Partnerships and Fiduciaries*.

MOTOR FUEL TAX

You will need to register to the Michigan Motor Fuel Tax if you:

- operate a terminal or refinery for gasoline, diesel or aviation fuel or import from a foreign country;

- acquire or sell tax-free diesel or gasoline;

- transport fuel across a Michigan border;

- sell diesel fuel of liquefied propane gas (LPG) to an end user; or

- operate a diesel-powered road tractor, or straight truck having more than two axles.

If you have any questions about the Motor Fuel Tax, call the Michigan Department of Treasury at 517-373-3180.

TOBACCO PRODUCTS TAX

If you sell cigarettes or other tobacco products for resale (i.e., as a wholesaler), or if you purchase tobacco products from an unlicensed out-of-state source, you will need to register for the Michigan Tobacco Products Tax. If you have any questions about the Tobacco Products Tax, call the Michigan Department of Treasury at 517-373-3180.

MICHIGAN UNEMPLOYMENT TAX

For more information, including various forms and publications, about Michigan unemployment taxes, contact:

Michigan Unemployment Agency
Cadillac Place
3024 W. Grand Blvd.
Detroit, MI 48202
800-638-3994
Website: http://www.cis.state.mi.us/ua/home.htm

If you have employees, you are required to file an Employer Registration Report (MESC-1009), which is an eight-page form. You will then be sent reporting forms to complete and file each quarter.

MICHIGAN INCOME TAX WITHHOLDING

You must register for withholding of Michigan income tax from the paychecks of your employees, just as you withhold Federal income tax and social security. For information about registering, contact one of the field offices listed below, the Department of Treasury's main office (Michigan Department of Treasury, Lansing, MI 48922; phone 517-373-0884), or visit their website at:

http://www.treas.state.mi.us

MICHIGAN DEPARTMENT OF TREASURY TAX OFFICES

The Department of Treasury maintains offices in the following locations:

Detroit
State of Michigan Plaza Bldg
1200 6th Street
Detroit, MI 48226

Escanaba
State Office Bldg., Rm. 7
305 Ludington St.
Escanaba, MI 49829
(open 8am-12noon)

Flint
State Office Bldg., 7th Floor
125 E. Union St.
Flint, MI 48502

Grand Rapids:
State Office Bldg.
350 Ottawa, NW
Grand Rapids, MI 49503-2340

Kalamazoo
535 S. Burdick St., Ste. 197
Kalamazoo, MI 49005-0286
(closed 12 - 1)

Lansing
Treasury Building
430 W. Allegan St.
Lansing, MI 48922

Marquette (forms only):
1055 W. Baraga
Marquette, MI 49855

Pontiac
100 N. Saginaw St.
Pontiac, MI 48342

Saginaw (forms only):
State Office Building
411-I E. Genesee St.
Saginaw, MI 48607
(open 8am-12noon)

Sterling Heights:
43100 Dequindre, Suite 200
Sterling Heights, MI 48314

Traverse City:
701 S. Elmwood Ave., Ste. 1
Traverse City, MI 49684
(open 8 - 12 only)

A few Michigan cities and counties (such as Detroit and Wayne County) also have income taxes, so be sure to check with your city or county government also.

Out-of-State Taxes 19

In addition to federal and Michigan taxes, you may also need to be concerned with taxes that other states, and Canada, seek to impose in certain circumstances.

State Sales Taxes

In 1992, the United States Supreme Court struck a blow for the rights of small businesses by ruling that state tax authorities cannot force them to collect sales taxes on interstate mail orders (*Quill Corporation v. North Dakota*).

Unfortunately, the court left open the possibility that Congress could allow interstate taxation of mail order sales, and since then several bills have been introduced that would do so. One, introduced by Arkansas senator Dale Bumpers was given the *1984*-style "newspeak" title, *The Consumer and Main Street Protection Act*.

At present, companies are only required to collect sales taxes for states in which they *do business*. Exactly what business is enough to trigger taxation is a legal question and some states try to define it as broadly as possible.

If you have an office in a state, clearly you are doing business there and any goods shipped to consumers in the state are subject to sales taxes. If you have a full time employee working in the state much of the year many states will consider you doing business there. In some states attending a two-day trade show is enough business to trigger taxation for the entire year for every order shipped to the state. One loophole that often works is to be represented at shows by persons who are not your employees.

Because the laws are different in each state you will have to do some research on a state-by-state basis to find out how much business you can do in a state without being subject to their taxation. You can request a state's rules from its department of revenue, but keep in mind that what a department of revenue wants the law to be is not always what the courts will rule that it is.

BUSINESS TAXES

Even worse than being subject to a state's sales taxes is to be subject to their income or other business taxes. For example, California charges every company doing business in the state a minimum $800 a year fee and charges income tax on a portion of the company's worldwide income. Doing a small amount of business in the state is clearly not worth getting mired in California taxation.

For this reason some trade shows have been moved from the state and this has resulted in a review of the tax policies and some "safe-harbor" guidelines to advise companies on what they can do without becoming subject to taxation.

Write to the department of revenue of any state with which you have business contacts to see what might trigger your taxation.

INTERNET TAXES

State revenue departments are drooling at the prospect of taxing commerce on the Internet. Theories have already been proposed that web sites available to state residents mean a company is doing business in a state.

Fortunately, Congress has passed a moratorium on taxation of the Internet. Hopefully this will be extended and will give us a new tax-free world, but do not count on it. It would take a tremendous outcry to keep the Internet tax-free. Keep an eye out for any news stories on proposals to tax the Internet and petition your representatives against them.

CANADIAN TAXES

Apparently oblivious to the logic of the U.S. Supreme Court, the Canadian government expects American companies that sell goods by mail order to Canadians to collect taxes for them and file returns with Revenue Canada, their tax department.

Those that receive an occasional unsolicited order are not expected to register, and Canadian customers who order things from the U.S. pay the tax plus a $5 fee upon receipt of the goods. But companies that solicit Canadian orders are expected to be registered if their worldwide income is $30,000 or more per year. In some cases a company may be required to post a bond and to pay for the cost of Canadian auditors visiting its premises and auditing its books. For these reasons you may notice that some companies decline to accept orders from Canada.

THE END...AND THE BEGINNING 20

If you have read through this whole book you know more about the rules and laws for operating a Michigan business than most people in business today. But after learning about all of the governmental regulations you may become discouraged. You are probably wondering how you can keep track of all the laws and how you will have any time left to make money after complying with the laws. But its not that bad. People are starting businesses every day and they are making money. At least we do not have laws like some countries which have marginal tax rates as high as 105%.

The regulations that exist right now are enough to strangle some businesses. Consider the case of the Armour meat-packing plant. The Federal Meat Inspection Service required that an opening be made in a conveyor to allow inspection or they would shut down the plant. OSHA told them that if they made that opening they would be shut down for safety reasons. Government regulations made it impossible for that plant to be in business!

But what you have to realize is that the same bureaucrats who are creating laws to slow down businesses are the ones who are responsible for enforcing the laws. And just as most government programs cost more than expected and fail to achieve their goals, most government regulations cannot be enforced against millions of people.

In a pure democracy, fifty-one percent of the voters can decide that all left-handed people must wear green shirts and that everyone must go to church three days a week. It is the Bill of Rights in our constitution which protects us from the tyrannical whims of the majority.

In America today, there are no laws regarding left-handed people or going to church, but there are laws controlling minute aspects of our personal and business lives. Does a majority have the right to decide what hours you can work, what you can sell, or where you can sell it? You must decide for yourself.

One way to avoid problems with the government is to keep a low profile and avoid open confrontation. For a lawyer it can be fun going to appeals court over an unfair parking ticket or making a federal case out of a $25 fine. But for most people the expenses of a fight with the government are unbearable. If you start a mass protest against the IRS or OSHA they will have to make an example of you.

Congratulations on deciding to start a business in Michigan! If you have any unusual experiences along the way, drop us a line at the following address. The information may be useful for a future book.

Sphinx Publishing
P. O. Box 4410
Naperville, IL 60567-4410

GLOSSARY

A

acceptance. Agreeing to the terms of an offer and creating a contract.

articles of incorporation. A legal document filed with the state government to set up a corporation.

articles of organization. A legal document filed with the state government to set up a limited liability company.

assumed name. A name under which a person, corporation, or other business entity conducts business.

B

bait and switch. An illegal business practice where one item is advertised for sale to entice a customer into the store, then telling the customer that product is no longer available and trying to sell the customer another (usually more expensive) product.

blue sky laws. A common name for laws regulating investments and securities.

bulk sales. Selling substantially all of a company's inventory.

C

C corporation. A corporation that pays taxes on its profits.

certificate of limited partnership. A legal document filed with the state government to register a limited partnership.

collections. The collection of money owed to a business.

common law. Laws that are determined in court cases rather than statutes.

consideration. The exchange of value or promises in a contract.

contract. A legally binding agreement between two or more parties.

copyright. Legal protection given to "original works of authorship."

corporation. An artificial person that is set up to conduct a business owned by shareholders and run by officers and directors.

D

d/b/a. Abbreviation for doing business as.

deceptive pricing. Pricing goods or services in a manner intended to deceive the customers.

discrimination. The choosing among various options based on their characteristics.

domain name. A name used and registered for conducting business on the Internet.

E

employee. Person who works for another under that person's control and direction.

endorsements. Positive statements about goods or services.

excise tax. A tax paid on the sale or consumption of goods or services.

express warranty. A specific guarantee of a product or service.

F

fictitious name. *See* assumed name.

G

general partner. A partner in a limited partnership who has authority to engage in operating the business.

goods. Items of personal property.

guarantee/guaranty. A promise of quality of a good or service.

H

home solicitation. When a salesman comes to a customer's home seeking to sell products or services.

I

implied warranty. A guarantee of a product or service that is not specifically made, but can be implied from the circumstances of the sale.

independent contractor. Person who works for another as a separate business, not as an employee.

intellectual property. Legal rights to the products of the mind, such as writings, musical compositions, formulas and designs.

L

liability. The legal responsibility to pay for an injury.

limited liability company. An entity recognized as a legal "person" that is set up to conduct a business owned and run by members.

limited liability partnership. An entity recognized as a legal "person" that is set up to conduct a business owned and run by members that is set up for professionals such as attorneys or doctors.

limited partner. A partner in a limited partnership who is in the position of an investor, and has no authority to engage in operating the business.

limited warranty. A guarantee covering certain aspects of a good or service.

M

merchant. A person who is in business.

merchant's firm offer. An offer by a business made under specific terms.

N

nonprofit corporation. An entity recognized as a legal "person" that is set up to run an operation in which none of the profits are distributed to controlling members.

O

occupational license. A government-issued permit to transact business.

offer. A proposal to enter into a contract.

P

partnership. A business formed by two or more persons.

patent. Protection given to inventions, discoveries and designs.

personal property. Any type of property other than land and the structures attached to it.

R

real property. Land and the structures attached to it.

Regulation Z. A complex Federal regulation governing interest rate disclosures by lenders to borrowers.

S

sale on approval. Selling an item with the agreement that it may be brought back and the sale cancelled.

service mark. A mark used to identify the provider of certain services.

SCORE. Acronym for Service Corps of Retired Executives, which is a group of retired business executives who volunteer to give advice to new small business owners.

S corporation. A corporation which is taxed as a partnership under IRS rules.

securities. Interests in a business such as stocks or bonds.

sexual harassment. Activity that causes an employee to feel or be sexually threatened.

shares. Units of stock in a corporation.

sole proprietorship. A business owned by an individual.

statute of frauds. Laws requiring that certain types of contracts be in writing in order to be binding on the parties.

sublease. An agreement to rent premises from an existing tenant.

T

trade name. A name used to identify the manufacturer of a product or group of products.

trademark. A distinguishing mark used to identify the manufacturer of a product or group of products.

U

UCC. Abbreviation for Uniform Commercial Code.

unemployment compensation. Payments to a former employee who was terminated from a job for a reason not based on his or her fault.

Uniform Commercial Code. A set of laws which apply to commercial business transactions.

usury. An illegally high rate of interest charged on a loan.

W

whistleblower. An employee who reports a violation of law or regulation by his or her employer to a government agency.

withholding. Money taken out of an employee's salary and remitted to the government.

workers' compensation. A system of compensating employees for job-related injuries.

FOR FURTHER REFERENCE

The following books will provide valuable information to those who are starting new businesses. Some are out of print, but they are classics that are worth tracking down.

For inspiration to give you the drive to succeed:

Hill, Napoleon, *Think and Grow Rich*. New York: Fawcett Books, 1990.

Karbo, Joe, *The Lazy Man's Way to Riches*. Sunset Beach: F P Publishing, 1974.

Schwartz, David J., *The Magic of Thinking Big*. Fireside, 1987.

For hints on what it takes to be successful:

Carnegie, Dale, *How to Win Friends and Influence People*. New York: Pocket Books, 1994.

Ringer, Robert J., *Looking Out for #1*. New York: Fawcett Books, 1993.

Ringer, Robert J., *Million Dollar Habits*. New York: Fawcett Books, 1991.

Ringer, Robert J., *Winning Through Intimidation*. New York: Fawcett Books, 1993.

For advice on bookkeeping and organization:

Kamoroff, Bernard, *Small Time Operator (25th Edition)*. Bell Springs Publishing, 2000.

For a very practical guide to investing:

Tobias, Andrew, *The Only Investment Guide You'll Ever Need*. Harvest Books, 1999.

For advice on how to avoid problems with government agencies:

Browne, Harry, *How I Found Freedom in an Unfree World*. Great Falls: Liam Works, 1998.

The following are other books published by **Sphinx Publishing** that may be helpful to your business:

Eckert, W. Kelsea, Sartorius, Arthur, III, & Warda, Mark, *How to Form Your Own Corporation*. 2001.

Haman, Edward A., *How to Form Your Own Partnership*. 1999.

Ray, James C., *The Most Valuable Business Legal Forms You'll Ever Need*. 2001.

Ray, James C., *The Complete Book of Corporate Forms*. 2001.

Warda, Mark, *How to Form a Delaware Corporation from Any State*. 1999.

Warda, Mark, *Incorporate in Nevada from Any State*. 2001.

Warda, Mark, *How to Form a Limited Liability Company*. 1999.

Warda, Mark, *How to Register Your Own Copyright*. 2000.

Warda, Mark, *How to Register Your Own Trademark.*. 1999.

The following are books published by **Sourcebooks, Inc.** that may be helpful to your business:

Fleury, Robert E., *The Small Business Survival Guide.*. 1995.

Gutman, Jean E., *Accounting Made Easy*. 1998.

Milling, Bryan E., *How to Get a Small Business Loan (2nd Edition)*. 1998.

The following websites provide information that may be useful to you in starting your business:

Internal Revenue Service: http://www.irs.gov

Small Business Administration: http://www.sba.gov

Social Security Administration: http://www.ssa.gov

U. S. Business Advisor: http://www.business.gov

APPENDIX A
BUSINESS START-UP
CHECKLIST

This checklist will help you to organize your start-up procedures. Refer to the text of the chapters if you have any questions on the items appearing here.

Business Start-up Checklist

- ❏ Make your plan
    - ❏ Obtain and read all relevant publications on your type of business.
    - ❏ Obtain and read all laws and regulations affecting your business
    - ❏ Calculate plan to produce a profit
    - ❏ Plan sources of capital
    - ❏ Plan sources of goods or services
    - ❏ Plan marketing efforts
- ❏ Choose the form of your business
    - ❏ Prepare and file organizational papers (incorporation, LLC, etc.)
    - ❏ Prepare and file assumed name registration
- ❏ Choose your business name
    - ❏ Check other business names and trademarks
    - ❏ Register your business name, trademark, etc.
- ❏ Choose the location
    - ❏ Check competitors
    - ❏ Check zoning
- ❏ Obtain necessary licenses
    - ❏ City   ❏ County   ❏ State   ❏ Federal
- ❏ Arrange for telephone service
- ❏ Choose a bank
    - ❏ Checking account
    - ❏ Credit card processing
    - ❏ Loans
- ❏ Obtain necessary or desired insurance
    - ❏ Workers' compensation   ❏ Automobile
    - ❏ Liability   ❏ Health
    - ❏ Hazard   ❏ Life/disability
- ❏ File necessary federal and state tax registrations
- ❏ Set up bookkeeping system
- ❏ Plan your hiring
    - ❏ Obtain required posters
    - ❏ Prepare employment application
    - ❏ Prepare employment policies
    - ❏ Determine compliance with health and safety laws
- ❏ Plan your opening
    - ❏ Obtain necessary equipment and supplies
    - ❏ Obtain necessary inventory
    - ❏ Marketing and publicity
    - ❏ Obtain necessary forms, agreements, etc.
    - ❏ Prepare company policies on refunds, exchanges, returns, etc.

The following forms are samples of some of the forms that appear in Appendix C.

TAX TIMETABLE

MICHIGAN   FEDERAL

	SUW*	SBT**	Unemploy.	Est. Tax	Est. Tax	Annual Return	Form 941***	Misc.
JAN.	15th		25th	15th	15th		31st	31st 940 W-2 508 1099
FEB.	15th							28th W-3
MAR.	15th					15th		
APR.	15th	30th Ann. Ret.	25th	15th	15th	15th	30th	30th 508
MAY	15th							
JUN.	15th			15th	15th			
JUL.	15th		25th				31st	31st 508
AUG.	15th							
SEP.	15th			15th	15th			
OCT.	15th		25th				31st	31st 508
NOV.	15th							
DEC.	15th							

*   SUW = Sales, Use & Withholding taxes; a combined return is filed.

**   SBT = Single Business Tax. Based on calendar year. If fiscal year, due 15th day of 4th month after end of fiscal year, Quarterly returns are required if you expect annual liability greater than $600.

*** In addition to Form 941, deposits must be made regularly if withholding exceeds $500 in any month.

Form **SS-4**

(Rev. April 2000)

Department of the Treasury
Internal Revenue Service

Application for Employer Identification Number

(For use by employers, corporations, partnerships, trusts, estates, churches, government agencies, certain individuals, and others. See instructions.)

▶ Keep a copy for your records.

EIN

OMB No. 1545-0003

Please type or print clearly.

1 Name of applicant (legal name) (see instructions) Doe Company	

2 Trade name of business (if different from name on line 1)	**3** Executor, trustee, "care of" name

4a Mailing address (street address) (room, apt., or suite no.) 123 Main Street	**5a** Business address (if different from address on lines 4a and 4b)
4b City, state, and ZIP code Lansing, MI 48910	**5b** City, state, and ZIP code

6 County and state where principal business is located
Lansing, Michigan

7 Name of principal officer, general partner, grantor, owner, or trustor—SSN or ITIN may be required (see instructions) ▶
John Doe   123-45-6789

8a Type of entity (Check only one box.) (see instructions)

Caution: *If applicant is a limited liability company, see the instructions for line 8a.*

☐ Sole proprietor (SSN) _____
☒ Partnership   ☐ Personal service corp.
☐ REMIC   ☐ National Guard
☐ State/local government   ☐ Farmers' cooperative
☐ Church or church-controlled organization
☐ Other nonprofit organization (specify) ▶ _____
☐ Other (specify) ▶

☐ Estate (SSN of decedent) _____
☐ Plan administrator (SSN) _____
☐ Other corporation (specify) ▶ _____
☐ Trust
☐ Federal government/military
(enter GEN if applicable) _____

8b If a corporation, name the state or foreign country (if applicable) where incorporated

State	Foreign country

9 Reason for applying (Check only one box.) (see instructions)

☒ Started new business (specify type) ▶ _____
   clothing manufacturing
☐ Hired employees (Check the box and see line 12.)
☐ Created a pension plan (specify type) ▶

☐ Banking purpose (specify purpose) ▶ _____
☐ Changed type of organization (specify new type) ▶ _____
☐ Purchased going business
☐ Created a trust (specify type) ▶ _____
☐ Other (specify) ▶

10 Date business started or acquired (month, day, year) (see instructions)
10-15-01

11 Closing month of accounting year (see instructions)
December

12 First date wages or annuities were paid or will be paid (month, day, year). **Note:** *If applicant is a withholding agent, enter date income will first be paid to nonresident alien. (month, day, year)* . . . . ▶   10-22-01

13 Highest number of employees expected in the next 12 months. **Note:** *If the applicant does not expect to have any employees during the period, enter -0-. (see instructions)* . . . . ▶	Nonagricultural	Agricultural	Household
	3		

14 Principal activity (see instructions) ▶   clothing manufacturing

15 Is the principal business activity manufacturing? . . . .   ☒ Yes   ☐ No
If "Yes," principal product and raw material used ▶   fabric

16 To whom are most of the products or services sold? Please check one box.   ☒ Business (wholesale)
☐ Public (retail)   ☐ Other (specify) ▶   ☐ N/A

17a Has the applicant ever applied for an employer identification number for this or any other business? . . . . ☐ Yes   ☒ No
Note: *If "Yes," please complete lines 17b and 17c.*

17b If you checked "Yes" on line 17a, give applicant's legal name and trade name shown on prior application, if different from line 1 or 2 above.
Legal name ▶   Trade name ▶

17c Approximate date when and city and state where the application was filed. Enter previous employer identification number if known.

Approximate date when filed (mo., day, year)	City and state where filed	Previous EIN

Under penalties of perjury, I declare that I have examined this application, and to the best of my knowledge and belief, it is true, correct, and complete.

Business telephone number (include area code)
(517) 555-0000

Fax telephone number (include area code)
(   )

Name and title (Please type or print clearly.) ▶   John Doe, Partner

Signature ▶ *John Doe*   Date ▶ **10/15/01**

Note: *Do not write below this line. For official use only.*

Please leave blank ▶	Geo.	Ind.	Class	Size	Reason for applying

For Privacy Act and Paperwork Reduction Act Notice, see page 4.   Cat. No. 16055N   Form **SS-4** (Rev. 4-2000)

U.S. Department of Justice
Immigration and Naturalization Service

OMB No. 1115-0136

Employment Eligibility Verification

Please read instructions carefully before completing this form. The instructions must be available during completion of this form. ANTI-DISCRIMINATION NOTICE: It is illegal to discriminate against work eligible individuals. Employers CANNOT specify which document(s) they will accept from an employee. The refusal to hire an individual because of a future expiration date may also constitute illegal discrimination.

Section 1. Employee Information and Verification. To be completed and signed by employee at the time employment begins.

Print Name: Last	First	Middle Initial	Maiden Name
REDDENBACHER	MARY	J.	HASSENFUSS

Address (Street Name and Number)	Apt. #	Date of Birth (month/day/year)
1234 LIBERTY LANE		1/26/69

City	State	Zip Code	Social Security #
LANSING	MI	12345	123-45-6789

I am aware that federal law provides for imprisonment and/or fines for false statements or use of false documents in connection with the completion of this form.

I attest, under penalty of perjury, that I am (check one of the following):
- [ ] A citizen or national of the United States
- [ ] A Lawful Permanent Resident (Alien # A_____)
- [ ] An alien authorized to work until ___/___/___
  (Alien # or Admission #) _____

Employee's Signature *Mary J. Reddenbacher*	Date (month/day/year) 1/29/00

Preparer and/or Translator Certification. *(To be completed and signed if Section 1 is prepared by a person other than the employee.) I attest, under penalty of perjury, that I have assisted in the completion of this form and that to the best of my knowledge the information is true and correct.*

Preparer's/Translator's Signature	Print Name
Address (Street Name and Number, City, State, Zip Code)	Date (month/day/year)

Section 2. Employer Review and Verification. To be completed and signed by employer. Examine one document from List A OR examine one document from List B and one from List C, as listed on the reverse of this form, and record the title, number and expiration date, if any, of the document(s)

List A	OR	List B	AND	List C
Document title: PASSPORT				
Issuing authority: PASSPORT AGENCY NYC				
Document #: 123456789				
Expiration Date (if any): 10/5/06		___/___/___		___/___/___
Document #:				
Expiration Date (if any): ___/___/___				

CERTIFICATION - I attest, under penalty of perjury, that I have examined the document(s) presented by the above-named employee, that the above-listed document(s) appear to be genuine and to relate to the employee named, that the employee began employment on (month/day/year) ___/___/___ and that to the best of my knowledge the employee is eligible to work in the United States. (State employment agencies may omit the date the employee began employment.)

Signature of Employer or Authorized Representative	Print Name	Title
Business or Organization Name	Address (Street Name and Number, City, State, Zip Code)	Date (month/day/year)

Section 3. Updating and Reverification. To be completed and signed by employer.

A. New Name (if applicable)	B. Date of rehire (month/day/year) (if applicable)

C. If employee's previous grant of work authorization has expired, provide the information below for the document that establishes current employment eligibility.

Document Title:_____ Document #:_____ Expiration Date (if any): ___/___/___

I attest, under penalty of perjury, that to the best of my knowledge, this employee is eligible to work in the United States, and if the employee presented document(s), the document(s) I have examined appear to be genuine and to relate to the individual.

Signature of Employer or Authorized Representative	Date (month/day/year)

Form I-9 (Rev. 11-21-91)N Page 2

Form W-4 (2001)

Purpose. Complete Form W-4 so your employer can withhold the correct Federal income tax from your pay. Because your tax situation may change, you may want to refigure your withholding each year.

Exemption from withholding. If you are exempt, complete only lines 1, 2, 3, 4, and 7, and sign the form to validate it. Your exemption for 2001 expires February 18, 2002.

Note: *You cannot claim exemption from withholding if (1) your income exceeds $750 and includes more than $250 of unearned income (e.g., interest and dividends) and (2) another person can claim you as a dependent on their tax return.*

Basic instructions. If you are not exempt, complete the **Personal Allowances Worksheet** below. The worksheets on page 2 adjust your withholding allowances based on itemized deductions, certain credits, adjustments to

income, or two-earner/two-job situations. Complete all worksheets that apply. They will help you figure the number of withholding allowances you are entitled to claim. **However, you may claim fewer (or zero) allowances.**

Head of household. Generally, you may claim head of household filing status on your tax return only if you are unmarried and pay more than 50% of the costs of keeping up a home for yourself and your dependent(s) or other qualifying individuals. See line E below.

Tax credits. You can take projected tax credits into account in figuring your allowable number of withholding allowances. Credits for child or dependent care expenses and the child tax credit may be claimed using the **Personal Allowances Worksheet** below. See **Pub. 919,** How Do I Adjust My Tax Withholding? for information on converting your other credits into withholding allowances.

Nonwage income. If you have a large amount of nonwage income, such as interest or dividends,

consider making estimated tax payments using **Form 1040-ES,** Estimated Tax for Individuals. Otherwise, you may owe additional tax.

Two earners/two jobs. If you have a working spouse or more than one job, figure the total number of allowances you are entitled to claim on all jobs using worksheets from only one Form W-4. Your withholding usually will be most accurate when all allowances are claimed on the Form W-4 for the highest paying job and zero allowances are claimed on the others.

Check your withholding. After your Form W-4 takes effect, use Pub. 919 to see how the dollar amount you are having withheld compares to your projected total tax for 2001. Get Pub. 919 especially if you used the **Two-Earner/Two-Job Worksheet** on page 2 and your earnings exceed $150,000 (Single) or $200,000 (Married).

Recent name change? If your name on line 1 differs from that shown on your social security card, call 1-800-772-1213 for a new social security card.

Personal Allowances Worksheet (Keep for your records.)

A Enter "1" for **yourself** if no one else can claim you as a dependent . . . . **A** ____

B Enter "1" if: {
- You are single and have only one job; or
- You are married, have only one job, and your spouse does not work; or
- Your wages from a second job or your spouse's wages (or the total of both) are $1,000 or less. } . . **B** ____

C Enter "1" for your **spouse.** But, you may choose to enter -0- if you are married and have either a working spouse or more than one job. (Entering -0- may help you avoid having too little tax withheld.) . . . . **C** ____

D Enter number of **dependents** (other than your spouse or yourself) you will claim on your tax return . . . **D** ____

E Enter "1" if you will file as **head of household** on your tax return (see conditions under **Head of household** above) . **E** ____

F Enter "1" if you have at least $1,500 of **child or dependent care expenses** for which you plan to claim a credit . . **F** ____

(**Note:** Do **not** include child support payments. See **Pub. 503,** Child and Dependent Care Expenses, for details.)

G **Child Tax Credit** (including additional child tax credit):
- If your total income will be between $18,000 and $50,000 ($23,000 and $63,000 if married), enter "1" for each eligible child.
- If your total income will be between $50,000 and $80,000 ($63,000 and $115,000 if married), enter "1" if you have two eligible children, enter "2" if you have three or four eligible children, or enter "3" if you have five or more eligible children. **G** ____

H Add lines A through G and enter total here. (**Note:** This may be different from the number of exemptions you claim on your tax return.) ▶ **H** ____

{ For accuracy, complete all worksheets that apply. }
- If you plan to **itemize or claim adjustments to income** and want to reduce your withholding, see the **Deductions and Adjustments Worksheet** on page 2.
- If you are **single,** have **more than one job** and your combined earnings from all jobs exceed $35,000, **or** if you are **married** and have a **working spouse or more than one job** and the combined earnings from all jobs exceed $60,000, see the **Two-Earner/Two-Job Worksheet** on page 2 to avoid having too little tax withheld.
- If **neither** of the above situations applies, **stop here** and enter the number from line H on line 5 of Form W-4 below.

- - - - - - - - - - Cut here and give Form W-4 to your employer. Keep the top part for your records. - - - - - - - - - -

---

| Form **W-4** Department of the Treasury Internal Revenue Service | **Employee's Withholding Allowance Certificate** ▶ For Privacy Act and Paperwork Reduction Act Notice, see page 2. | OMB No. 1545-0010 **2001** |

1 Type or print your first name and middle initial: John A. Last name: Smith **2** Your social security number: 123 45 6789

Home address (number and street or rural route): 567 Wharf Blvd.

City or town, state, and ZIP code: Lansing, MI 48910

3 ☒ Single ☐ Married ☐ Married, but withhold at higher Single rate.
Note: If married, but legally separated, or spouse is a nonresident alien, check the Single box.

4 If your last name differs from that on your social security card, check here. You must call 1-800-772-1213 for a new card. ▶ ☐

5 Total number of allowances you are claiming (from line **H** above **or** from the applicable worksheet on page 2) **5** | 1

6 Additional amount, if any, you want withheld from each paycheck . . . . **6** $ 0

7 I claim exemption from withholding for 2001, and I certify that I meet **both** of the following conditions for exemption:
- Last year I had a right to a refund of **all** Federal income tax withheld because I had **no** tax liability **and**
- This year I expect a refund of **all** Federal income tax withheld because I expect to have **no** tax liability.

If you meet both conditions, write "Exempt" here . . . . ▶ **7**

Under penalties of perjury, I certify that I am entitled to the number of withholding allowances claimed on this certificate, or I am entitled to claim exempt status.

Employee's signature
(Form is not valid unless you sign it.) ▶ *John Smith*

Date ▶ *John Smith*

8 Employer's name and address (Employer: Complete lines 8 and 10 only if sending to the IRS.)   **9** Office code (optional)   **10** Employer identification number

Cat. No. 10220Q

Deductions and Adjustments Worksheet

Note: *Use this worksheet only if you plan to itemize deductions, claim certain credits, or claim adjustments to income on your 2001 tax return.*

1	Enter an estimate of your 2001 itemized deductions. These include qualifying home mortgage interest, charitable contributions, state and local taxes, medical expenses in excess of 7.5% of your income, and miscellaneous deductions. (For 2001, you may have to reduce your itemized deductions if your income is over $132,950 ($66,475 if married filing separately). See **Worksheet 3** in Pub. 919 for details.) . . .	1	$ _____
2	Enter: { $7,600 if married filing jointly or qualifying widow(er) / $6,650 if head of household / $4,550 if single / $3,800 if married filing separately }	2	$ _____
3	**Subtract** line 2 from line 1. If line 2 is greater than line 1, enter -0-	3	$ _____
4	Enter an estimate of your 2001 adjustments to income, including alimony, deductible IRA contributions, and student loan interest	4	$ _____
5	**Add** lines 3 and 4 and enter the total (Include any amount for credits from **Worksheet 7** in Pub. 919.) .	5	$ _____
6	Enter an estimate of your 2001 nonwage income (such as dividends or interest)	6	$ _____
7	**Subtract** line 6 from line 5. Enter the result, but not less than -0-	7	$ _____
8	**Divide** the amount on line 7 by $3,000 and enter the result here. Drop any fraction	8	_____
9	Enter the number from the **Personal Allowances Worksheet,** line H, page 1	9	_____
10	**Add** lines 8 and 9 and enter the total here. If you plan to use the **Two-Earner/Two-Job Worksheet,** also enter this total on line 1 below. Otherwise, **stop here** and enter this total on Form W-4, line 5, page 1 .	10	_____

Two-Earner/Two-Job Worksheet

Note: *Use this worksheet only if the instructions under line H on page 1 direct you here.*

1	Enter the number from line H, page 1 (or from line 10 above if you used the **Deductions and Adjustments Worksheet**)	1	_____
2	Find the number in **Table 1** below that applies to the **lowest** paying job and enter it here	2	_____
3	If line 1 is **more than or equal to** line 2, subtract line 2 from line 1. Enter the result here (if zero, enter -0-) and on Form W-4, line 5, page 1. **Do not** use the rest of this worksheet	3	_____

Note: *If line 1 is **less than** line 2, enter -0- on Form W-4, line 5, page 1. Complete lines 4–9 below to calculate the additional withholding amount necessary to avoid a year end tax bill.*

4	Enter the number from line 2 of this worksheet	4	_____
5	Enter the number from line 1 of this worksheet	5	_____
6	**Subtract** line 5 from line 4	6	_____
7	Find the amount in **Table 2** below that applies to the **highest** paying job and enter it here	7	$ _____
8	**Multiply** line 7 by line 6 and enter the result here. This is the additional annual withholding needed . .	8	$ _____
9	**Divide** line 8 by the number of pay periods remaining in 2001. For example, divide by 26 if you are paid every two weeks and you complete this form in December 2000. Enter the result here and on Form W-4, line 6, page 1. This is the additional amount to be withheld from each paycheck	9	$ _____

Table 1: Two-Earner/Two-Job Worksheet

Married Filing Jointly				All Others			
If wages from **LOWEST** paying job are—	Enter on line 2 above	If wages from **LOWEST** paying job are—	Enter on line 2 above	If wages from **LOWEST** paying job are—	Enter on line 2 above	If wages from **LOWEST** paying job are—	Enter on line 2 above
$0 - $4,000	0	42,001 - 47,000	8	$0 - $6,000	0	65,001 - 80,000	8
4,001 - 8,000	1	47,001 - 55,000	9	6,001 - 12,000	1	80,001 - 105,000	9
8,001 - 14,000	2	55,001 - 65,000	10	12,001 - 17,000	2	105,001 and over	10
14,001 - 19,000	3	65,001 - 70,000	11	17,001 - 22,000	3		
19,001 - 25,000	4	70,001 - 90,000	12	22,001 - 28,000	4		
25,001 - 32,000	5	90,001 - 105,000	13	28,001 - 40,000	5		
32,001 - 38,000	6	105,001 - 115,000	14	40,001 - 50,000	6		
38,001 - 42,000	7	115,001 and over	15	50,001 - 65,000	7		

Table 2: Two-Earner/Two-Job Worksheet

Married Filing Jointly		All Others	
If wages from **HIGHEST** paying job are—	Enter on line 7 above	If wages from **HIGHEST** paying job are—	Enter on line 7 above
$0 - $50,000	$440	$0 - $30,000	$440
50,001 - 100,000	800	30,001 - 60,000	800
100,001 - 130,000	900	60,001 - 120,000	900
130,001 - 250,000	1,000	120,001 - 270,000	1,000
250,001 and over	1,100	270,001 and over	1,100

form 7

Michigan Department of Treasury and Unemployment Agency
518 (Rev. 6-99). Formerly C-3400.

REGISTRATION FOR MICHIGAN TAXES

1. Federal Employer Identification Number (Required for UA)
If you do not have an FEIN, call the IRS at 1-800-829-1040.

1a. UA No.   59-123456

2. Complete Company Name or Owner's Full Name (include, if applicable, Corp., Inc., P.C., L.C., L.L.C., L.L.P., etc.)

Doe Security Systems

3. Business Name, Assumed Name or DBA (as registered with the county)

Legal Address

4A. This address is for all legal contacts. Enter number and street (no P.O. boxes).

423 Cass Ave.

Business Telephone

City, State, ZIP

Mt. Clemens, MI 48043

County

Mailing Address

4B. This address is where all tax forms will be sent unless otherwise instructed.

Same as 4A

City, State, ZIP

If this address is for an accountant, bookkeeper or other representative, attach a Power of Attorney.

Physical Address

4C. This address is the actual location of the business in Michigan. Enter number and street (cannot be a P.O. box number).

Same as 4A

City, State, ZIP

County

5. Type of Business Ownership (check one only)

- [X] (1) Individual (Sole Proprietorship)
- [ ] (2) Husband/Wife
- [ ] (3) Partnership
- [ ] (3) Registered Partnership, Agreement Date:_____
- [ ] (3) Limited Partnership - Identify all general partners below
- [ ] (34) Limited Liability Co. or Partnership
  - [ ] Domestic (Mich)
  - [ ] Professional
  - [ ] Foreign (Non-Mich)

- [ ] (4) Michigan Corporation
  - [ ] (1) Subchapter S
  - [ ] (2) Professional
- [ ] (5) Non-Mich. Corporation
  - [ ] (1) Subchapter S

- [ ] (6) Trust or Estate (Fiduciary)
- [ ] (7) Joint Stock Club or Investment Co
- [ ] (8) Social Club or Fraternal Org.
- [ ] (9) Other (Explain)

Date of Incorporation
Mo.   Day   Year

State of Incorporation

Michigan Department of Consumer & Industry Services Identification No.

6. Which taxes do you expect to owe?   What date will that liability begin?   How much of each tax do you estimate you will owe each month?

[X] Sales Tax	7 / 1 / 02 (Mo. Day Year)	[ ] Up to $65 [X] Up to $300 [ ] Over $300	
[ ] Use Tax	__ / __ / __ (Mo. Day Year)	[ ] Up to $65 [ ] Up to $300 [ ] Over $300	
[X] Income Tax Withholding	7 / 1 / 02 (Mo. Day Year)	[ ] Up to $65 [X] Up to $300 [ ] Over $300	
[ ] Single Business Tax	__ / __ / __ (Mo. Day Year)	How many people will you employ who are subject to Michigan withholding? 1 to 3	

- [ ] Motor Fuel Taxes .... Treasury will review your registration and send you any necessary tax application forms.
- [ ] Tobacco Products Tax .... Treasury will review your registration and send you any necessary tax application forms.
- [ ] UA Unemployment Tax .... **Attach Schedules A, B (if successor) and C. Enclose a copy of your Articles of Incorporation or Organization.**

7. Estimated annual Michigan gross receipts?

- [X] Up to $250,000
- [ ] Over $250,000

GROSS RECEIPTS are from (a) sales of inventory items, (b) rental or leases, (c) performance of services, interest, royalties, etc., to the extent they are derived from business activity.

8A. Name (Last, First, Middle, Jr./Sr./III)

Doe, John

Social Security Number
123-45-678

Title

owner

Date of Birth
2-19-40

Residence Address (Number, Street)
19499 Liberty

Driver License/Michigan Identification
D-999-99-999-98

City, State, ZIP
Mt. Clemens, MI 48043

Home Telephone
(810) 555-1234

8B. Name (Last, First, Middle, Jr./Sr./III)

Social Security Number

Title

Date of Birth

Residence Address (Number, Street)

Driver License/Michigan Identification

City, State, ZIP

Home Telephone

PLEASE DETACH BEFORE MAILING.

Complete all information for each owner, partner, member or corporate officer. Attach a separate list if necessary.

Multiple Locations

Seasonal Business

Fiscal Year

Payroll Service

9. How many business locations will you operate in Michigan? If more than one, attach a list of names and addresses.

10. Month Business Opens   Month Business Closes

11. Do you close your tax books on Dec. 31?   If no, give month of closing.

[X] Yes [ ] No

12. If your withholding taxes are paid by a payroll service, enter the payroll service name and address.

13A. Describe your business activity.

Sale and installation of home security systems.

13B. What retail products, if any, do you sell (sold to final consumer)?

Electronic security equipment

13C. What wholesale products, if any, do you sell?

None

13D. Do you have employees entering Michigan or representatives acting as your agent in Michigan to solicit orders, describe products or provide service? [ ] Yes [X] No

14A. What is the reason for this application?

[X] Started a new business

[ ] Incorporated an existing business

[ ] Purchased an existing business. Complete item 15 below.

[ ] Other (explain):

14B. List any previous account numbers

15A. If you purchased or acquired a business, what assets did you acquire? Check the boxes that apply and complete **UA Schedule B.**

[ ] Land [ ] Building [ ] Furniture & Fixtures [ ] Equipment [ ] Inventory [ ] Goodwill

15B. Name of previous owner(s) or corporation

15C. Previous Owner's Account Number (if known)

15D. Will the previous owner continue to make retail sales or have employees in Mich.

[ ] Yes [ ] No

15E. What was your total purchase price?

16A. Gasoline Stations: Name of Distributor

16B. Brand

16C. Address of Distributor (No., Street, City, State, ZIP)

17. Motor Fuel and Tobacco Tax Information

	Yes	No
Will you sell gasoline or diesel fuel for exempt purposes?	[ ]	[ ]
Will you sell diesel fuel from bulk storage into highway vehicles?	[ ]	[ ]
Will you operate a terminal or refinery?		
Do you own a diesel-powered vehicle with 3 or more axles or 2 axles and gross vehicle wt., over 26,000 lbs.?	[ ]	[ ]
Will you transport fuel across Michigan's borders?	[ ]	[ ]

	Yes	No
Will you sell tobacco products for resale?	[ ]	[ ]
Will you operate a tobacco products vending machine?	[ ]	[ ]
If yes, do you supply tobacco products for the machine?	[ ]	[ ]
If no, please give the supplier's name.		

SIGNATURE OF OWNERS. This registration must be signed by the owner(s), two partners, two corporate officers, member(s) of a limited liability company or their authorized representative. Applications without signatures will be returned.

I declare, under penalty of perjury, that I have examined this registration and its attachments and they are true and complete to the best of my knowledge.

Type or print name of owner or officer responsible for filing returns and making tax payments

John Doe

Title: owner

Signature

John Doe

Phone   Date 6/15/02

Type or print name of second owner; partner; officer or member

Title   Phone   Date

Signature

Preparer's name and address if different from above.   Phone   Date

If your business is liable for Sales and/or Use Tax only, you may register your business over the telephone by calling (517) 373-0888. If your business is liable for Income Withholding Tax, you must complete and mail this application to: Michigan Department of Treasury, Treasury Building, Lansing, MI 48922

Sales Tax Registrants Only - Enclose $1 License Fee

$ __1.00__

BCS/CD-600 (Rev. 07/01)

MICHIGAN DEPARTMENT OF CONSUMER & INDUSTRY SERVICES
BUREAU OF COMMERCIAL SERVICES

Date Received	(FOR BUREAU USE ONLY)

This registration will expire 10 years from the stamped registration date.

MARK IDENTIFICATION NUMBER	**M**			**-**			

APPLICATION FOR REGISTRATION OF TRADEMARK/SERVICE MARK

(Please read information and instructions on last page)

Pursuant to the provisions of Act 242, Public Acts of 1969, as amended, the undersigned executes the following Application:

1. This Application is for the purpose of registering a: (check one)

   [X] Trademark   [ ] Service mark

2. The mark: (Complete only one of the following)

   a) **WORDS ONLY:**
   If the mark is only words, the words in the mark are: (Include type style if it is an inherent part of the mark)

   Doe Boy

   b) **DESIGN ONLY:**
   If the mark is a design only, describe the design: (Include colors if they are an inherent part of the mark)

   c) **WORDS AND DESIGN:**
   Describe the design and list the words in the mark: (Include color and type style if they are an inherent part of the mark)

Please note: Complete either Item 3 **or** Item 4. Designate only one mark and one classification code per application.

Trademarks only

3. a) List the goods in connection with which the mark is used.

   Clothing

   b) The mode or manner in which the trademark is used in connection with the goods.

   Labels are sewn on the goods.

   c) Numerical classification of goods: 39

Service marks only

4. a) List the services in connection with which the mark is used.

   b) The mode or manner in which the mark is used in connection with the services.

   c) Numerical classification of services: _____

5. a) The mark was first used in Michigan by the applicant, or a predecessor, in _Detroit_____
      on _3/4/01_____ .   (city)
          (month / day / year)

   b) The mark was first used in the United States by the applicant, or a predecessor, in _Detroit_____
                                                                              (city)
      _Michigan_____ on _3/4/01_____ .
          (state)   (month / day / year)

6. a) The name of the individual or other entity applying for the registration is:

      John Doe

   b) The business name of the applicant, if different than 6(a):

      Doe Boy Sportwear

   c) The business address of the applicant is: 423 Cass Ave.

      Mt. Clemens, MI 48043

7. a) The applicant is a: (check one)

   ☐ Corporation   ☐ Partnership   ☒ Individual   ☐ Limited Liability Company   ☐ Other

   b) If a corporation, the state where incorporated: _____

8. Two copies, photographs, facsimiles or specimens of the mark, as actually in use must accompany this Application. The sample should be 8.5 x 11 inches or smaller so it may be scanned to optical disk media.

State of _Michigan_____

County of _Macomb_____ } SS

I, being first sworn, hereby depose and say that I have read the above application, including any attached papers, and the facts set out therein are true; the applicant is the owner of the mark and none other has the right to use the mark in Michigan either in the identical form or in a form which so nearly resembles the mark as to be likely to deceive or to be mistaken for the mark; the specimens of the mark as filed herewith are true and correct. FURTHER, the Bureau of Commercial Services, Michigan Department of Consumer & Industry Services, is hereby appointed as the applicant's agent for service of process only in actions relating to the registration or the application for registration of this mark.

Signature	Type or Print Name	Type or Print Title
John Doe	John Doe	owner

Subscribed and sworn to before me this _24th_____ day of _September_____ , _2001_____ .

I.M. Witness
_____
(Signature of Notary)

I.M. Witness
_____
(Type or Print Name of Notary)

Notary Public for _Macomb_____ County,

State of _Michigan_____

(Notary Seal)

My Commission expires _8/3/04_____

Preparer's name __John Doe__

Business telephone number __(810) 555-9999__

INFORMATION AND INSTRUCTIONS

1. This application must be used to register a Trademark/Service Mark. A document required or permitted to be filed under this act cannot be filed unless it contains the minimum information required by the act. This is a legal document and agency staff cannot provide legal advice.

2. Submit one original of this document. Upon filing, a Certificate of Registration will be mailed to the applicant or his/her representative to the address provided on this Application.

    Since this application will be maintained on electronic format, it is important that the filing be legible. Documents with poor black and white contrast, or otherwise illegible, will be rejected.

3. This Application is to be used pursuant to Section 3(1) of Act 242, P.A. of 1969 for the purpose of registering a trademark or service mark. A trademark is any word, name, symbol, or device, or any combination thereof, other than a trade name in its entirety, adopted and used by a person to identify goods made or sold by him or her and to distinguish them from similar goods made or sold by others. Similarly, a service mark is a mark used by a person in the sale or advertising of services to identify his or her services and distinguish them from the similar services of others. The term person, as used above, means an individual, firm, partnership, corporation, association, union, or other organization. A mark is not registrable until it has actually been adopted and used in Michigan. The registration is effective for ten years and is renewable for successive terms of 10 years upon the filing of an application for renewal, on a form provided by the Bureau, within six months prior to the expiration date.

4. The Department of Consumer & Industry Services, Bureau of Commercial Services is appointed as the applicant's agent for service of process in actions relating to the registration or application for registration if: (1) the applicant is or becomes a nonresident individual, partnership or association, (2) the applicant is or becomes a foreign corporation or limited liability company without a certificate of authority to transact business in Michigan, or (3) the applicant cannot be found in Michigan.

5. Item 2 - Complete section (a), (b) or (c) depending on the type of mark that is being registered.

6. Trademarks only:
    Item 3(a) - List the good(s) on which the mark is used.
    Item 3(b) - List how the mark is used on the good(s) i.e. tag, label, etc.
    Item 3(c) - List the classification of the good, but be aware that only one classification can be designated per application.
       A list of the classification codes can be found on the back of this Application.

7. Service marks only:
    Item 4(a) - List the service(s) in connection with which the mark is used.
    Item 4(b) - List how the mark is used i.e. in advertising, signs, letterhead, etc.
    Item 4(c) - List the classification of the good, but be aware that only one classification can be designated per application.
       A list of the classification codes can be found on the back of this Application.

8. Item 5 - A trademark is considered "used in Michigan" when affixed to the product, container, tags or labels and sold in Michigan. For services, the mark must be used or displayed in this state in the sale or advertising of services rendered in Michigan.

9. Item 8 - Two copies, photographs, facsimiles or specimens of the mark, as actually in use must accompany this Application. The sample should be 8.5 x 11 inches or smaller so it may be maintained on electronic format.

10. This Application must be signed by:
    Individual - by the applicant
    Corporation - by an authorized officer or agent.
    Limited Liability Company - by a manager if management is vested in one or more managers or by a member if
       management is reserved for members.
    Partnership - by a partner.

11. NONREFUNDABLE FEE: Make remittance payable to the State of Michigan $50.00

To submit by mail:	To submit in person:
Michigan Department of Consumer & Industry Services Bureau of Commercial Services Corporation Division 7150 Harris Drive P.O. Box 30054 Lansing, MI 48909	6546 Mercantile Way Lansing, MI Telephone: (517) 241-6400 Fees may be paid by VISA or Mastercard when delivered in person to our office.

SAMPLE FORM 8109-B: FEDERAL TAX DEPOSIT COUPONS

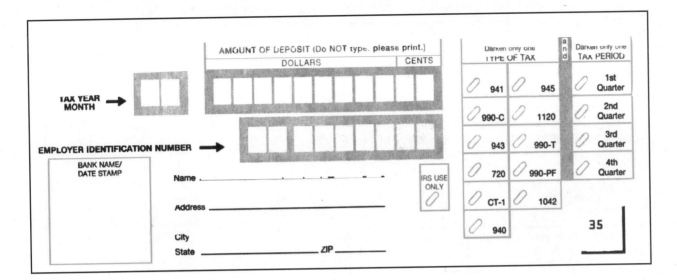

Sample Form 1040-ES: Estimated Tax Payment Voucher

Cat. No. 61900V

OMB No. 1545-0087

Form 1040-ES (OCR)

2000 Estimated Tax

Payment Voucher **4**

Calendar year—
Due Jan. 15, 2001

Department of the Treasury
Internal Revenue Service

Cross out any errors and print the correct information. Get **Form 8822** to report a new address (see instructions). For Paperwork Reduction Act Notice, see instructions.

0746497

07 234-56-7890 DC 9712

234-56-7890 DC WARD 30 0 9712 430 07

**JOHN DOE
123 ANYWHERE STREET
LANSING, MI 48908**

LANSING MI 48900-0001

| Enter the amount of your payment. File this voucher only if you are making a payment of **estimated** tax. | $ | ▸ Make your check or money order payable to **"Internal Revenue Service."** ▸ Write your social security number and "1997 Form 1040-ES" on your payment. ▸ Send your payment and payment voucher to the address above. ▸ Do not send cash. Do not staple your payment to the voucher. |

SAMPLE FORM W-2: WAGE AND TAX STATEMENT

a Control number	22222	Void ☐	For Official Use Only ▶ OMB No. 1545-0008		
b Employer's identification number 59-123456			**1** Wages, tips, other compensation 25,650.00		**2** Federal income tax withheld 5,050.00
c Employer's name, address, and ZIP code Doe Company 123 Main Street Lansing, MI 48910			**3** Social security wages 25,650.00		**4** Social security tax withheld 1,590.30
			5 Medicare wages and tips 25,650.00		**6** Medicare tax withheld 371.93
			7 Social security tips 0		**8** Allocated tips 0
d Employee's social security number 123-45-6789			**9** Advance EIC payment 0		**10** Dependent care benefits 0
e Employee's name (first, middle initial, last) John A. Smith 567 Wharf Boulevard Lansing, MI 48910			**11** Nonqualified plans 0		**12** Benefits included in box 1 0
			13 See Instrs. for box 13		**14** Other

15 Statutory employee ☐	Deceased ☐	Pension plan ☐	Legal rep. ☐	Hshld. emp. ☐	Subtotal ☐	Deferred compensation ☐

f Employee's address and ZIP code

16 State	Employer's state I.D. No.	**17** State wages, tips, etc.	**18** State income tax	**19** Locality name	**20** Local wages, tips, etc.	**21** Local income tax
MI	98765432	25,650.00	565.00			

Cat. No. 10134D

Department of the Treasury—Internal Revenue Service

Form W-2 Wage and Tax Statement 2000

Copy A For Social Security Administration

For Paperwork Reduction Act Notice, see separate instructions.

SAMPLE FORM 1099: MISCELLANEOUS INCOME

9595	☐ VOID	☐ CORRECTED			
PAYER'S name, street address, city, state, and ZIP code Doe Company 123 Main Street Lansing, MI 48910	1 Rents $ 12,000.00	OMB No. 1545-0115 20**00** Form **1099-MISC**	**Miscellaneous Income**		
	2 Royalties $				
	3 Other income $				
PAYER'S Federal identification number 59-123456	RECIPIENT'S identification number 9876532	4 Federal income tax withheld $	5 Fishing boat proceeds $	Copy A	
RECIPIENT'S name John A. Smith		6 Medical and health care payments $	7 Nonemployee compensation $ 21,000	For **Internal Revenue Service Center**	
Street address (including apt. no.) 567 Wharf Boulevard		8 Substitute payments in lieu of dividends or interest $	9 Payer made direct sales of $5,000 or more of consumer products to a buyer (recipient) for resale ▶ ☐	**File with Form 1096.** For Paperwork Reduction Act Notice and instructions for completing this form, see **Instructions for Forms 1099, 1098, 5498, and W-2G.**	
City, state, and ZIP code Lansing, MI 48910		10 Crop insurance proceeds $	11 State income tax withheld $ 00.00		
Account number (optional)	2nd TIN Not. ☐	12 State/Payer's state number 8884444			

Form **1099-MISC**   Cat. No. 14425J   Department of the Treasury - Internal Revenue Service

Do NOT Cut or Separate Forms on This Page

SAMPLE FORM 1096: MISCELLANEOUS INCOME

DO NOT STAPLE 6969

Form **1096**	**Annual Summary and Transmittal of U.S. Information Returns**	OMB No. 1545-0108
Department of the Treasury Internal Revenue Service		2000

ATTACH IRS LABEL HERE

FILER'S name

Doe Company

Street address (including room or suite number)

123 Main Street

City, state, and ZIP code

Lansing, MI 48910

If you are not using a preprinted label, enter in box 1 or 2 below the identification number you used as the filer on the information returns being transmitted. Do not fill in both boxes 1 and 2.

Name of person to contact if the IRS needs more information

John Doe
Telephone number
(517) 5550000

For Official Use Only

1 Employer identification number	2 Social security number	3 Total number of forms	4 Federal income tax withheld	5 Total amount reported with this Form 1096
59-123456		3	$ 0	$ $63,000

If this is your FINAL return, enter an "X" here . . . ▶ ☒

W-2G 32	1098 81	1099-A 80	1099-B 79	1099-C 85	1099-DIV 91	1099-G 86	1099-INT 92	1099-MISC 95	1099-OID 96	1099-PATR 97	1099-R 98	1099-S 75	5498 28
☐	☐	☐	☐	☐	☐	☐	☐	☒	☐	☐	☐	☐	☐

201

Appendix C
Blank Forms

The following forms may be photocopied or removed from this book and used immediately. Some of the tax forms explained in this book are not included here because you should use original forms provided by the IRS, the Michigan Department of Treasury, or some other agency as explained in the portion of this book where the particular form was discussed.

TAX TIMETABLE

	MICHIGAN				FEDERAL			
	SUW*	SBT**	Unemploy.	Est. Tax	Est. Tax	Annual Return	Form 941***	Misc.
JAN.	15th		25th	15th	15th		31st	31st 940 W-2 508 1099
FEB.	15th							28th W-3
MAR.	15th					15th		
APR.	15th	30th Ann. Ret.	25th	15th	15th	15th	30th	30th 508
MAY	15th							
JUN.	15th			15th	15th			
JUL.	15th		25th				31st	31st 508
AUG.	15th							
SEP.	15th			15th	15th			
OCT.	15th		25th				31st	31st 508
NOV.	15th							
DEC.	15th							

*   SUW = Sales, Use & Withholding taxes; a combined return is filed.

**   SBT = Single Business Tax. Based on calendar year. If fiscal year, due 15th day of 4th month after end of fiscal year, Quarterly returns are required if you expect annual liability greater than $600.

*** In addition to Form 941, deposits must be made regularly if withholding exceeds $500 in any month.

This page intentionally left blank.

Form **SS-4**

(Rev. April 2000)

Department of the Treasury
Internal Revenue Service

Application for Employer Identification Number

(For use by employers, corporations, partnerships, trusts, estates, churches, government agencies, certain individuals, and others. See instructions.)

▶ **Keep a copy for your records.**

EIN

OMB No. 1545-0003

Please type or print clearly.

1 Name of applicant (legal name) (see instructions)	
2 Trade name of business (if different from name on line 1)	**3** Executor, trustee, "care of" name
4a Mailing address (street address) (room, apt., or suite no.)	**5a** Business address (if different from address on lines 4a and 4b)
4b City, state, and ZIP code	**5b** City, state, and ZIP code
6 County and state where principal business is located	
7 Name of principal officer, general partner, grantor, owner, or trustor—SSN or ITIN may be required (see instructions) ▶	

8a Type of entity (Check only one box.) (see instructions)

Caution: *If applicant is a limited liability company, see the instructions for line 8a.*

☐ Sole proprietor (SSN) _____

☐ Partnership   ☐ Personal service corp.

☐ REMIC   ☐ National Guard

☐ State/local government   ☐ Farmers' cooperative

☐ Church or church-controlled organization

☐ Other nonprofit organization (specify) ▶ _____

☐ Other (specify) ▶

☐ Estate (SSN of decedent) _____

☐ Plan administrator (SSN) _____

☐ Other corporation (specify) ▶ _____

☐ Trust

☐ Federal government/military

(enter GEN if applicable) _____

8b If a corporation, name the state or foreign country (if applicable) where incorporated

State	Foreign country

9 Reason for applying (Check only one box.) (see instructions)

☐ Started new business (specify type) ▶ _____

☐ Hired employees (Check the box and see line 12.)

☐ Created a pension plan (specify type) ▶

☐ Banking purpose (specify purpose) ▶ _____

☐ Changed type of organization (specify new type) ▶ _____

☐ Purchased going business

☐ Created a trust (specify type) ▶ _____

☐ Other (specify) ▶ _____

10 Date business started or acquired (month, day, year) (see instructions)

11 Closing month of accounting year (see instructions)

12 First date wages or annuities were paid or will be paid (month, day, year). **Note:** *If applicant is a withholding agent, enter date income will first be paid to nonresident alien. (month, day, year)* . . . . ▶

	Nonagricultural	Agricultural	Household
13 Highest number of employees expected in the next 12 months. **Note:** *If the applicant does not expect to have any employees during the period, enter -0-. (see instructions)* . . . . ▶			

14 Principal activity (see instructions) ▶

15 Is the principal business activity manufacturing? . . . .   ☐ Yes   ☐ No

If "Yes," principal product and raw material used ▶

16 To whom are most of the products or services sold? Please check one box.   ☐ Business (wholesale)   ☐ N/A

☐ Public (retail)   ☐ Other (specify) ▶

17a Has the applicant ever applied for an employer identification number for this or any other business? . . . .   ☐ Yes   ☐ No

Note: *If "Yes," please complete lines 17b and 17c.*

17b If you checked "Yes" on line 17a, give applicant's legal name and trade name shown on prior application, if different from line 1 or 2 above.

Legal name ▶   Trade name ▶

17c Approximate date when and city and state where the application was filed. Enter previous employer identification number if known.

Approximate date when filed (mo., day, year)	City and state where filed	Previous EIN

Under penalties of perjury, I declare that I have examined this application, and to the best of my knowledge and belief, it is true, correct, and complete.

Business telephone number (include area code)

( )

Fax telephone number (include area code)

( )

Name and title (Please type or print clearly.) ▶

Signature ▶   Date ▶

Note: *Do not write below this line. For official use only.*

Please leave blank ▶	Geo.	Ind.	Class	Size	Reason for applying

For Privacy Act and Paperwork Reduction Act Notice, see page 4.   Cat. No. 16055N   Form **SS-4** (Rev. 4-2000)

General Instructions

Section references are to the Internal Revenue Code unless otherwise noted.

Purpose of Form

Use Form SS-4 to apply for an employer identification number (EIN). An EIN is a nine-digit number (for example, 12-3456789) assigned to sole proprietors, corporations, partnerships, estates, trusts, and other entities for tax filing and reporting purposes. The information you provide on this form will establish your business tax account.

Caution: *An EIN is for use in connection with your business activities only. Do **not** use your EIN in place of your social security number (SSN).*

Who Must File

You must file this form if you have not been assigned an EIN before and:

• You pay wages to one or more employees including household employees.

• You are required to have an EIN to use on any return, statement, or other document, even if you are not an employer.

• You are a withholding agent required to withhold taxes on income, other than wages, paid to a nonresident alien (individual, corporation, partnership, etc.). A withholding agent may be an agent, broker, fiduciary, manager, tenant, or spouse, and is required to file **Form 1042,** Annual Withholding Tax Return for U.S. Source Income of Foreign Persons.

• You file **Schedule C,** Profit or Loss From Business, **Schedule C-EZ,** Net Profit From Business, or **Schedule F,** Profit or Loss From Farming, of **Form 1040,** U.S. Individual Income Tax Return, **and** have a Keogh plan or are required to file excise, employment, or alcohol, tobacco, or firearms returns.

The following must use EINs even if they do not have any employees:

• State and local agencies who serve as tax reporting agents for public assistance recipients, under Rev. Proc. 80-4, 1980-1 C.B. 581, should obtain a separate EIN for this reporting. See **Household employer** on page 3.

• Trusts, except the following:

1. Certain grantor-owned trusts. (See the **Instructions for Form 1041,** U.S. Income Tax Return for Estates and Trusts.)

2. Individual retirement arrangement (IRA) trusts, unless the trust has to file **Form 990-T,** Exempt Organization Business Income Tax Return. (See the **Instructions for Form 990-T.**)

• Estates

• Partnerships

• REMICs (real estate mortgage investment conduits) (See the **Instructions for Form 1066,** U.S. Real Estate Mortgage Investment Conduit (REMIC) Income Tax Return.)

• Corporations

• Nonprofit organizations (churches, clubs, etc.)

• Farmers' cooperatives

• Plan administrators (A plan administrator is the person or group of persons specified as the administrator by the instrument under which the plan is operated.)

When To Apply for a New EIN

New Business. If you become the new owner of an existing business, **do not** use the EIN of the former owner. **If you already have an EIN, use that number.** If you do not have an EIN, apply for one on this form. If you become the "owner" of a corporation by acquiring its stock, use the corporation's EIN.

Changes in Organization or Ownership. If you already have an EIN, you may need to get a new one if either the organization or ownership of your business changes. If you incorporate a sole proprietorship or form a partnership, you must get a new EIN. However, **do not** apply for a new EIN if:

• You change only the name of your business,

• You elected on **Form 8832,** Entity Classification Election, to change the way the entity is taxed, or

• A partnership terminates because at least 50% of the total interests in partnership capital and profits were sold or exchanged within a 12-month period. (See Regulations section 301.6109-1(d)(2)(iii).) The EIN for the terminated partnership should continue to be used.

Note: *If you are electing to be an "S corporation," be sure you file **Form 2553,** Election by a Small Business Corporation.*

File Only One Form SS-4. File only one Form SS-4, regardless of the number of businesses operated or trade names under which a business operates. However, each corporation in an affiliated group must file a separate application.

EIN Applied for, But Not Received. If you do not have an EIN by the time a return is due, write "Applied for" and the date you applied in the space shown for the number. **Do not** show your social security number (SSN) as an EIN on returns.

If you do not have an EIN by the time a tax deposit is due, send your payment to the Internal Revenue Service Center for your filing area. (See **Where To Apply** below.) Make your check or money order payable to "United States Treasury" and show your name (as shown on Form SS-4), address, type of tax, period covered, and date you applied for an EIN. Send an explanation with the deposit.

For more information about EINs, see **Pub. 583,** Starting a Business and Keeping Records, and **Pub. 1635,** Understanding Your EIN.

How To Apply

You can apply for an EIN either by mail or by telephone. You can get an EIN immediately by calling the Tele-TIN number for the service center for your state, or you can send the completed Form SS-4 directly to the service center to receive your EIN by mail.

Application by Tele-TIN. Under the Tele-TIN program, you can receive your EIN by telephone and use it immediately to file a return or make a payment. To receive an EIN by telephone, complete Form SS-4, then call the Tele-TIN number listed for your state under **Where To Apply.** The person making the call must be authorized to sign the form. (See **Signature** on page 4.)

An IRS representative will use the information from the Form SS-4 to establish your account and assign you an EIN. Write the number you are given on the upper right corner of the form and sign and date it.

Mail or fax (facsimile) the signed Form SS-4 **within 24 hours** to the Tele-TIN Unit at the service center address for your state. The IRS representative will give you the fax number. The fax numbers are also listed in Pub. 1635.

Taxpayer representatives can receive their client's EIN by telephone if they first send a fax of a completed **Form 2848,** Power of Attorney and Declaration of Representative, or **Form 8821,** Tax Information Authorization, to the Tele-TIN unit. The Form 2848 or Form 8821 will be used solely to release the EIN to the representative authorized on the form.

Application by Mail. Complete Form SS-4 at least 4 to 5 weeks before you will need an EIN. Sign and date the application and mail it to the service center address for your state. You will receive your EIN in the mail in approximately 4 weeks.

Where To Apply

The Tele-TIN numbers listed below will involve a long-distance charge to callers outside of the local calling area and can be used only to apply for an EIN. **The numbers may change without notice.** Call 1-800-829-1040 to verify a number or to ask about the status of an application by mail.

If your principal business, office or agency, or legal residence in the case of an individual, is located in:	Call the Tele-TIN number shown or file with the Internal Revenue Service Center at:
Florida, Georgia, South Carolina	Attn: Entity Control Atlanta, GA 39901 770-455-2360
New Jersey, New York (New York City and counties of Nassau, Rockland, Suffolk, and Westchester)	Attn: Entity Control Holtsville, NY 00501 631-447-4955
New York (all other counties), Connecticut, Maine, Massachusetts, New Hampshire, Rhode Island, Vermont	Attn: Entity Control Andover, MA 05501 978-474-9717
Illinois, Iowa, Minnesota, Missouri, Wisconsin	Attn: Entity Control Stop 6800 2306 E. Bannister Rd. Kansas City, MO 64999 816-823-7777
Delaware, District of Columbia, Maryland, Pennsylvania, Virginia	Attn: Entity Control Philadelphia, PA 19255 215-516-6999
Indiana, Kentucky, Michigan, Ohio, West Virginia	Attn: Entity Control Cincinnati, OH 45999 859-292-5467

Kansas, New Mexico, Oklahoma, Texas	Attn: Entity Control Austin, TX 73301 512-460-7843
Alaska, Arizona, California (counties of Alpine, Amador, Butte, Calaveras, Colusa, Contra Costa, Del Norte, El Dorado, Glenn, Humboldt, Lake, Lassen, Marin, Mendocino, Modoc, Napa, Nevada, Placer, Plumas, Sacramento, San Joaquin, Shasta, Sierra, Siskiyou, Solano, Sonoma, Sutter, Tehama, Trinity, Yolo, and Yuba), Colorado, Idaho, Montana, Nebraska, Nevada, North Dakota, Oregon, South Dakota, Utah, Washington, Wyoming	Attn: Entity Control Mail Stop 6271 P.O. Box 9941 Ogden, UT 84201 801-620-7645
California (all other counties), Hawaii	Attn: Entity Control Fresno, CA 93888 559-452-4010
Alabama, Arkansas, Louisiana, Mississippi, North Carolina, Tennessee	Attn: Entity Control Memphis, TN 37501 901-546-3920
If you have no legal residence, principal place of business, or principal office or agency in any state	Attn: Entity Control Philadelphia, PA 19255 215-516-6999

Specific Instructions

The instructions that follow are for those items that are not self-explanatory. Enter N/A (nonapplicable) on the lines that do not apply.

Line 1. Enter the legal name of the entity applying for the EIN exactly as it appears on the social security card, charter, or other applicable legal document.

Individuals. Enter your first name, middle initial, and last name. If you are a sole proprietor, enter your individual name, not your business name. Enter your business name on line 2. Do not use abbreviations or nicknames on line 1.

Trusts. Enter the name of the trust.

Estate of a decedent. Enter the name of the estate.

Partnerships. Enter the legal name of the partnership as it appears in the partnership agreement. **Do not** list the names of the partners on line 1. See the specific instructions for line 7.

Corporations. Enter the corporate name as it appears in the corporation charter or other legal document creating it.

Plan administrators. Enter the name of the plan administrator. A plan administrator who already has an EIN should use that number.

Line 2. Enter the trade name of the business if different from the legal name. The trade name is the "doing business as" name.

Note: *Use the full legal name on line 1 on all tax returns filed for the entity. However, if you enter a trade name on line 2 and choose to use the trade name instead of the legal name, enter the trade name on all returns you file. To prevent processing delays and errors, **always** use either the legal name only or the trade name only on all tax returns.*

Line 3. Trusts enter the name of the trustee. Estates enter the name of the executor, administrator, or other fiduciary. If the entity applying has a designated person to receive tax information, enter that person's name as the "care of" person. Print or type the first name, middle initial, and last name.

Line 7. Enter the first name, middle initial, last name, and SSN of a principal officer if the business is a corporation; of a general partner if a partnership; of the owner of a single member entity that is disregarded as an entity separate from its owner; or of a grantor, owner, or trustor if a trust. If the person in question is an alien individual with a previously assigned individual taxpayer identification number (ITIN), enter the ITIN in the space provided, instead of an SSN. You are not required to enter an SSN or ITIN if the reason you are applying for an EIN is to make an entity classification election (see Regulations section 301.7701-1 through 301.7701-3), and you are a nonresident alien with no effectively connected income from sources within the United States.

Line 8a. Check the box that best describes the type of entity applying for the EIN. If you are an alien individual with an ITIN previously assigned to you, enter the ITIN in place of a requested SSN.

Caution: *This is not an election for a tax classification of an entity. See "Limited liability company (LLC)" below.*

If not specifically mentioned, check the "Other" box, enter the type of entity and the type of return that will be filed (for example, common trust fund, Form 1065). Do not enter N/A. If you are an alien individual applying for an EIN, see the **Line 7** instructions above.

Sole proprietor. Check this box if you file Schedule C, C-EZ, or F (Form 1040) and have a qualified plan, or are required to file excise, employment, or alcohol, tobacco, or firearms returns, or are a payer of gambling winnings. Enter your SSN (or ITIN) in the space provided. If you are a nonresident alien with are a nonresident alien with no effectively connected income from sources within the United States, you do not need to enter an SSN or ITIN.

REMIC. Check this box if the entity has elected to be treated as a real estate mortgage investment conduit (REMIC). See the Instructions for Form 1066 for more information.

Other nonprofit organization. Check this box if the nonprofit organization is other than a church or church-controlled organization and specify the type of nonprofit organization (for example, an educational organization).

If the organization also seeks tax-exempt status, you must file either **Package 1023**, Application for Recognition of Exemption, or **Package 1024**, Application for Recognition of Exemption Under Section 501(a). Get **Pub. 557**, Tax Exempt Status for Your Organization, for more information.

Group exemption number (GEN). If the organization is covered by a group exemption letter, enter the four-digit GEN. (Do not confuse the GEN with the nine-digit EIN.) If you do not know the GEN, contact the parent organization. Get Pub. 557 for more information about group exemption numbers.

Withholding agent. If you are a withholding agent required to file Form 1042, check the "Other" box and enter "Withholding agent."

Personal service corporation. Check this box if the entity is a personal service corporation. An entity is a personal service corporation for a tax year only if:

● The principal activity of the entity during the testing period (prior tax year) for the tax year is the performance of personal services substantially by employee-owners, and

● The employee-owners own at least 10% of the fair market value of the outstanding stock in the entity on the last day of the testing period.

Personal services include performance of services in such fields as health, law, accounting, or consulting. For more information about personal service corporations, see the **Instructions for Forms 1120 and 1120-A**, and **Pub. 542**, Corporations.

Limited liability company (LLC). See the definition of limited liability company in the **Instructions for Form 1065**, U.S. Partnership Return of Income. An LLC with two or more members can be a partnership or an association taxable as a corporation. An LLC with a single owner can be an association taxable as a corporation or an entity disregarded as an entity separate from its owner. See Form 8832 for more details.

Note: *A domestic LLC with at least two members that does not file Form 8832 is classified as a partnership for Federal income tax purposes.*

● If the entity is classified as a partnership for Federal income tax purposes, check the "partnership" box.

● If the entity is classified as a corporation for Federal income tax purposes, check the "Other corporation" box and write "limited liability co." in the space provided.

● If the entity is disregarded as an entity separate from its owner, check the "Other" box and write in "disregarded entity" in the space provided.

Plan administrator. If the plan administrator is an individual, enter the plan administrator's SSN in the space provided.

Other corporation. This box is for any corporation other than a personal service corporation. If you check this box, enter the type of corporation (such as insurance company) in the space provided.

Household employer. If you are an individual, check the "Other" box and enter "Household employer" and your SSN. If you are a state or local agency serving as a tax reporting agent for public assistance recipients who become household employers, check the "Other" box and enter "Household employer agent." If you are a trust that qualifies as a household employer, you do not need a separate EIN for reporting tax information relating to household employees; use the EIN of the trust.

QSub. For a qualified subchapter S subsidiary (QSub) check the "Other" box and specify "QSub."

Line 9. Check only **one** box. Do not enter N/A.

Started new business. Check this box if you are starting a new business that requires an EIN. If you check this box, enter the type of business being started. **Do not** apply if you already have an EIN and are only adding another place of business.

Hired employees. Check this box if the existing business is requesting an EIN because it has hired or is hiring employees and is therefore required to file employment tax returns. **Do not** apply if you already have an EIN and are only hiring employees. For information on the applicable employment taxes for family members, see **Circular E**, Employer's Tax Guide (Publication 15).

Created a pension plan. Check this box if you have created a pension plan and need an EIN for reporting purposes. Also, enter the type of plan.

Note: *Check this box if you are applying for a trust EIN when a new pension plan is established.*

Banking purpose. Check this box if you are requesting an EIN for banking purposes only, and enter the banking purpose (for example, a bowling league for depositing dues or an investment club for dividend and interest reporting).

Changed type of organization. Check this box if the business is changing its type of organization, for example, if the business was a sole proprietorship and has been incorporated or has become a partnership. If you check this box, specify in the space provided the type of change made, for example, "from sole proprietorship to partnership."

Purchased going business. Check this box if you purchased an existing business. **Do not** use the former owner's EIN. **Do not** apply for a new EIN if you already have one. Use your own EIN.

Created a trust. Check this box if you created a trust, and enter the type of trust created. For example, indicate if the trust is a nonexempt charitable trust or a split-interest trust.

Note: *Do not check this box if you are applying for a trust EIN when a new pension plan is established. Check "Created a pension plan."*

Exception. Do **not** file this form for certain grantor-type trusts. The trustee does not need an EIN for the trust if the trustee furnishes the name and TIN of the grantor/owner and the address of the trust to all payors. See the Instructions for Form 1041 for more information.

Other (specify). Check this box if you are requesting an EIN for any other reason, and enter the reason.

Line 10. If you are starting a new business, enter the starting date of the business. If the business you acquired is already operating, enter the date you acquired the business. Trusts should enter the date the trust was legally created. Estates should enter the date of death of the decedent whose name appears on line 1 or the date when the estate was legally funded.

Line 11. Enter the last month of your accounting year or tax year. An accounting or tax year is usually 12 consecutive months, either a calendar year or a fiscal year (including a period of 52 or 53 weeks). A calendar year is 12 consecutive months ending on December 31. A fiscal year is either 12 consecutive months ending on the last day of any month other than December or a 52-53 week year. For more information on accounting periods, see Pub. 538, Accounting Periods and Methods.

Individuals. Your tax year generally will be a calendar year.

Partnerships. Partnerships generally must adopt one of the following tax years:
- The tax year of the majority of its partners,
- The tax year common to all of its principal partners,
- The tax year that results in the least aggregate deferral of income, or
- In certain cases, some other tax year.

See the Instructions for Form 1065 for more information.

REMIC. REMICs must have a calendar year as their tax year.

Personal service corporations. A personal service corporation generally must adopt a calendar year unless:
- It can establish a business purpose for having a different tax year, or
- It elects under section 444 to have a tax year other than a calendar year.

Trusts. Generally, a trust must adopt a calendar year except for the following:
- Tax-exempt trusts,
- Charitable trusts, and
- Grantor-owned trusts.

Line 12. If the business has or will have employees, enter the date on which the business began or will begin to pay wages. If the business does not plan to have employees, enter N/A.

Withholding agent. Enter the date you began or will begin to pay income to a nonresident alien. This also applies to individuals who are required to file Form 1042 to report alimony paid to a nonresident alien.

Line 13. For a definition of agricultural labor (farmwork), see **Circular A,** Agricultural Employer's Tax Guide (Publication 51).

Line 14. Generally, enter the exact type of business being operated (for example, advertising agency, farm, food or beverage establishment, labor union, real estate agency, steam laundry, rental of coin-operated vending machine, or investment club). Also state if the business will involve the sale or distribution of alcoholic beverages.

Governmental. Enter the type of organization (state, county, school district, municipality, etc.).

Nonprofit organization (other than governmental). Enter whether organized for religious, educational, or humane purposes, and the principal activity (for example, religious organization—hospital, charitable).

Mining and quarrying. Specify the process and the principal product (for example, mining bituminous coal, contract drilling for oil, or quarrying dimension stone).

Contract construction. Specify whether general contracting or special trade contracting. Also, show the type of work normally performed (for example, general contractor for residential buildings or electrical subcontractor).

Food or beverage establishments. Specify the type of establishment and state whether you employ workers who receive tips (for example, lounge—yes).

Trade. Specify the type of sales and the principal line of goods sold (for example, wholesale dairy products, manufacturer's representative for mining machinery, or retail hardware).

Manufacturing. Specify the type of establishment operated (for example, sawmill or vegetable cannery).

Signature. The application must be signed by (a) the individual, if the applicant is an individual, (b) the president, vice president, or other principal officer, if the applicant is a corporation, (c) a responsible and duly authorized member or officer having knowledge of its affairs, if the applicant is a partnership or other unincorporated organization, or (d) the fiduciary, if the applicant is a trust or an estate.

How To Get Forms and Publications

Phone. You can order forms, instructions, and publications by phone 24 hours a day, 7 days a week. Just call 1-800-TAX-FORM (1-800-829-3676). You should receive your order or notification of its status within 10 workdays.

Personal computer. With your personal computer and modem, you can get the forms and information you need using IRS's Internet Web Site at **www.irs.gov** or File Transfer Protocol at **ftp.irs.gov.**

CD-ROM. For small businesses, return preparers, or others who may frequently need tax forms or publications, a CD-ROM containing over 2,000 tax products (including many prior year forms) can be purchased from the National Technical Information Service (NTIS).

To order **Pub. 1796,** Federal Tax Products on CD-ROM, call **1-877-CDFORMS** (1-877-233-6767) toll free or connect to **www.irs.gov/cdorders**

Form **2553**
(Rev. January 2001)

Department of the Treasury
Internal Revenue Service

Election by a Small Business Corporation
(Under section 1362 of the Internal Revenue Code)
▶ See Parts II and III on back and the separate instructions.
▶ The corporation may either send or fax this form to the IRS. See page 1 of the instructions.

OMB No. 1545-0146

Notes: 1. *This election to be an S corporation can be accepted only if all the tests are met under* **Who May Elect** *on page 1 of the instructions; all signatures in Parts I and III are originals (no photocopies); and the exact name and address of the corporation and other required form information are provided.*

2. *Do not file* **Form 1120S,** *U.S. Income Tax Return for an S Corporation, for any tax year before the year the election takes effect.*

3. *If the corporation was in existence before the effective date of this election, see* **Taxes an S Corporation May Owe** *on page 1 of the instructions.*

Part I	Election Information

Please Type or Print

Name of corporation (see instructions)	**A**	Employer identification number
Number, street, and room or suite no. (If a P.O. box, see instructions.)	**B**	Date incorporated
City or town, state, and ZIP code	**C**	State of incorporation

D Election is to be effective for tax year beginning (month, day, year) . . . . ▶   /   /

E Name and title of officer or legal representative who the IRS may call for more information   **F** Telephone number of officer or legal representative

(   )

G If the corporation changed its name or address after applying for the EIN shown in **A** above, check this box . . . . ▶ ☐

H If this election takes effect for the first tax year the corporation exists, enter month, day, and year of the **earliest** of the following: (1) date the corporation first had shareholders, (2) date the corporation first had assets, or (3) date the corporation began doing business . . . . ▶   /   /

I Selected tax year: Annual return will be filed for tax year ending (month and day) ▶ . . . .

If the tax year ends on any date other than December 31, except for an automatic 52-53-week tax year ending with reference to the month of December, you **must** complete Part II on the back. If the date you enter is the ending date of an automatic 52-53-week tax year, write "52-53-week year" to the right of the date. See Temporary Regulations section 1.441-2T(e)(3).

J Name and address of each shareholder; shareholder's spouse having a community property interest in the corporation's stock; and each tenant in common, joint tenant, and tenant by the entirety. (A husband and wife (and their estates) are counted as one shareholder in determining the number of shareholders without regard to the manner in which the stock is owned.)	K Shareholders' Consent Statement. Under penalties of perjury, we declare that we consent to the election of the above-named corporation to be an S corporation under section 1362(a) and that we have examined this consent statement, including accompanying schedules and statements, and to the best of our knowledge and belief, it is true, correct, and complete. We understand our consent is binding and may not be withdrawn after the corporation has made a valid election. (Shareholders sign and date below.)		L Stock owned		M Social security number or employer identification number (see instructions)	N Share-holder's tax year ends (month and day)
	Signature	Date	Number of shares	Dates acquired		

Under penalties of perjury, I declare that I have examined this election, including accompanying schedules and statements, and to the best of my knowledge and belief, it is true, correct, and complete.

Signature of officer ▶   Title ▶   Date ▶

For Paperwork Reduction Act Notice, see page 4 of the instructions.   Cat. No. 18629R   Form **2553** (Rev. 1-2001)

Part II   Selection of Fiscal Tax Year (All corporations using this part must complete item O and item P, Q, or R.)

O   Check the applicable box to indicate whether the corporation is:

1. ☐ A new corporation adopting the tax year entered in item I, Part I.

2. ☐ An existing corporation retaining the tax year entered in item I, Part I.

3. ☐ An existing corporation changing to the tax year entered in item I, Part I.

P   Complete item P if the corporation is using the expeditious approval provisions of Rev. Proc. 87-32, 1987-2 C.B. 396, to request **(1)** a natural business year (as defined in section 4.01(1) of Rev. Proc. 87-32) or **(2)** a year that satisfies the ownership tax year test in section 4.01(2) of Rev. Proc. 87-32. Check the applicable box below to indicate the representation statement the corporation is making as required under section 4 of Rev. Proc. 87-32.

1. Natural Business Year ▶ ☐ I represent that the corporation is retaining or changing to a tax year that coincides with its natural business year as defined in section 4.01(1) of Rev. Proc. 87-32 and as verified by its satisfaction of the requirements of section 4.02(1) of Rev. Proc. 87-32. In addition, if the corporation is changing to a natural business year as defined in section 4.01(1), I further represent that such tax year results in less deferral of income to the owners than the corporation's present tax year. I also represent that the corporation is not described in section 3.01(2) of Rev. Proc. 87-32. (See instructions for additional information that must be attached.)

2. Ownership Tax Year ▶ ☐ I represent that shareholders holding more than half of the shares of the stock (as of the first day of the tax year to which the request relates) of the corporation have the same tax year or are concurrently changing to the tax year that the corporation adopts, retains, or changes to per item I, Part I. I also represent that the corporation is not described in section 3.01(2) of Rev. Proc. 87-32.

Note: If you do not use item P and the corporation wants a fiscal tax year, complete either item Q or R below. Item Q is used to request a fiscal tax year based on a business purpose and to make a back-up section 444 election. Item R is used to make a regular section 444 election.

Q   Business Purpose—To request a fiscal tax year based on a business purpose, you must check box Q1 and pay a user fee. See instructions for details. You may also check box Q2 and/or box Q3.

1. Check here ▶ ☐ if the fiscal year entered in item I, Part I, is requested under the provisions of section 6.03 of Rev. Proc. 87-32. Attach to Form 2553 a statement showing the business purpose for the requested fiscal year. See instructions for additional information that must be attached.

2. Check here ▶ ☐ to show that the corporation intends to make a back-up section 444 election in the event the corporation's business purpose request is not approved by the IRS. (See instructions for more information.)

3. Check here ▶ ☐ to show that the corporation agrees to adopt or change to a tax year ending December 31 if necessary for the IRS to accept this election for S corporation status in the event (1) the corporation's business purpose request is not approved and the corporation makes a back-up section 444 election, but is ultimately not qualified to make a section 444 election, or (2) the corporation's business purpose request is not approved and the corporation did not make a back-up section 444 election.

R   Section 444 Election—To make a section 444 election, you must check box R1 and you may also check box R2.

1. Check here ▶ ☐ to show the corporation will make, if qualified, a section 444 election to have the fiscal tax year shown in item I, Part I. To make the election, you must complete **Form 8716**, Election To Have a Tax Year Other Than a Required Tax Year, and either attach it to Form 2553 or file it separately.

2. Check here ▶ ☐ to show that the corporation agrees to adopt or change to a tax year ending December 31 if necessary for the IRS to accept this election for S corporation status in the event the corporation is ultimately not qualified to make a section 444 election.

Part III   Qualified Subchapter S Trust (QSST) Election Under Section 1361(d)(2)*

Income beneficiary's name and address	Social security number
Trust's name and address	Employer identification number

Date on which stock of the corporation was transferred to the trust (month, day, year) . . . . ▶   /   /

In order for the trust named above to be a QSST and thus a qualifying shareholder of the S corporation for which this Form 2553 is filed, I hereby make the election under section 1361(d)(2). Under penalties of perjury, I certify that the trust meets the definitional requirements of section 1361(d)(3) and that all other information provided in Part III is true, correct, and complete.

Signature of income beneficiary or signature and title of legal representative or other qualified person making the election   Date

*Use Part III to make the QSST election only if stock of the corporation has been transferred to the trust on or before the date on which the corporation makes its election to be an S corporation. The QSST election must be made and filed separately if stock of the corporation is transferred to the trust after the date on which the corporation makes the S election.

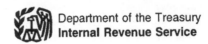
Department of the Treasury
Internal Revenue Service

Election by a Small Business Corporation

Section references are to the Internal Revenue Code unless otherwise noted.

A Change To Note

Corporations may be mailing forms and elections to different service centers in 2001 and again in 2002 because the IRS has changed the filing location for several areas.

General Instructions

Purpose

To elect to be an S corporation, a corporation must file Form 2553. The election permits the income of the S corporation to be taxed to the shareholders of the corporation rather than to the corporation itself, except as noted below under **Taxes an S Corporation May Owe.**

Who May Elect

A corporation may elect to be an S corporation only if it meets all of the following tests:

1. It is a domestic corporation.

2. It has no more than 75 shareholders. A husband and wife (and their estates) are treated as one shareholder for this requirement. All other persons are treated as separate shareholders.

3. Its only shareholders are individuals, estates, exempt organizations described in section 401(a) or 501(c)(3), or certain trusts described in section 1361(c)(2)(A). See the instructions for Part III regarding qualified subchapter S trusts (QSSTs).

A trustee of a trust wanting to make an election under section 1361(e)(3) to be an electing small business trust (ESBT) should see Notice 97-12, 1997-1 C.B. 385. Also see Rev. Proc. 98-23, 1998-1 C.B. 662, for guidance on how to convert a QSST to an ESBT. If there was an inadvertent failure to timely file an ESBT election, see the relief provisions under Rev. Proc. 98-55, 1998-2 C.B. 643.

4. It has no nonresident alien shareholders.

5. It has only one class of stock (disregarding differences in voting rights). Generally, a corporation is treated as having only one class of stock if all outstanding shares of the corporation's stock confer identical rights to distribution and liquidation proceeds. See Regulations section 1.1361-1(l) for details.

6. It is not one of the following ineligible corporations:

a. A bank or thrift institution that uses the reserve method of accounting for bad debts under section 585,

b. An insurance company subject to tax under the rules of subchapter L of the Code,

c. A corporation that has elected to be treated as a possessions corporation under section 936, or

d. A domestic international sales corporation (DISC) or former DISC.

7. It has a permitted tax year as required by section 1378 or makes a section 444 election to have a tax year other than a permitted tax year. Section 1378 defines a permitted tax year as a tax year ending December 31, or any other tax year for which the corporation establishes a business purpose to the satisfaction of the IRS. See Part II for details on requesting a fiscal tax year based on a business purpose or on making a section 444 election.

8. Each shareholder consents as explained in the instructions for column K.

See sections 1361, 1362, and 1378 for additional information on the above tests.

A parent S corporation can elect to treat an eligible wholly-owned subsidiary as a qualified subchapter S subsidiary (QSub). If the election is made, the assets, liabilities, and items of income, deduction, and credit of the QSub are treated as those of the parent. To make the election, get **Form 8869,** Qualified Subchapter S Subsidiary Election. If the QSub election was not timely filed, the corporation may be entitled to relief under Rev. Proc. 98-55.

Taxes an S Corporation May Owe

An S corporation may owe income tax in the following instances:

1. If, at the end of any tax year, the corporation had accumulated earnings and profits, and its passive investment income under section 1362(d)(3) is more than 25% of its gross receipts, the corporation may owe tax on its excess net passive income.

2. A corporation with net recognized built-in gain (as defined in section 1374(d)(2)) may owe tax on its built-in gains.

3. A corporation that claimed investment credit before its first year as an S corporation will be liable for any investment credit recapture tax.

4. A corporation that used the LIFO inventory method for the year immediately preceding its first year as an S corporation may owe an additional tax due to LIFO recapture. The tax is paid in four equal installments, the first of which must be paid by the due date (not including extensions) of the corporation's income tax return for its last tax year as a C corporation.

For more details on these taxes, see the Instructions for Form 1120S.

Where To File

Send or fax this election to the Internal Revenue Service Center listed on page 2. If the corporation files this election by fax, keep the original Form 2553 with the corporation's permanent records.

Cat. No. 49978N

Use the list below if filing the election before January 1, 2002. Use the list in the second column if filing the election after December 31, 2001.

If the corporation's principal business, office, or agency is located in ▼	Use the following Internal Revenue Service Center address or fax number ▼
New York (New York City and counties of Nassau, Rockland, Suffolk, and Westchester)	Holtsville, NY 00501 (631) 654-6567
New York (all other counties), Connecticut, Maine, Massachusetts, New Hampshire, Rhode Island, Vermont	Andover, MA 05501 (978) 474-5633
Florida, Georgia	Atlanta, GA 39901 (770) 454-1607
Delaware, District of Columbia, Indiana, Kentucky, Maryland, Michigan, New Jersey, North Carolina, Ohio, Pennsylvania, South Carolina, West Virginia, Wisconsin	Cincinnati, OH 45999 (859) 292-5289
Kansas, New Mexico, Oklahoma	Austin, TX 73301 (512) 460-4046
Alaska, Arizona, Arkansas, California (counties of Alpine, Amador, Butte, Calaveras, Colusa, Contra Costa, Del Norte, El Dorado, Glenn, Humboldt, Lake, Lassen, Marin, Mendocino, Modoc, Napa, Nevada, Placer, Plumas, Sacramento, San Joaquin, Shasta, Sierra, Siskiyou, Solano, Sonoma, Sutter, Tehama, Trinity, Yolo, and Yuba), Colorado, Hawaii, Idaho, Iowa, Louisiana, Minnesota, Mississippi, Missouri, Montana, Nebraska, Nevada, North Dakota, Oregon, South Dakota, Texas, Utah, Washington, Wyoming	Ogden, UT 84201 (801) 620-7116
California (all other counties)	Fresno, CA 93888 (559) 443-5030
Illinois	Kansas City, MO 64999 (816) 823-7861
Alabama, Tennessee	Memphis, TN 37501 (901) 546-3900
Virginia	Philadelphia, PA 19255 (215) 516-3048

 *Use the list below **only** for elections filed after December 31, 2001.*

If the corporation's principal business, office, or agency is located in ▼	Use the following Internal Revenue Service Center address or fax number ▼
Connecticut, Delaware, District of Columbia, Illinois, Indiana, Kentucky, Maine, Maryland, Massachusetts, Michigan, New Hampshire, New Jersey, New York, North Carolina, Ohio, Pennsylvania, Rhode Island, South Carolina, Vermont, Virginia, West Virginia, Wisconsin	Cincinnati, OH 45999 (859) 292-5289
Alabama, Alaska, Arizona, Arkansas, California, Colorado, Florida, Georgia, Hawaii, Idaho, Iowa, Kansas, Louisiana, Minnesota, Mississippi, Missouri, Montana, Nebraska, Nevada, New Mexico, North Dakota, Oklahoma, Oregon, South Dakota, Tennessee, Texas, Utah, Washington, Wyoming	Ogden, UT 84201 (801) 620-7116

When To Make the Election

Complete and file Form 2553 **(a)** at any time before the 16th day of the 3rd month of the tax year, if filed during the tax year the election is to take effect, or **(b)** at any time during the preceding tax year. An election made no later than 2 months and 15 days after the beginning of a tax year that is less than 2½ months long is treated as timely made for that tax year. An election made after the 15th day of the 3rd month but before the end of the tax year is effective for the next year. For example, if a calendar tax year corporation makes the election in April 2001, it is effective for the corporation's 2002 calendar tax year.

However, an election made after the due date will be accepted as timely filed if the corporation can show that the failure to file on time was due to reasonable cause. To request relief for a late election, the corporation generally must request a private letter ruling and pay a user fee in accordance with Rev. Proc. 2000-1, 2000-1 I.R.B. 4 (or its successor). But if the election is filed within 12 months of its due date and the original due date for filing the corporation's initial Form 1120S has not passed, the ruling and user fee requirements do not apply. To request relief in this case, write "FILED PURSUANT TO REV. PROC. 98-55" at the top of page 1 of Form 2553, attach a statement explaining the reason for failing to file the election on time, and file Form 2553 as otherwise instructed. See Rev. Proc. 98-55 for more details.

See Regulations section 1.1362-6(b)(3)(iii) for how to obtain relief for an inadvertent invalid election if the corporation filed a timely election, but one or more shareholders did not file a timely consent.

Acceptance or Nonacceptance of Election

The service center will notify the corporation if its election is accepted and when it will take effect. The corporation will also be notified if its election is not accepted. The corporation should generally receive a determination on

Page 2

its election within 60 days after it has filed Form 2553. If box Q1 in Part II is checked on page 2, the corporation will receive a ruling letter from the IRS in Washington, DC, that either approves or denies the selected tax year. When box Q1 is checked, it will generally take an additional 90 days for the Form 2553 to be accepted.

Do not file Form 1120S for any tax year before the year the election takes effect. If the corporation is now required to file **Form 1120**, U.S. Corporation Income Tax Return, or any other applicable tax return, continue filing it until the election takes effect.

Care should be exercised to ensure that the IRS receives the election. If the corporation is not notified of acceptance or nonacceptance of its election within 3 months of the date of filing (date mailed), or within 6 months if box Q1 is checked, take follow-up action by corresponding with the service center where the corporation filed the election.

If the IRS questions whether Form 2553 was filed, an acceptable proof of filing is **(a)** certified or registered mail receipt (timely postmarked) from the U.S. Postal Service, or its equivalent from a designated private delivery service (see Notice 99-41, 1999–35 I.R.B. 325); **(b)** Form 2553 with accepted stamp; **(c)** Form 2553 with stamped IRS received date; or **(d)** IRS letter stating that Form 2553 has been accepted.

End of Election

Once the election is made, it stays in effect until it is terminated. If the election is terminated in a tax year beginning after 1996, IRS consent is generally required for another election by the corporation (or a successor corporation) on Form 2553 for any tax year before the 5th tax year after the first tax year in which the termination took effect. See Regulations section 1.1362-5 for details.

Specific Instructions

Part I (*All corporations must complete.*)

Name and Address of Corporation

Enter the true corporate name as stated in the corporate charter or other legal document creating it. If the corporation's mailing address is the same as someone else's, such as a shareholder's, enter "c/o" and this person's name following the name of the corporation. Include the suite, room, or other unit number after the street address. If the Post Office does not deliver to the street address and the corporation has a P.O. box, show the box number instead of the street address. If the corporation changed its name or address after applying for its employer identification number, be sure to check the box in item G of Part I.

Item A. Employer Identification Number (EIN)

If the corporation has applied for an EIN but has not received it, enter "applied for." If the corporation does not have an EIN, it should apply for one on **Form SS-4,** Application for Employer Identification Number. You can order Form SS-4 by calling 1-800-TAX-FORM (1-800-829-3676).

Item D. Effective Date of Election

Enter the beginning effective date (month, day, year) of the tax year requested for the S corporation. Generally, this will be the beginning date of the tax year for which the ending effective date is required to be shown in item I, Part I. For a new corporation (first year the corporation exists) it will generally be the date required to be shown in item H, Part I. The tax year of a new corporation starts on the date that it has shareholders, acquires assets, or begins doing business, whichever happens first. If the effective date for item D for a newly formed corporation is later than the date in item H, the corporation should file Form 1120 or Form 1120-A for the tax period between these dates.

Column K. Shareholders' Consent Statement

Each shareholder who owns (or is deemed to own) stock at the time the election is made must consent to the election. If the election is made during the corporation's tax year for which it first takes effect, any person who held stock at any time during the part of that year that occurs before the election is made, must consent to the election, even though the person may have sold or transferred his or her stock before the election is made.

An election made during the first 2½ months of the tax year is effective for the following tax year if any person who held stock in the corporation during the part of the tax year before the election was made, and who did not hold stock at the time the election was made, did not consent to the election.

Each shareholder consents by signing and dating in column K or signing and dating a separate consent statement described below. The following special rules apply in determining who must sign the consent statement.

● If a husband and wife have a community interest in the stock or in the income from it, both must consent.

● Each tenant in common, joint tenant, and tenant by the entirety must consent.

● A minor's consent is made by the minor, legal representative of the minor, or a natural or adoptive parent of the minor if no legal representative has been appointed.

● The consent of an estate is made by the executor or administrator.

● The consent of an electing small business trust is made by the trustee.

● If the stock is owned by a trust (other than an electing small business trust), the deemed owner of the trust must consent. See section 1361(c)(2) for details regarding trusts that are permitted to be shareholders and rules for determining who is the deemed owner.

Continuation sheet or separate consent statement. If you need a continuation sheet or use a separate consent statement, attach it to Form 2553. The separate consent statement must contain the name, address, and EIN of the corporation and the shareholder information requested in columns J through N of Part I. If you want, you may combine all the shareholders' consents in one statement.

Column L

Enter the number of shares of stock each shareholder owns and the dates the stock was acquired. If the election

Page 3

is made during the corporation's tax year for which it first takes effect, do not list the shares of stock for those shareholders who sold or transferred all of their stock before the election was made. However, these shareholders must still consent to the election for it to be effective for the tax year.

Column M

Enter the social security number of each shareholder who is an individual. Enter the EIN of each shareholder that is an estate, a qualified trust, or an exempt organization.

Column N

Enter the month and day that each shareholder's tax year ends. If a shareholder is changing his or her tax year, enter the tax year the shareholder is changing to, and attach an explanation indicating the present tax year and the basis for the change (e.g., automatic revenue procedure or letter ruling request).

Signature

Form 2553 must be signed by the president, treasurer, assistant treasurer, chief accounting officer, or other corporate officer (such as tax officer) authorized to sign.

Part II

Complete Part II if you selected a tax year ending on any date other than December 31 (other than a 52-53-week tax year ending with reference to the month of December).

Box P1

Attach a statement showing separately for each month the amount of gross receipts for the most recent 47 months as required by section 4.03(3) of Rev. Proc. 87-32, 1987-2 C.B. 396. A corporation that does not have a 47-month period of gross receipts cannot establish a natural business year under section 4.01(1).

Box Q1

For examples of an acceptable business purpose for requesting a fiscal tax year, see Rev. Rul. 87-57, 1987-2 C.B. 117.

In addition to a statement showing the business purpose for the requested fiscal year, you must attach the other information necessary to meet the ruling request requirements of Rev. Proc. 2000-1 (or its successor). Also attach a statement that shows separately the amount of gross receipts from sales or services (and inventory costs, if applicable) for each of the 36 months preceding the effective date of the election to be an S corporation. If the corporation has been in existence for fewer than 36 months, submit figures for the period of existence.

If you check box Q1, you will be charged a user fee of up to $600 (subject to change—see Rev. Proc. 2000-1 or its successor). Do not pay the fee when filing Form 2553. The service center will send Form 2553 to the IRS in Washington, DC, who, in turn, will notify the corporation that the fee is due.

Box Q2

If the corporation makes a back-up section 444 election for which it is qualified, then the election will take effect in the event the business purpose request is not approved.

In some cases, the tax year requested under the back-up section 444 election may be different than the tax year requested under business purpose. See **Form 8716,** Election To Have a Tax Year Other Than a Required Tax Year, for details on making a back-up section 444 election.

Boxes Q2 and R2

If the corporation is not qualified to make the section 444 election after making the item Q2 back-up section 444 election or indicating its intention to make the election in item R1, and therefore it later files a calendar year return, it should write "Section 444 Election Not Made" in the top left corner of the first calendar year Form 1120S it files.

Part III

Certain qualified subchapter S trusts (QSSTs) may make the QSST election required by section 1361(d)(2) in Part III. Part III may be used to make the QSST election only if corporate stock has been transferred to the trust on or before the date on which the corporation makes its election to be an S corporation. However, a statement can be used instead of Part III to make the election. If there was an inadvertent failure to timely file a QSST election, see the relief provisions under Rev. Proc. 98-55.

Note: *Use Part III **only** if you make the election in Part I (i.e., Form 2553 cannot be filed with only Part III completed).*

The deemed owner of the QSST must also consent to the S corporation election in column K, page 1, of Form 2553. See section 1361(c)(2).

Paperwork Reduction Act Notice. We ask for the information on this form to carry out the Internal Revenue laws of the United States. You are required to give us the information. We need it to ensure that you are complying with these laws and to allow us to figure and collect the right amount of tax.

You are not required to provide the information requested on a form that is subject to the Paperwork Reduction Act unless the form displays a valid OMB control number. Books or records relating to a form or its instructions must be retained as long as their contents may become material in the administration of any Internal Revenue law. Generally, tax returns and return information are confidential, as required by section 6103.

The time needed to complete and file this form will depend on individual circumstances. The estimated average time is:

Recordkeeping	8 hr., 37 min.
Learning about the law or the form	3 hr., 11 min.
Preparing, copying, assembling, and sending the form to the IRS	3 hr., 28 min.

If you have comments concerning the accuracy of these time estimates or suggestions for making this form simpler, we would be happy to hear from you. You can write to the Tax Forms Committee, Western Area Distribution Center, Rancho Cordova, CA 95743-0001. **Do not** send the form to this address. Instead, see **Where To File** on page 1.

Page 4

OMB No. 1115-0136

U.S. Department of Justice
Immigration and Naturalization Service

Employment Eligibility Verification

INSTRUCTIONS
PLEASE READ ALL INSTRUCTIONS CAREFULLY BEFORE COMPLETING THIS FORM.

Anti-Discrimination Notice. It is illegal to discriminate against any individual (other than an alien not authorized to work in the U.S.) in hiring, discharging, or recruiting or referring for a fee because of that individual's national origin or citizenship status. It is illegal to discriminate against work eligible individuals. Employers **CANNOT** specify which document(s) they will accept from an employee. The refusal to hire an individual because of a future expiration date may also constitute illegal discrimination.

Section 1 - Employee. All employees, citizens and noncitizens, hired after November 6, 1986, must complete Section 1 of this form at the time of hire, which is the actual beginning of employment. **The employer is responsible for ensuring that Section 1 is timely and properly completed.**

Preparer/Translator Certification. The Preparer/Translator Certification must be completed if Section 1 is prepared by a person other than the employee. A preparer/translator may be used only when the employee is unable to complete Section 1 on his/her own. However, the employee must still sign Section 1.

Section 2 - Employer. For the purpose of completing this form, the term "employer" includes those recruiters and referrers for a fee who are agricultural associations, agricultural employers or farm labor contractors.

Employers must complete Section 2 by examining evidence of identity and employment eligibility within three (3) business days of the date employment begins. If employees are authorized to work, but are unable to present the required document(s) within three business days, they must present a receipt for the application of the document(s) within three business days and the actual document(s) within ninety (90) days. However, if employers hire individuals for a duration of less than three business days, Section 2 must be completed at the time employment begins. **Employers must record: 1)** document title; 2) issuing authority; 3) document number, 4) expiration date, if any; and 5) the date employment begins. Employers must sign and date the certification. Employees must present original documents. Employers may, but are not required to, photocopy the document(s) presented. These photocopies may only be used for the verification process and must be retained with the I-9. **However, employers are still responsible for completing the I-9.**

Section 3 - Updating and Reverification. Employers must complete Section 3 when updating and/or reverifying the I-9. Employers must reverify employment eligibility of their employees on or before the expiration date recorded in Section 1. Employers **CANNOT** specify which document(s) they will accept from an employee.

- If an employee's name has changed at the time this form is being updated/ reverified, complete Block A.

- If an employee is rehired within three (3) years of the date this form was originally completed and the employee is still eligible to be employed on the same basis as previously indicated on this form (updating), complete Block B and the signature block.

- If an employee is rehired within three (3) years of the date this form was originally completed and the employee's work authorization has expired or if a current employee's work authorization is about to expire (reverification), complete Block B and:
  - examine any document that reflects that the employee is authorized to work in the U.S. (see List A or C).
  - record the document title, document number and expiration date (if any) in Block C, and complete the signature block.

Photocopying and Retaining Form I-9. A blank I-9 may be reproduced, provided both sides are copied. The Instructions must be available to all employees completing this form. Employers must retain completed I-9s for three (3) years after the date of hire or one (1) year after the date employment ends, whichever is later.

For more detailed information, you may refer to the INS Handbook for Employers, (Form M-274). You may obtain the handbook at your local INS office.

Privacy Act Notice. The authority for collecting this information is the Immigration Reform and Control Act of 1986, Pub. L. 99-603 (8 USC 1324a).

This information is for employers to verify the eligibility of individuals for employment to preclude the unlawful hiring, or recruiting or referring for a fee, of aliens who are not authorized to work in the United States.

This information will be used by employers as a record of their basis for determining eligibility of an employee to work in the United States. The form will be kept by the employer and made available for inspection by officials of the U.S. Immigration and Naturalization Service, the Department of Labor and the Office of Special Counsel for Immigration Related Unfair Employment Practices.

Submission of the information required in this form is voluntary. However, an individual may not begin employment unless this form is completed, since employers are subject to civil or criminal penalties if they do not comply with the Immigration Reform and Control Act of 1986.

Reporting Burden. We try to create forms and instructions that are accurate, can be easily understood and which impose the least possible burden on you to provide us with information. Often this is difficult because some immigration laws are very complex. Accordingly, the reporting burden for this collection of information is computed as follows: 1) learning about this form, 5 minutes; 2) completing the form, 5 minutes; and 3) assembling and filing (recordkeeping) the form, 5 minutes, for an average of 15 minutes per response. If you have comments regarding the accuracy of this burden estimate, or suggestions for making this form simpler, you can write to the Immigration and Naturalization Service, HQPDI, 425 I Street, N.W., Room 4307r, Washington, DC 20536. OMB No. 1115-0136.

EMPLOYERS MUST RETAIN COMPLETED FORM I-9
PLEASE DO NOT MAIL COMPLETED FORM I-9 TO INS

Form I-9 (Rev. 11-21-91)N

OMB No. 1115-0136

Employment Eligibility Verification

Please read instructions carefully before completing this form. The instructions must be available during completion of this form. **ANTI-DISCRIMINATION NOTICE:** It is illegal to discriminate against work eligible individuals. Employers CANNOT specify which document(s) they will accept from an employee. The refusal to hire an individual because of a future expiration date may also constitute illegal discrimination.

Section 1. Employee Information and Verification. To be completed and signed by employee at the time employment begins.

Print Name: Last	First	Middle Initial	Maiden Name

Address (Street Name and Number)	Apt. #	Date of Birth (month/day/year)

City	State	Zip Code	Social Security #

I am aware that federal law provides for imprisonment and/or fines for false statements or use of false documents in connection with the completion of this form.

I attest, under penalty of perjury, that I am (check one of the following):
- ☐ A citizen or national of the United States
- ☐ A Lawful Permanent Resident (Alien # A_____)
- ☐ An alien authorized to work until ___/___/___
  (Alien # or Admission #) _____

Employee's Signature

Date (month/day/year)

Preparer and/or Translator Certification. (To be completed and signed if Section 1 is prepared by a person other than the employee.) I attest, under penalty of perjury, that I have assisted in the completion of this form and that to the best of my knowledge the information is true and correct.

Preparer's/Translator's Signature	Print Name

Address (Street Name and Number, City, State, Zip Code)	Date (month/day/year)

Section 2. Employer Review and Verification. To be completed and signed by employer. Examine one document from List A OR examine one document from List B and one from List C, as listed on the reverse of this form, and record the title, number and expiration date, if any, of the document(s)

List A	OR	List B	AND	List C
Document title: _____		_____		_____
Issuing authority: _____		_____		_____
Document #: _____		_____		_____
Expiration Date (if any): ___/___/___		___/___/___		___/___/___
Document #: _____				
Expiration Date (if any): ___/___/___				

CERTIFICATION - I attest, under penalty of perjury, that I have examined the document(s) presented by the above-named employee, that the above-listed document(s) appear to be genuine and to relate to the employee named, that the employee began employment on (month/day/year) ___/___/___ **and that to the best of my knowledge the employee is eligible to work in the United States. (State employment agencies may omit the date the employee began employment.)**

Signature of Employer or Authorized Representative	Print Name	Title

Business or Organization Name	Address (Street Name and Number, City, State, Zip Code)	Date (month/day/year)

Section 3. Updating and Reverification. To be completed and signed by employer.

A. New Name (if applicable)	B. Date of rehire (month/day/year) (if applicable)

C. If employee's previous grant of work authorization has expired, provide the information below for the document that establishes current employment eligibility.

Document Title:_____ Document #:_____ Expiration Date (if any): ___/___/___

I attest, under penalty of perjury, that to the best of my knowledge, this employee is eligible to work in the United States, and if the employee presented document(s), the document(s) I have examined appear to be genuine and to relate to the individual.

Signature of Employer or Authorized Representative	Date (month/day/year)

LISTS OF ACCEPTABLE DOCUMENTS

LIST A

Documents that Establish Both Identity and Employment Eligibility

OR

1. U.S. Passport (unexpired or expired)

2. Certificate of U.S. Citizenship (INS Form N-560 or N-561)

3. Certificate of Naturalization (INS Form N-550 or N-570)

4. Unexpired foreign passport, with I-551 stamp or attached INS Form I-94 indicating unexpired employment authorization

5. Alien Registration Receipt Card with photograph (INS Form I-151 or I-551)

6. Unexpired Temporary Card (INS Form I-688)

7. Unexpired Employment Authorization Card (INS Form I-688A)

8. Unexpired Reentry Permit (INS Form I-327)

9. Unexpired Refugee Travel Document (INS Form I-571)

10. Unexpired Employment Authorization Document issued by the INS which contains a photograph (INS Form I-688B)

LIST B

Documents that Establish Identity

AND

1. Driver's license or ID card issued by a state or outlying possession of the United States provided it contains a photograph or information such as name, date of birth, sex, height, eye color and address

2. ID card issued by federal, state or local government agencies or entities, provided it contains a photograph or information such as name, date of birth, sex, height, eye color and address

3. School ID card with a photograph

4. Voter's registration card

5. U.S. Military card or draft record

6. Military dependent's ID card

7. U.S. Coast Guard Merchant Mariner Card

8. Native American tribal document

9. Driver's license issued by a Canadian government authority

For persons under age 18 who are unable to present a document listed above:

10. School record or report card

11. Clinic, doctor or hospital record

12. Day-care or nursery school record

LIST C

Documents that Establish Employment Eligibility

1. U.S. social security card issued by the Social Security Administration (other than a card stating it is not valid for employment)

2. Certification of Birth Abroad issued by the Department of State (Form FS-545 or Form DS-1350)

3. Original or certified copy of a birth certificate issued by a state, county, municipal authority or outlying possession of the United States bearing an official seal

4. Native American tribal document

5. U.S. Citizen ID Card (INS Form I-197)

6. ID Card for use of Resident Citizen in the United States (INS Form I-179)

7. Unexpired employment authorization document issued by the INS (other then those listed under List A)

Illustrations of many of these documents appear in Part 8 of the Handbook for Employers (M-274)

This page intentionally left blank.

Form W-4 (2001)

Purpose. Complete Form W-4 so your employer can withhold the correct Federal income tax from your pay. Because your tax situation may change, you may want to refigure your withholding each year.

Exemption from withholding. If you are exempt, complete only lines 1, 2, 3, 4, and 7, and sign the form to validate it. Your exemption for 2001 expires February 18, 2002.

Note: *You cannot claim exemption from withholding if (1) your income exceeds $750 and includes more than $250 of unearned income (e.g., interest and dividends) and (2) another person can claim you as a dependent on their tax return.*

Basic instructions. If you are not exempt, complete the **Personal Allowances Worksheet** below. The worksheets on page 2 adjust your withholding allowances based on itemized deductions, certain credits, adjustments to income, or two-earner/two-job situations. Complete all worksheets that apply. They will help you figure the number of withholding allowances you are entitled to claim. **However, you may claim fewer (or zero) allowances.**

Head of household. Generally, you may claim head of household filing status on your tax return only if you are unmarried and pay more than 50% of the costs of keeping up a home for yourself and your dependent(s) or other qualifying individuals. See line E below.

Tax credits. You can take projected tax credits into account in figuring your allowable number of withholding allowances. Credits for child or dependent care expenses and the child tax credit may be claimed using the **Personal Allowances Worksheet** below. See **Pub. 919,** How Do I Adjust My Tax Withholding? for information on converting your other credits into withholding allowances.

Nonwage income. If you have a large amount of nonwage income, such as interest or dividends, consider making estimated tax payments using **Form 1040-ES,** Estimated Tax for Individuals. Otherwise, you may owe additional tax.

Two earners/two jobs. If you have a working spouse or more than one job, figure the total number of allowances you are entitled to claim on all jobs using worksheets from only one Form W-4. Your withholding usually will be most accurate when all allowances are claimed on the Form W-4 for the highest paying job and zero allowances are claimed on the others.

Check your withholding. After your Form W-4 takes effect, use Pub. 919 to see how the dollar amount you are having withheld compares to your projected total tax for 2001. Get Pub. 919 especially if you used the **Two-Earner/Two-Job Worksheet** on page 2 and your earnings exceed $150,000 (Single) or $200,000 (Married).

Recent name change? If your name on line 1 differs from that shown on your social security card, call 1-800-772-1213 for a new social security card.

Personal Allowances Worksheet (Keep for your records.)

A Enter "1" for **yourself** if no one else can claim you as a dependent . . . . **A** _____

B Enter "1" if: {
- You are single and have only one job; or
- You are married, have only one job, and your spouse does not work; or
- Your wages from a second job or your spouse's wages (or the total of both) are $1,000 or less.
} . . **B** _____

C Enter "1" for your **spouse.** But, you may choose to enter -0- if you are married and have either a working spouse or more than one job. (Entering -0- may help you avoid having too little tax withheld.) . . . . **C** _____

D Enter number of **dependents** (other than your spouse or yourself) you will claim on your tax return . . . . **D** _____

E Enter "1" if you will file as **head of household** on your tax return (see conditions under **Head of household** above) . **E** _____

F Enter "1" if you have at least $1,500 of **child or dependent care expenses** for which you plan to claim a credit . . **F** _____
(**Note:** *Do not include child support payments. See **Pub. 503**, Child and Dependent Care Expenses, for details.*)

G **Child Tax Credit** (including additional child tax credit):
- If your total income will be between $18,000 and $50,000 ($23,000 and $63,000 if married), enter "1" for each eligible child.
- If your total income will be between $50,000 and $80,000 ($63,000 and $115,000 if married), enter "1" if you have two eligible children, enter "2" if you have three or four eligible children, or enter "3" if you have five or more eligible children. **G** _____

H Add lines A through G and enter total here. (**Note:** *This may be different from the number of exemptions you claim on your tax return.*) ▶ **H** _____

For accuracy, complete all worksheets that apply. {
- If you plan to **itemize or claim adjustments to income** and want to reduce your withholding, see the **Deductions and Adjustments Worksheet** on page 2.
- If you are **single,** have **more than one job** and your combined earnings from all jobs exceed $35,000, **or** if you are **married** and have a **working spouse or more than one job** and the combined earnings from all jobs exceed $60,000, see the **Two-Earner/Two-Job Worksheet** on page 2 to avoid having too little tax withheld.
- If **neither** of the above situations applies, **stop here** and enter the number from line H on line 5 of Form W-4 below.
}

- - - - - - - - - - - **Cut here and give Form W-4 to your employer. Keep the top part for your records.** - - - - - - - - - - -

---

| Form **W-4**
 Department of the Treasury
 Internal Revenue Service | **Employee's Withholding Allowance Certificate**
 ▶ **For Privacy Act and Paperwork Reduction Act Notice, see page 2.** | OMB No. 1545-0010
 2001 |

1 Type or print your first name and middle initial	Last name		2 Your social security number
Home address (number and street or rural route)		3 ☐ Single ☐ Married ☐ Married, but withhold at higher Single rate. **Note:** *If married, but legally separated, or spouse is a nonresident alien, check the Single box.*	
City or town, state, and ZIP code		4 If your last name differs from that on your social security card, check here. You must call 1-800-772-1213 for a new card. ▶ ☐	

5 Total number of allowances you are claiming (from line **H** above **or** from the applicable worksheet on page 2) | **5** _____

6 Additional amount, if any, you want withheld from each paycheck . . . . | **6** $ _____

7 I claim exemption from withholding for 2001, and I certify that I meet **both** of the following conditions for exemption:
- Last year I had a right to a refund of **all** Federal income tax withheld because I had **no** tax liability **and**
- This year I expect a refund of **all** Federal income tax withheld because I expect to have **no** tax liability.

If you meet both conditions, write "Exempt" here . . . . ▶ | **7** _____

Under penalties of perjury, I certify that I am entitled to the number of withholding allowances claimed on this certificate, or I am entitled to claim exempt status.

Employee's signature
 (Form is not valid <br> unless you sign it.) ▶ _____ Date ▶ _____

8 Employer's name and address (Employer: Complete lines 8 and 10 only if sending to the IRS.)	9 Office code (optional)	10 Employer identification number

Cat. No. 10220Q

Deductions and Adjustments Worksheet

Note: *Use this worksheet only if you plan to itemize deductions, claim certain credits, or claim adjustments to income on your 2001 tax return.*

1 Enter an estimate of your 2001 itemized deductions. These include qualifying home mortgage interest, charitable contributions, state and local taxes, medical expenses in excess of 7.5% of your income, and miscellaneous deductions. (For 2001, you may have to reduce your itemized deductions if your income is over $132,950 ($66,475 if married filing separately). See **Worksheet 3** in Pub. 919 for details.) . . . **1** $ _____

2 Enter: { $7,600 if married filing jointly or qualifying widow(er)
$6,650 if head of household
$4,550 if single
$3,800 if married filing separately } . . . . **2** $ _____

3 **Subtract** line 2 from line 1. If line 2 is greater than line 1, enter -0- . . . . **3** $ _____

4 Enter an estimate of your 2001 adjustments to income, including alimony, deductible IRA contributions, and student loan interest **4** $ _____

5 **Add** lines 3 and 4 and enter the total (Include any amount for credits from **Worksheet 7** in Pub. 919.) . **5** $ _____

6 Enter an estimate of your 2001 nonwage income (such as dividends or interest) . . . . **6** $ _____

7 **Subtract** line 6 from line 5. Enter the result, but not less than -0- . . . . **7** $ _____

8 **Divide** the amount on line 7 by $3,000 and enter the result here. Drop any fraction . . . . **8** _____

9 Enter the number from the **Personal Allowances Worksheet,** line H, page 1 . . . . . . **9** _____

10 **Add** lines 8 and 9 and enter the total here. If you plan to use the **Two-Earner/Two-Job Worksheet,** also enter this total on line 1 below. Otherwise, **stop here** and enter this total on Form W-4, line 5, page 1. **10** _____

Two-Earner/Two-Job Worksheet

Note: *Use this worksheet only if the instructions under line H on page 1 direct you here.*

1 Enter the number from line H, page 1 (or from line 10 above if you used the **Deductions and Adjustments Worksheet**) **1** _____

2 Find the number in **Table 1** below that applies to the **lowest** paying job and enter it here . . . . . **2** _____

3 If line 1 is **more than or equal to** line 2, subtract line 2 from line 1. Enter the result here (if zero, enter -0-) and on Form W-4, line 5, page 1. **Do not** use the rest of this worksheet . . . . **3** _____

Note: *If line 1 is less than line 2, enter -0- on Form W-4, line 5, page 1. Complete lines 4–9 below to calculate the additional withholding amount necessary to avoid a year end tax bill.*

4 Enter the number from line 2 of this worksheet . . . . **4** _____

5 Enter the number from line 1 of this worksheet . . . . **5** _____

6 **Subtract** line 5 from line 4 . . . . **6** _____

7 Find the amount in **Table 2** below that applies to the **highest** paying job and enter it here . . . . . **7** $ _____

8 **Multiply** line 7 by line 6 and enter the result here. This is the additional annual withholding needed . . **8** $ _____

9 Divide line 8 by the number of pay periods remaining in 2001. For example, divide by 26 if you are paid every two weeks and you complete this form in December 2000. Enter the result here and on Form W-4, line 6, page 1. This is the additional amount to be withheld from each paycheck . . . . **9** $ _____

Table 1: Two-Earner/Two-Job Worksheet

Married Filing Jointly				All Others			
If wages from LOWEST paying job are—	Enter on line 2 above	If wages from LOWEST paying job are—	Enter on line 2 above	If wages from LOWEST paying job are—	Enter on line 2 above	If wages from LOWEST paying job are—	Enter on line 2 above
$0 - $4,000	0	42,001 - 47,000	8	$0 - $6,000	0	65,001 - 80,000	8
4,001 - 8,000	1	47,001 - 55,000	9	6,001 - 12,000	1	80,001 - 105,000	9
8,001 - 14,000	2	55,001 - 65,000	10	12,001 - 17,000	2	105,001 and over	10
14,001 - 19,000	3	65,001 - 70,000	11	17,001 - 22,000	3		
19,001 - 25,000	4	70,001 - 90,000	12	22,001 - 28,000	4		
25,001 - 32,000	5	90,001 - 105,000	13	28,001 - 40,000	5		
32,001 - 38,000	6	105,001 - 115,000	14	40,001 - 50,000	6		
38,001 - 42,000	7	115,001 and over	15	50,001 - 65,000	7		

Table 2: Two-Earner/Two-Job Worksheet

Married Filing Jointly		All Others	
If wages from HIGHEST paying job are—	Enter on line 7 above	If wages from HIGHEST paying job are—	Enter on line 7 above
$0 - $50,000	$440	$0 - $30,000	$440
50,001 - 100,000	800	30,001 - 60,000	800
100,001 - 130,000	900	60,001 - 120,000	900
130,001 - 250,000	1,000	120,001 - 270,000	1,000
250,001 and over	1,100	270,001 and over	1,100

Michigan Department of Treasury
22 (Rev. 11-00); Formerly C-1030

ORDER FOR MICHIGAN TAX FORMS

Issued under authority of the Income Tax Act and Single Business Tax Act.

Mail to:
Individual Taxes Division - WPU
Michigan Department of Treasury
Lansing, MI 48922

OFFICE USE (Date Stamp)

Check here if this is a second order. ☐

PLEASE PRINT OR TYPE	NAME OF PERSON ORDER SHOULD BE SENT TO
	NAME OF BUSINESS OR ORGANIZATION
	SHIPPING ADDRESS
	CITY, STATE, ZIP
	TELEPHONE (Include extension number if applicable) ( ) Extension

ORDER IS FOR: (Check one)
☐ Tax Practitioner
☐ Local Government
☐ State Government
☐ Educational
☐ Financial Institution
☐ Library
☐ Post Office
☐ Volunteer Group
☐ Other

No. of Repro Packets or CDs   23   28

REPRODUCIBLE PACKETS OR CDs OF INCOME AND SINGLE BUSINESS TAX FORMS. Packets/CDs include a photographic master quality copy of each form highlighted below by a gray screen. Packets/CDs also include one of each of the following form and instruction booklets: MI-1040 and CR, MI-1040CR-7, Single Business Tax Combined booklet, Michigan Estate Tax and two MI-1040ES forms. Forms not in the packet or CD may be ordered below. **ONE PACKET OR CD IS FREE. ADDITIONAL COPIES ARE $5 EACH. Mark your choice in the appropriate box.** ☐ Reproducible Packet   ☐ Compact Disk   Make your check payable to "State of Michigan."   23   28

SHADED AREA IDENTIFIES REPRODUCIBLE FORMS.

Income Tax

Quantity	Office Use	Form Number	Style	Description
	00	MI-1040 and CR	Form, Instruction Booklet	Income Tax Return, Property Tax Credit Claim
	25	MI-1040EZ	Form, Instruction Booklet	Michigan Individual Income Tax Easy Return
	03	MI-1040 & Sch. 1	Flat Sheet	Michigan Individual Income Tax Return & Schedule 1
	09	Schedule NR	Flat Sheet	Michigan Nonresident and Part-Year Resident Schedule
	04	MI-1040EZ	Flat Sheet	Michigan Individual Income Tax Easy Return
	05	MI-1040CR	Flat Sheet	Michigan Homestead Property Tax Credit Claim
	01	MI-1040CR-2	Form, Instruction Booklet	Property Tax Credit Claim for Veterans and Blind People
	06	MI-1040CR-2	Flat Sheet	Property Tax Credit Claim for Veterans and Blind People
	24	MI-1040CR-5	Form, Instruction Booklet	Farmland Preservation Tax Credit Claim and Instructions
	02	MI-1040CR-7	Form, Instruction Booklet	Michigan Home Heating Credit Claim and Instructions
	07	MI-1040CR-7	Flat Sheet	Michigan Home Heating Credit Claim
	13	MI-1040CR-9	Flat Sheet	Michigan Senior Citizen Prescription Drug Credit Claim
	18	Schedule CT	Flat Sheet	Michigan College Tuition and Fees Credit
	11	MI-1040D	Form and Instructions	Adjustments of Capital Gains and Losses
	08	MI-1040ES	4 - coupon set	Quarterly Income Tax Estimate Voucher
	14	MI-1040H	Form and Instructions	Schedule of Apportionment
	10	MI-1040X	Form and Instructions	Amended Michigan Income Tax Return and Instructions
	19	MI-1045	Form and Instructions	Application for Net Operating Loss Refund
	20	MI-1310	Flat Sheet	Claim for Refund Due a Deceased Taxpayer
	21	MI-2210	Flat Sheet	Underpayment of Estimated Income Tax
	12	MI-4797	Form and Instructions	Adj. of Gains & Losses from Sales of Business Property

Fiduciary Income Tax

Quantity	Office Use	Form Number	Style	Description
	15	MI-1041	Flat Sheet	Michigan Fiduciary Income Tax Return
	16	MI-1041	Instructions	Instructions for Fiduciary Income Tax Return
	17	MI-1041D	Form and Instructions	Fiduciary Adjustments of Capital Gains and Losses
	26	MI-1041ES	4 - coupon set	Quarterly Fiduciary Income Tax Estimate Voucher

OVER

Income Tax Withholding

Quantity	Office Use	Form Number	Style	Description
	82	MI-W4	Flat Sheet	Employee's Withholding Exemption Certificate
	80	446 (C-3260)	Booklet	Employers Withholding Tax Guide

Single Business Tax

Quantity	Office Use	Form Number	Style	Description
	31	C-8000	Forms, Instruction Booklet	Combined Returns and Instructions (Individual, Corporations, Partnerships, Fiduciaries)
	32	C-8000	Flat Sheet	Single Business Tax Annual Return
	42	C-8044	Flat Sheet	SBT Simplified Return
	43	C-8044X	Flat Sheet	SBT Amended Simplified Return
	33	C-8000C	Flat Sheet	SBT Credit for Small Businesses and Contribution Credits
	34	C-8000D	Flat Sheet	SBT Recapture of Capital Acquisition Deduction
	35	C-8000G	Flat Sheet	SBT Statutory Exemption/Business Income Averaging
	36	C-8000H	Flat Sheet	SBT Apportionment Formula
	30	C-8000ITC	Flat Sheet	SBT Investment Tax Credit
	37	C-8000KC	Flat Sheet	SBT Schedule of Shareholders and Officers
	38	C-8000KP	Flat Sheet	SBT Schedule of Partners
	47	C-8000MC	Flat Sheet	SBT Miscellaneous Credits
	39	C-8000S	Flat Sheet	SBT Reductions to Adjusted Tax Base
	40	C-8000X	Flat Sheet	SBT Amended Annual Return
	41	C-8002	4 - Coupon Set	SBT Quarterly Return (maximum 5)
	44	C-8009	Flat Sheet	SBT Alloc. of Exemptions/Small Bus. Credit/Cont. Groups
	45	C-8010AGR	Flat Sheet	SBT Adjusted Gross Receipts For Controlled Groups
	46	C-8020	Flat Sheet	SBT Penalty, Interest Computation for Underpaid Est. Tax
	48	C-8030	Flat Sheet	SBT Notice of No SBT Return Required
	50	C-8043	Flat Sheet	SBT Statutory Exemption Schedule

Miscellaneous or Multiple-tax Forms

Quantity	Office Use	Form Number	Style	Description
	84	151 (C-1029)	Flat Sheet	Authorization for Power of Attorney Representation
	85	22 (C-1030)	Flat Sheet	Order for Michigan Tax Forms
	86	74 (C-1036)	Flat Sheet	Taxpayer Information Release
	87	2325 (C-3179)	Brochure	What is the Michigan Use Tax?
	65	518 (C-3400)	Form and Instructions	Registration for Michigan Taxes
	66	163 (C-3479)	Flat Sheet	Notice of Change or Discontinuance
	22	4 (C-4267)	Flat Sheet	Appl. for Extension of Time to File Michigan Tax Returns
	76	3174	Flat Sheet	Direct Deposit of Refund
	27	3581	Form and Instructions	Historic Preservation Tax Credit
	29	3614	Flat Sheet	Historic Preservation Tax Credit Assignment

MICHIGAN BUSINESS TAXES
Registration Booklet

Dear New Business Owner:

Congratulations on your decision to do business in Michigan!

As part of the State's continuing effort to make doing business in Michigan easier, we have designed a single registration form for State of Michigan business taxes. Please read all the information and complete everything on the form that applies to your business.

It may be four to six weeks before you receive your tax returns, licenses and other information, depending on the time of year. Please submit your registration form at least six weeks before you plan to start your business so you are assured proper registration before opening your business.

I wish you success in your new business venture.

John Engler
Governor

STATE OF MICHIGAN

Your Responsibilities Concerning Taxes

Michigan Employers

If other people work for you, you have responsibilities to both the state and federal governments. The following is a list of your responsibilities.

Federal, State and Local Taxes

Employers must register with the Internal Revenue Service (IRS) and the Michigan Department of Treasury for Social Security Tax (federal) and income tax withholding (federal and state). These taxes must be withheld from each employee's wages and paid to the appropriate taxing agency. Some cities also levy a city income tax. Contact the city treasurer's office for information.

Employers must also comply with the Personal Responsibility and Work Opportunity Reconciliation Act of 1996 by reporting certain information on their newly-hired employees to the Michigan Department of Treasury starting October 1, 1997. For complete information, see your Michigan Income Tax Withholding Guide.

Federal Unemployment Tax (FUTA)

Employers must pay federal unemployment taxes. Unemployment taxes are paid by the employer; no deduction is allowed from any employee's wages. Contact the Internal Revenue Service toll-free at **800-829-1040** for more information.

State Unemployment Tax

Employers must also register with the Michigan Unemployment Agency (UA) and pay unemployment taxes. Unemployment taxes are paid entirely by the employer, with no deduction allowed from employee wages. Contact the UA Tax Office at 7310 Woodward Ave., Detroit, MI 48202; **313-876-5146** for more information.

Worker's Compensation

Most employers are required to provide workers' compensation coverage for their employees. A workers' compensation policy is purchased from a private insurance company. Contact the Workers' Compensation Bureau, Box 30016, Lansing, MI 48909, **517-322-1195** for more information.

Health and Safety Standards

Employers must comply with health and safety standards under the federal and state Occupational Safety and Health Act (OSHA), and the Right-to-Know laws. Contact the Department of Consumer & Industry Services, Box 30015, Lansing, MI 48909, **517-322-1845** for more information.

Immigration Law Compliance

Employers must verify the employment eligibility of all employees hired after November 6, 1986 by reviewing documents presented by employees and recording information on a verification form. Contact the Immigration and Naturalization Service at **313-568-6041** for information and forms.

New Businesses

Taxpayers are required to meet certain obligations under Michigan law, including filing tax returns on time and with the correct payment when required. You are responsible for the accuracy of your returns, no matter who you hire to prepare them. You must also keep accurate and complete records for determining tax liability properly, as required by law or department rule.

Selling your business. When you sell a business that is covered under the MES Act, you must complete the *Business Transferor's Notice to Transferee of Unemployment Tax Liability and Rate* (form UA 1027), and deliver the completed form to the purchaser of the business at least two business days before the transfer of the business. This obligation extends to the seller's real estate broker, other agent or attorney.

Delinquent taxes to the Department of Treasury must be paid with this registration. Submit a letter identifying the business name, address, Federal Employer Identification Number (FEIN), type of tax being paid and the period(s) the tax was due. Payment should include tax, penalty and interest owed. **Contact the specific tax division for help calculating penalty and interest.** Telephone numbers are listed on page 3 of this booklet.

Corporate officers may be held liable for Treasury tax debts incurred by their corporations.

Delinquent collections. Treasury and UA may both file tax liens against any taxpayer's real and personal property and issue a tax warrant or levy to seize and sell the property to pay delinquent taxes.

Successors (buyer or acquirer of a business). If you buy either an existing or discontinued business or its stock of goods, you can be held liable for tax debts incurred by the previous owner. You must withhold sufficient purchase money to cover these tax debts until the previous owner produces a receipt showing the taxes have been paid or a certificate stating that no taxes are due. This certificate may be obtained through the Department of Treasury, Collection Division, tax clearance. Upon the owner's written waiver of confidentiality, Treasury will release a business' known tax liability for purposes of establishing an escrow account.

For unemployment tax purposes, successors may also be held liable for tax debts incurred by the previous owner. In addition, the tax rate of the previous owner may be transferred to the successor. Clearance statements may be obtained through the Unemployment Agency's Tax Office.

CHECKLIST FOR STARTING A NEW BUSINESS

By reading and completing this *Michigan Business Taxes Registration Booklet*, you can be registered for all of the following business taxes and licenses:

- sales tax (includes license)
- use tax
- income tax withholding
- single business tax
- unemployment tax

Your unemployment taxes are paid to the UA. All other taxes are paid to the Michigan Department of Treasury.

If you need motor fuel and tobacco products licenses, please call **517-373-3180**. The following are some suggestions of other places to contact for further help.

1. Determine your business' legal structure

Contact an attorney, accountant or other business professional to determine the appropriate structure for your business. You may wish to contact the Michigan Economic Development Corporation at **517-373-9808** for more information about starting a business.

2. Register your business name

Depending on the legal structure chosen, the business name may be registered with the local county clerk's office or the State of Michigan. Sole-propietorships and Co-partnerships contact the county clerk's office. Corporations, Limited Partnerships and Limited Liability Companies, contact the Corporation, Securities and Land Development Bureau, Michigan Department of Consumer and Industry Services at **900-555-0031** or **517-334-7561**.

3. Obtain a Federal Employer Identification Number (FEIN)

This number is issued by the Internal Revenue Service (IRS) and is required if you will have employees. It is also mandatory on your UA registration. If you don't have a number yet, contact the IRS at **800-829-3676** and ask for form SS4. When you have completed the form, you may call **606-292-5467** and provide the information from the form to the agent. The agent will assign your FEIN while you are on the telephone. To complete your FEIN registration, you either mail the form to the address shown on the form or fax it to **606-292-5760**.

4. Obtain any special licenses

Some occupations, professions and business activities require certification or licensing at the state or local level. An abbreviated list of state licensing contacts is provided below.

Department of Agriculture

800-292-3939, Food Service

Department of Consumer & Industry Services

Health Services
517-335-0918

Commercial Services
517-373-9879

Insurance Bureau
517-373-9273

Liquor Control Commission
517-322-1400

Plumbing, Mechanical, Electrical Boiler or Elevator Licensing
517-241-9313

Health Facilities Licensing & Certification
517-335-8000

You may also contact your local library, chamber of commerce or the nearest Small Business Development Center for information about state licenses. Also check with your county and city clerks for information about local licenses.

REGISTRATION FOR MICHIGAN TAXES

It is important that you complete all items on this registration. Incomplete information will delay processing. Read all instructions carefully before you begin.

This form is provided under P. A. 122 of 1941 and the Michigan Employment Security Act of 1936. Filing is mandatory if you are required to pay business taxes in Michigan.

Complete this registration if you:
- are starting a new business or reinstating an old business.
- purchased or acquired an existing business.
- need to register for any of the Michigan taxes listed below.
- changed the type of ownership of your business (e.g.: from sole proprietorship to partnership, or incorporating a sole proprietorship or partnership).

Do **not** complete this registration if you:
- make sales at fewer than 3 events in Michigan. Call **800-FORM-2-ME** for a concessionaire's form.
- wish to apply for an ID number for your bank account. Use your Social Security number for this purpose.

Register for **sales tax** if you:
- sell tangible personal property to the end user from a Michigan location (wholesalers do not need to register).
Questions? Call **517-373-3190**, then press 14.

Register for **use tax** if you:
- lease tangible personal property in Michigan.
- sell telecommunication services.
- provide transient hotel or motel room rentals.
- buy goods for your own use from out-of-state unlicensed vendors.
- launder or clean textiles under a sole rental or service agreement with a term of at least five days.
Questions? Call **517-373-3190**, then press 14.

Register for **withholding** if you:
- are an employer withholding federal income tax from employee compensation (see Federal Employer's Tax Guide Circular E).

Individual owners and partners may not remit withholding on their wages through their business account number. They must file quarterly income tax estimates. For information about quarterly estimates, call **800-487-7000**.
Questions? Call **517-373-3190**, then press 14.

Register for **single business tax** if you:
- have apportioned gross receipts plus recapture of capital acquisition deduction greater than the filing requirement. The filing requirement is $250,000 in 1995 and beyond. Special circumstances apply for controlled groups effective for tax years ending after June 30, 1994.
Questions? Call **517-373-8030**, then press 15.

Register for **motor fuel tax** if you:
- operate a terminal or refinery for gasoline, diesel or aviation fuel or import from a foreign country.
- acquire or sell tax-free diesel or gasoline.
- transport fuel across a Michigan border.
- sell diesel fuel or LPG to an end user.

- operate a diesel-powered vehicle with three or more axles or with two axles and gross vehicle weight over 26,000 pounds.

Register for **tobacco products tax** if you:
- sell cigarettes or other tobacco products for resale.
- purchase any tobacco products from unlicensed out-of-state sources.
Questions on motor fuel or tobacco products taxes? Call **517-373-3180**. If, after reviewing your registration, Treasury determines that you will need to file motor fuel or tobacco products returns, we will send you the necessary applications.

Register for **UA unemployment tax** if you:
- have employees performing services in Michigan.
- plan to have employees working in Michigan.
- have acquired all or any part of the assets, organization or trade of an existing business having employees in Michigan. (You must also file *UA 518 Schedule B, Successorship Questionnaire*.)

All employers must also complete these UA forms which are included in this booklet:
- *Schedule A, Liability Questionnaire*
- *Schedule C, Michigan Business Activity and Location Information*.
Questions? In Michigan call **800-638-3994**. Out of state, call **(313) 876-6691**.

For specific information regarding missing UA payments, reports, penalties, and/or interest due call **313-876-5135**. A recorded message will offer you a number of options. Note the last three digits of your UA or FEIN number as you will be asked to make a menu selection based on those three digits.

Mail your completed registration and UA schedules to:

Michigan Department of Treasury
Lansing, MI 48922

Please mail your application at least six weeks before you intend to start your business to allow your registration to be processed. Treasury will forward your application to UA.

Treasury will mail your personalized sales, use and withholding taxes returns. UA will issue your unemployment account number. If you have forms or registration questions, contact the proper agency at the numbers below.

Registration questions:
Call **517-373-0888**, then press 13,
or fax questions on Registration to: **517-241-4311**.
Call **800-FORM-2-ME** for Treasury forms.
UA questions:
In Michigan, call **800-638-3994**.
Out of state, call **313-876-6691**,
or fax to **313-876-5678**.

Michigan Department of Treasury and Unemployment Agency
518 (Rev. 6-99). Formerly C-3400.

REGISTRATION FOR MICHIGAN TAXES

1. Federal Employer Identification Number (Required for UA)
If you do not have an FEIN, call the IRS at 1-800-829-1040.

1a. UA No.

2. Complete Company Name or Owner's Full Name (include, if applicable, Corp., Inc., P.C., L.C., L.L.C., L.L.P., etc.)

3. Business Name, Assumed Name or DBA (as registered with the county)

Legal Address

4A. This address is for all legal contacts. Enter number and street (no P.O. boxes).

Business Telephone

City, State, ZIP

County

Mailing Address

4B. This address is where all tax forms will be sent unless otherwise instructed.

If this address is for an accountant, bookkeeper or other representative, attach a Power of Attorney.

City, State, ZIP

Physical Address

4C. This address is the actual location of the business in Michigan. Enter number and street (cannot be a P.O. box number).

City, State, ZIP

County

5. Type of Business Ownership (check one only)

- [ ] (1) Individual (Sole Proprietorship)
- [ ] (2) Husband/Wife
- [ ] (3) Partnership
- [ ] (3) Registered Partnership, Agreement Date: _____
- [ ] (3) Limited Partnership - Identify all general partners below
- [ ] (34) Limited Liability Co. or Partnership
  - [ ] Domestic (Mich)
  - [ ] Professional
  - [ ] Foreign (Non-Mich)

- [ ] (4) Michigan Corporation
  - [ ] (1) Subchapter S
  - [ ] (2) Professional
- [ ] (5) Non-Mich. Corporation
  - [ ] (1) Subchapter S

- [ ] (6) Trust or Estate (Fiduciary)
- [ ] (7) Joint Stock Club or Investment Co
- [ ] (8) Social Club or Fraternal Org.
- [ ] (9) Other (Explain)

Date of Incorporation | Mo. | Day | Year

State of Incorporation

Michigan Department of Consumer & Industry Services Identification No.

6. Which taxes do you expect to owe?   What date will that liability begin?   How much of each tax do you estimate you will owe each month?

- [ ] Sales Tax — Mo. Day Year — [ ] Up to $65 [ ] Up to $300 [ ] Over $300
- [ ] Use Tax — Mo. Day Year — [ ] Up to $65 [ ] Up to $300 [ ] Over $300
- [ ] Income Tax Withholding — Mo. Day Year — [ ] Up to $65 [ ] Up to $300 [ ] Over $300
- [ ] Single Business Tax — Mo. Day Year

How many people will you employ who are subject to Michigan withholding? _____

- [ ] Motor Fuel Taxes .... Treasury will review your registration and send you any necessary tax application forms.
- [ ] Tobacco Products Tax .... Treasury will review your registration and send you any necessary tax application forms.
- [ ] UA Unemployment Tax .... **Attach Schedules A, B (if successor) and C. Enclose a copy of your Articles of Incorporation or Organization.**

7. Estimated annual Michigan gross receipts?   **GROSS RECEIPTS** are from (a) sales of inventory items, (b) rental or leases, (c) performance of services, interest, royalties, etc., to the extent they are derived from business activity.

- [ ] Up to $250,000
- [ ] Over $250,000

Complete all information for each owner, partner, member or corporate officer. Attach a separate list if necessary.

8A. Name (Last, First, Middle, Jr./Sr./III)

Social Security Number

Title

Date of Birth

Residence Address (Number, Street)

Driver License/Michigan Identification

City, State, ZIP

Home Telephone

8B. Name (Last, First, Middle, Jr./Sr./III)

Social Security Number

Title

Date of Birth

Residence Address (Number, Street)

Driver License/Michigan Identification

City, State, ZIP

Home Telephone

PLEASE DETACH BEFORE MAILING.

Multiple Locations	**9.** How many business locations will you operate in Michigan? If more than one, attach a list of names and addresses.

Seasonal Business	**10.** Month Business Opens Month Business Closes

Fiscal Year	**11.** Do you close your tax books on Dec. 31? If no, give month of closing. ☐ Yes ☐ No

Payroll Service	**12.** If your withholding taxes are paid by a payroll service, enter the payroll service name and address.

13A. Describe your business activity.

13B. What retail products, if any, do you sell (sold to final consumer)?	**13C.** What wholesale products, if any, do you sell?

13D. Do you have employees entering Michigan or representatives acting as your agent in Michigan to solicit orders, describe products or provide service?   ☐ Yes   ☐ No

14A. What is the reason for this application? ☐ Started a new business ☐ Incorporated an existing business ☐ Purchased an existing business. Complete item 15 below. ☐ Other (explain):	**14B. List any previous account numbers**

15A. If you purchased or acquired a business, what assets did you acquire? Check the boxes that apply and complete **UA *Schedule B.***
☐ Land   ☐ Building   ☐ Furniture & Fixtures   ☐ Equipment   ☐ Inventory   ☐ Goodwill

15B. Name of previous owner(s) or corporation	**15C.** Previous Owner's Account Number (if known)

15D. Will the previous owner continue to make retail sales or have employees in Mich. ☐ Yes ☐ No	**15E.** What was your total purchase price?

16A. Gasoline Stations: Name of Distributor	**16B.** Brand

16C. Address of Distributor (No., Street, City, State, ZIP)

17. Motor Fuel and Tobacco Tax Information

	Yes	No		Yes	No
Will you sell gasoline or diesel fuel for exempt purposes?	☐	☐	Will you sell tobacco products for resale?	☐	☐
Will you sell diesel fuel from bulk storage into highway vehicles?	☐	☐	Will you operate a tobacco products vending machine?	☐	☐
Will you operate a terminal or refinery?	☐	☐			
Do you own a diesel-powered vehicle with 3 or more axles or 2 axles and gross vehicle wt., over 26,000 lbs.?	☐	☐	If yes, do you supply tobacco products for the machine?	☐	☐
Will you transport fuel across Michigan's borders?	☐	☐	If no, please give the supplier's name.		

SIGNATURE OF OWNERS.
This registration must be signed by the owner(s), two partners, two corporate officers, member(s) of a limited liability company or their authorized representative. Applications without signatures will be returned.

I declare, under penalty of perjury, that I have examined this registration and its attachments and they are true and complete to the best of my knowledge.

Type or print name of owner or officer responsible for filing returns and making tax payments	Title
Signature	Phone Date
Type or print name of second owner; partner; officer or member	Title
Signature	Phone Date
Preparer's name and address if different from above.	Phone Date

If your business is liable for Sales and/or Use Tax only, you may register your business over the telephone by calling (517) 373-0888. If your business is liable for Income Withholding Tax, you must complete and mail this application to: Michigan Department of Treasury, Treasury Building, Lansing, MI 48922

Sales Tax Registrants Only - Enclose $1 License Fee

$ __1.00__

MICHIGAN DEPARTMENT OF CONSUMER & INDUSTRY SERVICES
BUREAU OF COMMERCIAL SERVICES

Date Received	(FOR BUREAU USE ONLY)

This registration will expire 10 years from the stamped registration date.

MARK IDENTIFICATION NUMBER **M** ☐ ☐ **-** ☐ ☐ ☐

APPLICATION FOR REGISTRATION OF TRADEMARK/SERVICE MARK
(Please read information and instructions on last page)

Pursuant to the provisions of Act 242, Public Acts of 1969, as amended, the undersigned executes the following Application:

1. This Application is for the purpose of registering a: (check one)

   ☐ Trademark   ☐ Service mark

2. The mark: (Complete only one of the following)

   a) **WORDS ONLY:**
      If the mark is only words, the words in the mark are: (Include type style if it is an inherent part of the mark)

   b) **DESIGN ONLY:**
      If the mark is a design only, describe the design: (Include colors if they are an inherent part of the mark)

   c) **WORDS AND DESIGN:**
      Describe the design and list the words in the mark: (Include color and type style if they are an inherent part of the mark)

Please note: Complete either Item 3 **or** Item 4. Designate only one mark and one classification code per application.

Trademarks only

3. a) List the goods in connection with which the mark is used.

   b) The mode or manner in which the trademark is used in connection with the goods.

   c) Numerical classification of goods:_____

Service marks only

4. a) List the services in connection with which the mark is used.

b) The mode or manner in which the mark is used in connection with the services.

c) Numerical classification of services: _____

5. a) The mark was first used in Michigan by the applicant, or a predecessor, in_____
   on_____ .
   (month / day / year)   (city)

b) The mark was first used in the United States by the applicant, or a predecessor, in_____
   (city)

_____ on _____ .
(state)   (month / day / year)

6. a) The name of the individual or other entity applying for the registration is:

b) The business name of the applicant, if different than 6(a):

c) The business address of the applicant is:

7. a) The applicant is a: (check one)

☐ Corporation   ☐ Partnership   ☐ Individual   ☐ Limited Liability Company   ☐ Other

b) If a corporation, the state where incorporated: _____

8. Two copies, photographs, facsimiles or specimens of the mark, as actually in use must accompany this Application. The sample should be 8.5 x 11 inches or smaller so it may be scanned to optical disk media.

State of_____

County of_____ } SS

I, being first sworn, hereby depose and say that I have read the above application, including any attached papers, and the facts set out therein are true; the applicant is the owner of the mark and none other has the right to use the mark in Michigan either in the identical form or in a form which so nearly resembles the mark as to be likely to deceive or to be mistaken for the mark; the specimens of the mark as filed herewith are true and correct. FURTHER, the Bureau of Commercial Services, Michigan Department of Consumer & Industry Services, is hereby appointed as the applicant's agent for service of process only in actions relating to the registration or the application for registration of this mark.

Signature	Type or Print Name	Type or Print Title

Subscribed and sworn to before me this _____ day of_____, _____ .

_____
(Signature of Notary)

_____
(Type or Print Name of Notary)

Notary Public for _____ County,

State of_____

(Notary Seal)   My Commission expires_____

INFORMATION AND INSTRUCTIONS

1. This application must be used to register a Trademark/Service Mark. A document required or permitted to be filed under this act cannot be filed unless it contains the minimum information required by the act. This is a legal document and agency staff cannot provide legal advice.

2. Submit one original of this document. Upon filing, a Certificate of Registration will be mailed to the applicant or his/her representative to the address provided on this Application.

   Since this application will be maintained on electronic format, it is important that the filing be legible. Documents with poor black and white contrast, or otherwise illegible, will be rejected.

3. This Application is to be used pursuant to Section 3(1) of Act 242, P.A. of 1969 for the purpose of registering a trademark or service mark. A trademark is any word, name, symbol, or device, or any combination thereof, other than a trade name in its entirety, adopted and used by a person to identify goods made or sold by him or her and to distinguish them from similar goods made or sold by others. Similarly, a service mark is a mark used by a person in the sale or advertising of services to identify his or her services and distinguish them from the similar services of others. The term person, as used above, means an individual, firm, partnership, corporation, association, union, or other organization. A mark is not registrable until it has actually been adopted and used in Michigan. The registration is effective for ten years and is renewable for successive terms of 10 years upon the filing of an application for renewal, on a form provided by the Bureau, within six months prior to the expiration date.

4. The Department of Consumer & Industry Services, Bureau of Commercial Services is appointed as the applicant's agent for service of process in actions relating to the registration or application for registration if: (1) the applicant is or becomes a nonresident individual, partnership or association, (2) the applicant is or becomes a foreign corporation or limited liability company without a certificate of authority to transact business in Michigan, or (3) the applicant cannot be found in Michigan.

5. Item 2 - Complete section (a), (b) or (c) depending on the type of mark that is being registered.

6. Trademarks only:
   Item 3(a) - List the good(s) on which the mark is used.
   Item 3(b) - List how the mark is used on the good(s) i.e. tag, label, etc.
   Item 3(c) - List the classification of the good, but be aware that only one classification can be designated per application.
       A list of the classification codes can be found on the back of this Application.

7. Service marks only:
   Item 4(a) - List the service(s) in connection with which the mark is used.
   Item 4(b) - List how the mark is used i.e. in advertising, signs, letterhead, etc.
   Item 4(c) - List the classification of the good, but be aware that only one classification can be designated per application.
       A list of the classification codes can be found on the back of this Application.

8. Item 5 - A trademark is considered "used in Michigan" when affixed to the product, container, tags or labels and sold in Michigan. For services, the mark must be used or displayed in this state in the sale or advertising of services rendered in Michigan.

9. Item 8 - Two copies, photographs, facsimiles or specimens of the mark, as actually in use must accompany this Application. The sample should be 8.5 x 11 inches or smaller so it may be maintained on electronic format.

10. This Application must be signed by:
    Individual - by the applicant
    Corporation - by an authorized officer or agent.
    Limited Liability Company - by a manager if management is vested in one or more managers or by a member if management is reserved for members.
    Partnership - by a partner.

11. NONREFUNDABLE FEE: Make remittance payable to the State of Michigan $50.00

To submit by mail:
   Michigan Department of Consumer & Industry Services
   Bureau of Commercial Services
   Corporation Division
   7150 Harris Drive
   P.O. Box 30054
   Lansing, MI 48909

To submit in person:
   6546 Mercantile Way
   Lansing, MI
   Telephone: (517) 241-6400

Fees may be paid by VISA or Mastercard when delivered in person to our office.

TRADEMARK UNIFORM CLASSIFICATION OF GOODS

1. Raw or partly prepared materials
2. Receptacles
3. Baggage, animal equipments, portfolios and pocketbooks
4. Abrasives and polishing materials
5. Adhesives
6. Chemicals and chemical compositions
7. Cordage
8. Smokers' articles, not including tobacco products
9. Explosives, firearms, equipments and projectiles
10. Fertilizers
11. Inks and inking materials
12. Construction materials
13. Hardware and plumbing and steam fitting supplies
14. Metals and metal castings and forgings
15. Oils and greases
16. Paints and painters' materials
17. Tobacco products
18. Medicines and pharmaceutical preparations
19. Vehicles
20. Linoleum and oiled cloth
21. Electrical apparatus, machines and supplies
22. Games, toys and sporting goods
23. Cutlery, machinery and tools, and parts thereof
24. Laundry appliances and machines
25. Locks and safes
26. Measuring and scientific appliances
27. Horological instruments
28. Jewelry and precious-metal ware
29. Brooms, brushes and dusters
30. Crockery, earthenware and porcelain
31. Filters and refrigerators
32. Furniture and upholstery
33. Glassware
34. Heating, lighting and ventilating apparatus
35. Belting, hose, machinery packing, and non-metallic tires
36. Musical instruments and supplies
37. Paper and stationery
38. Prints and publications
39. Clothing
40. Fancy goods, furnishings and notions
41. Canes, parasols and umbrellas
42. Knitted, netted and textile
43. Thread and yarn
44. Dental, medical and surgical appliances
45. Soft drinks and carbonated waters
46. Foods and ingredients of foods
47. Wines
48. Malt beverages and liquors
49. Distilled alcoholic liquors
50. Merchandise not otherwise classified
51. Cosmetics and toilet preparations
52. Detergents and soaps

SERVICE MARK UNIFORM CLASSIFICATION OF SERVICES

100. Miscellaneous
101. Advertising and business
102. Insurance and financial
103. Construction and repair
104. Communication
105. Transportation and storage
106. Material treatment
107. Education and entertainment

The Department of Consumer & Industry Services will not discriminate against any individual or group because of race, sex, religion, age, national origin, color, marital status, political beliefs or disability. If you need help with reading, writing, hearing, etc., under the Americans with Disabilities Act, you may make your needs known to this agency.

Form **SS-8**

(Rev. January 2001)

Department of the Treasury
Internal Revenue Service

Determination of Worker Status
for Purposes of Federal Employment Taxes
and Income Tax Withholding

OMB No. 1545-0004

Name of firm (or person) for whom the worker performed services	Worker's name

Firm's address (include street address, apt. or suite no., city, state, and ZIP code)	Worker's address (include street address, apt. or suite no., city, state, and ZIP code)

Trade name	Telephone number (include area code) ( )	Worker's social security number

Telephone number (include area code) ( )	Firm's employer identification number	Worker's employer identification number (if any)

Important Information Needed To Process Your Request

If this form is being completed by the worker, the IRS must have your permission to disclose your name to the firm. Do you object to disclosing your name and the information on this form to the firm? . . . . ☐ **Yes** ☐ **No**
If you answered "Yes" or did not check a box, stop here. The IRS cannot act on your request and a determination will not be issued.

You must answer ALL items OR mark them "Unknown" or "Does not apply." If you need more space, attach another sheet.

A This form is being completed by: ☐ Firm ☐ Worker; for services performed _____ to _____
(beginning date)   (ending date)

B Explain your reason(s) for filing this form (e.g., you received a bill from the IRS, you believe you received a Form 1099 or Form W-2 erroneously, you are unable to get worker's compensation benefits, you were audited or are being audited by the IRS). ------------------

----

C Total number of workers who performed or are performing the same or similar services _____ .

D How did the worker obtain the job? ☐ Application ☐ Bid ☐ Employment Agency ☐ Other (specify) _____

E Attach copies of all supporting documentation (contracts, invoices, memos, Forms W-2, Forms 1099, IRS closing agreements, IRS rulings, etc.). In addition, please inform us of any current or past litigation concerning the worker's status. If no income reporting forms (Form 1099-MISC or W-2) were furnished to the worker, enter the amount of income earned for the year(s) at issue $ _____ .

F Describe the firm's business. ------------------

G Describe the work done by the worker and provide the worker's job title. ------------------

----

H Explain why you believe the worker is an employee or an independent contractor. ------------------

----

I Did the worker perform services for the firm before getting this position? . . . . ☐ **Yes** ☐ **No** ☐ **N/A**
If "Yes," what were the dates of the prior service? ------------------
If "Yes," explain the differences, if any, between the current and prior service. ------------------

----

J If the work is done under a written agreement between the firm and the worker, attach a copy (preferably signed by both parties). Describe the terms and conditions of the work arrangement. ------------------

For Privacy Act and Paperwork Reduction Act Notice, see page 5.

Cat. No. 16106T

Form **SS-8** (Rev. 1-2001)

Part I — Behavioral Control

1 What specific training and/or instruction is the worker given by the firm? ....

2 How does the worker receive work assignments? ....

3 Who determines the methods by which the assignments are performed? ....

4 Who is the worker required to contact if problems or complaints arise and who is responsible for their resolution? ....

5 What types of reports are required from the worker? Attach examples. ....

6 Describe the worker's daily routine (i.e., schedule, hours, etc.). ....

7 At what location(s) does the worker perform services (e.g., firm's premises, own shop or office, home, customer's location, etc.)? ....

8 Describe any meetings the worker is required to attend and any penalties for not attending (e.g., sales meetings, monthly meetings, staff meetings, etc.). ....

9 Is the worker required to provide the services personally? . . . . ☐ Yes ☐ No

10 If substitutes or helpers are needed, who hires them? ....

11 If the worker hires the substitutes or helpers, is approval required? . . . . ☐ Yes ☐ No
If "Yes," by whom?

12 Who pays the substitutes or helpers? ....

13 Is the worker reimbursed if the worker pays the substitutes or helpers? . . . . ☐ Yes ☐ No
If "Yes," by whom? ....

Part II — Financial Control

1 List the supplies, equipment, materials, and property provided by each party:
The firm ....
The worker ....
Other party ....

2 Does the worker lease equipment? . . . . ☐ Yes ☐ No
If "Yes," what are the terms of the lease? (Attach a copy or explanatory statement.) ....

3 What expenses are incurred by the worker in the performance of services for the firm? ....

4 Specify which, if any, expenses are reimbursed by:
The firm ....
Other party ....

5 Type of pay the worker receives: ☐ Salary ☐ Commission ☐ Hourly Wage ☐ Piece Work
☐ Lump Sum ☐ Other (specify) ....
If type of pay is commission, and the firm guarantees a minimum amount of pay, specify amount $ _____ .

6 If the worker is paid by a firm other than the one listed on this form for these services, enter name, address, and employer identification number of the payer. ....

7 Is the worker allowed a drawing account for advances? . . . . ☐ Yes ☐ No
If "Yes," how often? ....
Specify any restrictions. ....

8 Whom does the customer pay? . . . . ☐ Firm ☐ Worker
If worker, does the worker pay the total amount to the firm? ☐ Yes ☐ No If "No," explain. ....

9 Does the firm carry worker's compensation insurance on the worker? . . . . ☐ Yes ☐ No

10 What economic loss or financial risk, if any, can the worker incur beyond the normal loss of salary (e.g., loss or damage of equipment, material, etc.)? ....

Part III Relationship of the Worker and Firm

1 List the benefits available to the worker (e.g., paid vacations, sick pay, pensions, bonuses). ----------

2 Can the relationship be terminated by either party without incurring liability or penalty? . . . . ☐ **Yes** ☐ **No**

 If "No," explain your answer. ----------

3 Does the worker perform similar services for others? . . . . ☐ **Yes** ☐ **No**

 If "Yes," is the worker required to get approval from the firm? . . . . ☐ **Yes** ☐ **No**

4 Describe any agreements prohibiting competition between the worker and the firm while the worker is performing services or during any later period. Attach any available documentation. ----------

5 Is the worker a member of a union? . . . . ☐ **Yes** ☐ **No**

6 What type of advertising, if any, does the worker do (e.g., a business listing in a directory, business cards, etc.)? Provide copies, if applicable.

7 If the worker assembles or processes a product at home, who provides the materials and instructions or pattern? ----------

8 What does the worker do with the finished product (e.g., return it to the firm, provide it to another party, or sell it)? ----------

9 How does the firm represent the worker to its customers (e.g., employee, partner, representative, or contractor)? ----------

10 If the worker no longer performs services for the firm, how did the relationship end? ----------

Part IV **For Service Providers or Salespersons-** Complete this part if the worker provided a service directly to customers or is a salesperson.

1 What are the worker's responsibilities in soliciting new customers? ----------

2 Who provides the worker with leads to prospective customers? ----------

3 Describe any reporting requirements pertaining to the leads. ----------

4 What terms and conditions of sale, if any, are required by the firm? ----------

5 Are orders submitted to and subject to approval by the firm? . . . . ☐ **Yes** ☐ **No**

6 Who determines the worker's territory? ----------

7 Did the worker pay for the privilege of serving customers on the route or in the territory? . . . . ☐ **Yes** ☐ **No**

 If "Yes," whom did the worker pay? ----------

 If "Yes," how much did the worker pay? . . . . $ _____

8 Where does the worker sell the product (e.g., in a home, retail establishment, etc.)? ----------

9 List the product and/or services distributed by the worker (e.g., meat, vegetables, fruit, bakery products, beverages, or laundry or dry cleaning services). If more than one type of product and/or service is distributed, specify the principal one. ----------

10 Does the worker sell life insurance full time? . . . . ☐ **Yes** ☐ **No**

11 Does the worker sell other types of insurance for the firm? . . . . ☐ **Yes** ☐ **No**

 If "Yes," enter the percentage of the worker's total working time spent in selling other types of insurance. . . . _____ %

12 If the worker solicits orders from wholesalers, retailers, contractors, or operators of hotels, restaurants, or other similar establishments, enter the percentage of the worker's time spent in the solicitation. . . . . _____ %

13 Is the merchandise purchased by the customers for resale or use in their business operations? . . . . . . ☐ **Yes** ☐ **No**

 Describe the merchandise and state whether it is equipment installed on the customers' premises. ----------

Part V Signature (see page 4)

Under penalties of perjury, I declare that I have examined this request, including accompanying documents, and to the best of my knowledge and belief, the facts presented are true, correct, and complete.

Signature ▶ _____ Title ▶ _____ Date ▶ _____

 (Type or print name below)

General Instructions

Section references are to the Internal Revenue Code unless otherwise noted.

Purpose

Firms and workers file Form SS-8 to request a determination of the status of a worker for purposes of Federal employment taxes and income tax withholding.

A Form SS-8 determination may be requested only in order to resolve Federal tax matters. The taxpayer requesting a determination must file an income tax return for the years under consideration before a determination can be issued. If Form SS-8 is submitted for a tax year for which the statute of limitations on the tax return has expired, a determination letter will not be issued. The statute of limitations expires 3 years from the due date of the tax return or the date filed, whichever is later.

The IRS does not issue a determination letter for proposed transactions or on hypothetical situations. We may, however, issue an information letter when it is considered appropriate.

Definition

Firm. For the purposes of this form, the term "firm" means any individual, business enterprise, organization, state, or other entity for which a worker has performed services. The firm may or may not have paid the worker directly for these services. **If the firm was not responsible for payment for services, please be sure to complete question 6 in Part II of Form SS-8.**

The SS-8 Determination Process

The IRS will acknowledge the receipt of your Form SS-8. Because there are usually two (or more) parties who could be affected by a determination of employment status, the IRS attempts to get information from all parties involved by sending those parties blank Forms SS-8 for completion. The case will be assigned to a technician who will review the facts, apply the law, and render a decision. The technician may ask for additional information before rendering a decision. The IRS will generally issue a formal determination to the firm or payer (if that is a different entity), and will send a copy to the worker. A determination letter applies only to a worker (or a class of workers) requesting it, and the decision is binding on the IRS. In certain cases, a formal determination will not be issued; instead, an information letter may be issued. Although an information letter is advisory only and is not binding on the IRS, it may be used to assist the worker to fulfill his or her Federal tax obligations. This process takes approximately 120 days.

Neither the SS-8 determination process nor the review of any records in connection with the determination constitutes an examination (audit) of any Federal tax return. If the periods under consideration have previously been examined, the SS-8 determination process will not constitute a reexamination under IRS reopening procedures. Because this is not an examination of any Federal tax return, the appeal rights available in connection with an examination do not apply to an SS-8 determination. However, if you disagree with a determination and you have additional information concerning the work relationship that you believe was not previously considered, you may request that the determining office reconsider the determination.

Completing Form SS-8

Please answer all questions as completely as possible. Attach additional sheets if you need more space. Provide information for all years the worker provided services for the firm. Determinations are based on the entire relationship between the firm and the worker.

Additional copies of this form may be obtained by calling 1-800-TAX-FORM (1-800-829-3676) or from the IRS Web Site at **www.irs.gov.**

Fee

There is no fee for requesting an SS-8 determination letter.

Signature

The Form SS-8 must be signed and dated by the taxpayer. A stamped signature will not be accepted.

The person who signs for a corporation must be an officer of the corporation who has personal knowledge of the facts. If the corporation is a member of an affiliated group filing a consolidated return, it must be signed by an officer of the common parent of the group.

The person signing for a trust, partnership, or limited liability company must be, respectively, a trustee, general partner, or member-manager who has personal knowledge of the facts.

Where To File

Send the completed Form SS-8 to the address listed below for the firm's location. However, for cases involving Federal agencies, send the form to the Internal Revenue Service, Attn: CC:CORP:T:C, Ben Franklin Station, P.O. Box 7604, Washington, DC 20044.

Firm's location:	Send to:
Alaska, Arizona, Arkansas, California, Colorado, Hawaii, Idaho, Illinois, Iowa, Kansas, Minnesota, Missouri, Montana, Nebraska, Nevada, New Mexico, North Dakota, Oklahoma, Oregon, South Dakota, Texas, Utah, Washington, Wisconsin, Wyoming, American Samoa, Guam, Puerto Rico, U.S. Virgin Islands	Internal Revenue Service SS-8 Determinations P.O. Box 1231 Stop 4106 AUCSC Austin, TX 78767
Alabama, Connecticut, Delaware, District of Columbia, Florida, Georgia, Indiana, Kentucky, Louisiana, Maine, Maryland, Massachusetts, Michigan, Mississippi, New Hampshire, New Jersey, New York, North Carolina, Ohio, Pennsylvania, Rhode Island, South Carolina, Tennessee, Vermont, Virginia, West Virginia, all other locations not listed	Internal Revenue Service SS-8 Determinations 40 Lakemont Road Newport, VT 05855-1555

Instructions for Workers

If you are requesting a determination for more than one firm, complete a separate Form SS-8 for each firm.

 Form SS-8 is not a claim for refund of social security and Medicare taxes or Federal income tax withholding.

If you are found to be an employee, you are responsible for filing an amended return for any corrections related to this decision. A determination that a worker is an employee does not necessarily reduce any current or prior tax liability. For more information, call 1-800-829-1040.

Time for filing a claim for refund. Generally, you must file your claim for a credit or refund within 3 years from the date your original return was filed or within 2 years from the date the tax was paid, whichever is later.

Form SS-8 does not prevent the expiration of the time in which a claim for a refund must be filed. If you are concerned about a refund, and the statute of limitations for filing a claim for refund for the year(s) at issue has not yet expired, you should file **Form 1040X,** Amended U.S. Individual Income Tax Return, to protect your statute of limitations. File a separate Form 1040X for each year.

On the Form 1040X you file, do not complete lines 1 through 24 on the form. Write "Protective Claim" at the top of the form, sign and date it. In addition, you should enter the following statement in Part II, Explanation of Changes to Income, Deductions, and Credits: "Filed Form SS-8 with the Internal Revenue Service Office in (Austin, TX; Newport, VT; or Washington, DC; as appropriate). By filing this protective claim, I reserve the right to file a claim for any refund that may be due after a determination of my employment tax status has been completed."

Filing Form SS-8 does not alter the requirement to timely file an income tax return. Do not delay filing your tax return in anticipation of an answer to your SS-8 request. You must file an income tax return for related tax years before a determination can be issued. In addition, if applicable, do not delay in responding to a request for payment while waiting for a determination of your worker status.

Instructions for Firms

If a **worker** has requested a determination of his or her status while working for you, you will receive a request from the IRS to complete a Form SS-8. In cases of this type, the IRS usually gives each party an opportunity to present a statement of the facts because any decision will affect the employment tax status of the parties. Failure to respond to this request will not prevent the IRS from issuing an information letter to the worker based on the information he or she has made available so that the worker may fulfill his or her Federal tax obligations. However, the information that you provide is extremely valuable in determining the status of the worker.

If **you** are requesting a determination for a particular class of worker, complete the form for **one** individual who is representative of the class of workers whose status is in question. If you want a written determination for more than one class of workers, complete a separate Form SS-8 for one worker from each class whose status is typical of that class. A written determination for any worker will apply to other workers of the same class if the facts are not materially different for these workers. Please provide a list of names and addresses of all workers potentially affected by this determination.

If you have a reasonable basis for not treating a worker as an employee, you may be relieved from having to pay employment taxes for that worker under section 530 of the 1978 Revenue Act. However, this relief provision cannot be considered in conjunction with a Form SS-8 determination because the determination does not constitute an examination of any tax return. For more information regarding section 530 of the 1978 Revenue Act and to determine if you qualify for relief under this section, you may visit the IRS Web Site at **www.irs.gov**.

Privacy Act and Paperwork Reduction Act Notice. We ask for the information on this form to carry out the Internal Revenue laws of the United States. This information will be used to determine the employment status of the worker(s) described on the form. Subtitle C, Employment Taxes, of the Internal Revenue Code imposes employment taxes on wages. Sections 3121(d), 3306(a), and 3401(c) and (d) and the related regulations define employee and employer for purposes of employment taxes imposed under Subtitle C. Section 6001 authorizes the IRS to request information needed to determine if a worker(s) or firm is subject to these taxes. Section 6109 requires you to provide your taxpayer identification number. Neither workers nor firms are required to request a status determination, but if you choose to do so, you must provide the information requested on this form. Failure to provide the requested information may prevent us from making a status determination. If any worker or the firm has requested a status determination, and you are being asked to provide information for use in that determination, you are not required to provide the requested information. However, failure to provide such information will prevent the IRS from considering it in making the status determination. Providing false or fraudulent information may subject you to penalties. Routine uses of this information include providing it to the Department of Justice for use in civil and criminal litigation, to the Social Security Administration for the administration of social security programs, and to cities, states, and the District of Columbia for the administration of their tax laws. We may also provide this information to the affected worker(s) or the firm as part of the status determination process.

You are not required to provide the information requested on a form that is subject to the Paperwork Reduction Act unless the form displays a valid OMB control number. Books or records relating to a form or its instructions must be retained as long as their contents may become material in the administration of any Internal Revenue law. Generally, tax returns and return information are confidential, as required by section 6103.

The time needed to complete and file this form will vary depending on individual circumstances. The estimated average time is: **Recordkeeping,** 22 hrs.; **Learning about the law or the form,** 47 min.; and **Preparing and sending the form to the IRS,** 1 hr., 11 min. If you have comments concerning the accuracy of these time estimates or suggestions for making this form simpler, we would be happy to hear from you. You can write to the Tax Forms Committee, Western Area Distribution Center, Rancho Cordova, CA 95743-0001. **Do not** send the tax form to this address. Instead, see **Where To File** on page 4.

This page intentionally left blank.

Form **8850**	Pre-Screening Notice and Certification Request for	
(Rev. November 1998)	the Work Opportunity and Welfare-to-Work Credits	OMB No. 1545-1500
Department of the Treasury Internal Revenue Service	▶ See separate instructions.	

Job applicant: Fill in the lines below and check any boxes that apply. Complete only this side.

Your name _____ Social security number ▶ _____

Street address where you live _____

City or town, state, and ZIP code _____

Telephone no. ( ) _____ - _____

If you are under age 25, enter your date of birth (month, day, year) _____ / _____ / _____

Work Opportunity Credit

1 ☐ Check here if you received a conditional certification from the state employment security agency (SESA) or a participating local agency for the work opportunity credit.

2 ☐ Check here if **any** of the following statements apply to you.

- I am a member of a family that has received assistance from Aid to Families with Dependent Children (AFDC) or its successor program, Temporary Assistance for Needy Families (TANF), for any 9 months during the last 18 months.

- I am a veteran and a member of a family that received food stamps for at least a 3-month period within the last 15 months.
- I was referred here by a rehabilitation agency approved by the state or the Department of Veterans Affairs.

- I am at least age 18 but **not** over age 24 and I am a member of a family that:
  a Received food stamps for the last 6 months, OR
  b Received food stamps for at least 3 of the last 5 months, BUT is no longer eligible to receive them.

- Within the past year, I was convicted of a felony or released from prison for a felony AND during the last 6 months I was a member of a low-income family.

- I received supplemental security income (SSI) benefits for any month ending within the last 60 days.

Welfare-to-Work Credit

3 ☐ Check here if you received a conditional certification from the SESA or a participating local agency for the welfare-to-work credit.

4 ☐ Check here if you are a member of a family that:
- Received AFDC or TANF payments for at least the last 18 months, OR
- Received AFDC or TANF payments for any 18 months beginning after August 5, 1997, OR
- Stopped being eligible for AFDC or TANF payments after August 5, 1997, because Federal or state law limited the maximum time those payments could be made.

All Applicants

Under penalties of perjury, I declare that I gave the above information to the employer on or before the day I was offered a job, and it is, to the best of my knowledge, true, correct, and complete.

Job applicant's signature ▶ _____ Date _____ / _____ / _____

For Privacy Act and Paperwork Reduction Act Notice, see page 2.   Cat. No. 22851L   Form **8850** (Rev. 11-98)

For Employer's Use Only

Employer's name _____ Telephone no. ( ) - _____ EIN ▶ _____

Street address _____

City or town, state, and ZIP code _____

Person to contact, if different from above _____ Telephone no. ( ) - _____

Street address _____

City or town, state, and ZIP code _____

If, based on the individual's age and home address, he or she is a member of group 4 or 6 (as described under **Members of Targeted Groups** in the separate instructions), enter that group number (4 or 6) . . . . ▶ _____

DATE APPLICANT:	Gave information	/ /	Was offered job	/ /	Was hired	/ /	Started job	/ /

Under penalties of perjury, I declare that I completed this form on or before the day a job was offered to the applicant and that the information I have furnished is, to the best of my knowledge, true, correct, and complete. Based on the information the job applicant furnished on page 1, I believe the individual is a member of a targeted group or a long-term family assistance recipient. I hereby request a certification that the individual is a member of a targeted group or a long-term family assistance recipient.

Employer's signature ▶ _____ **Title** _____ **Date** / /

Privacy Act and Paperwork Reduction Act Notice

Section references are to the Internal Revenue Code.

Section 51(d)(12) permits a prospective employer to request the applicant to complete this form and give it to the prospective employer. The information will be used by the employer to complete the employer's Federal tax return. Completion of this form is voluntary and may assist members of targeted groups and long-term family assistance recipients in securing employment. Routine uses of this form include giving it to the state employment security agency (SESA), which will contact appropriate sources to confirm that the applicant is a member of a targeted group or a long-term family

assistance recipient. This form may also be given to the Internal Revenue Service for administration of the Internal Revenue laws, to the Department of Justice for civil and criminal litigation, to the Department of Labor for oversight of the certifications performed by the SESA, and to cities, states, and the District of Columbia for use in administering their tax laws.

You are not required to provide the information requested on a form that is subject to the Paperwork Reduction Act unless the form displays a valid OMB control number. Books or records relating to a form or its instructions must be retained as long as their contents may become material in the administration of any Internal Revenue law. Generally, tax returns and return information are confidential, as required by section 6103.

The time needed to complete and file this form will vary depending on individual circumstances. The estimated average time is:

Recordkeeping . . . . 2 hr., 47 min.
Learning about the law or the form . . . . 28 min.
Preparing and sending this form to the SESA . . . . 36 min.

If you have comments concerning the accuracy of these time estimates or suggestions for making this form simpler, we would be happy to hear from you. You can write to the Tax Forms Committee, Western Area Distribution Center, Rancho Cordova, CA 95743-0001.

DO NOT send this form to this address. Instead, see **When and Where To File** in the separate instructions.

Form **8300**	**Report of Cash Payments Over $10,000 Received in a Trade or Business** ▶ See instructions for definition of cash. ▶ Use this form for transactions occurring after July 31, 1997. Please type or print.	OMB No. 1545-0892

Form **8300**
(Rev. August 1997)
Department of the Treasury
Internal Revenue Service

1 Check appropriate box(es) if: **a** ☐ Amends prior report;   **b** ☐ Suspicious transaction.

Part I   Identity of Individual From Whom the Cash Was Received

2 If more than one individual is involved, check here and see instructions . . . . ▶ ☐

3 Last name

4 First name

5 M.I.

6 Taxpayer identification number

7 Address (number, street, and apt. or suite no.)

8 Date of birth . ▶   M M   D D   Y Y Y Y (see instructions)

9 City

10 State

11 ZIP code

12 Country (if not U.S.)

13 Occupation, profession, or business

14 Document used to verify identity: **a** Describe identification ▶
b Issued by   **c** Number

Part II   Person on Whose Behalf This Transaction Was Conducted

15 If this transaction was conducted on behalf of more than one person, check here and see instructions . . . . ▶ ☐

16 Individual's last name or Organization's name

17 First name

18 M.I.

19 Taxpayer identification number

20 Doing business as (DBA) name (see instructions)

Employer identification number

21 Address (number, street, and apt. or suite no.)

22 Occupation, profession, or business

23 City

24 State

25 ZIP code

26 Country (if not U.S.)

27 Alien identification: **a** Describe identification ▶
b Issued by   **c** Number

Part III   Description of Transaction and Method of Payment

28 Date cash received   M M   D D   Y Y Y Y

29 Total cash received $ .00

30 If cash was received in more than one payment, check here . . . ▶ ☐

31 Total price if different from item 29 $ .00

32 Amount of cash received (in U.S. dollar equivalent) (must equal item 29) (see instructions):

   a U.S. currency $ _____ .00   (Amount in $100 bills or higher $ _____ .00)
   b Foreign currency $ _____ .00   (Country ▶ _____)
   c Cashier's check(s) $ _____ .00 ⎫ Issuer's name(s) and serial number(s) of the monetary instrument(s) ▶ ....
   d Money order(s) $ _____ .00 ⎪
   e Bank draft(s) $ _____ .00 ⎬ ....
   f Traveler's check(s) $ _____ .00 ⎭

33 Type of transaction

   a ☐ Personal property purchased
   b ☐ Real property purchased
   c ☐ Personal services provided
   d ☐ Business services provided
   e ☐ Intangible property purchased
   f ☐ Debt obligations paid
   g ☐ Exchange of cash
   h ☐ Escrow or trust funds
   i ☐ Bail bond
   j ☐ Other (specify) ▶

34 Specific description of property or service shown in 33. (Give serial or registration number, address, docket number, etc.) ▶
....
....

Part IV   Business That Received Cash

35 Name of business that received cash

36 Employer identification number

37 Address (number, street, and apt. or suite no.)

Social security number

38 City

39 State

40 ZIP code

41 Nature of your business

42 Under penalties of perjury, I declare that to the best of my knowledge the information I have furnished above is true, correct, and complete.

Signature of authorized official

Title of authorized official

43 Date of signature   M M   D D   Y Y Y Y

44 Type or print name of contact person

45 Contact telephone number   (   )

For Paperwork Reduction Act Notice, see page 4.   Cat. No. 62133S   Form **8300** (Rev. 8-97)

Multiple Parties
(Complete applicable parts below if box 2 or 15 on page 1 is checked)

Part I **Continued—Complete if box 2 on page 1 is checked**

3 Last name	4 First name	5 M.I.	6 Taxpayer identification number

7 Address (number, street, and apt. or suite no.)	8 Date of birth . ▶ (see instructions)	M M D D Y Y Y Y

9 City	10 State	11 ZIP code	12 Country (if not U.S.)	13 Occupation, profession, or business

14 Document used to verify identity: **a** Describe identification ▶ ....
b Issued by   **c** Number

3 Last name	4 First name	5 M.I.	6 Taxpayer identification number

7 Address (number, street, and apt. or suite no.)	8 Date of birth . ▶ (see instructions)	M M D D Y Y Y Y

9 City	10 State	11 ZIP code	12 Country (if not U.S.)	13 Occupation, profession, or business

14 Document used to verify identity: **a** Describe identification ▶ ....
b Issued by   **c** Number

Part II **Continued—Complete if box 15 on page 1 is checked**

16 Individual's last name or Organization's name	17 First name	18 M.I.	19 Taxpayer identification number

20 Doing business as (DBA) name (see instructions)	Employer identification number

21 Address (number, street, and apt. or suite no.)	22 Occupation, profession, or business

23 City	24 State	25 ZIP code	26 Country (if not U.S.)

27 Alien identification: **a** Describe identification ▶ ....
b Issued by   **c** Number

16 Individual's last name or Organization's name	17 First name	18 M.I.	19 Taxpayer identification number

20 Doing business as (DBA) name (see instructions)	Employer identification number

21 Address (number, street, and apt. or suite no.)	22 Occupation, profession, or business

23 City	24 State	25 ZIP code	26 Country (if not U.S.)

27 Alien identification: **a** Describe identification ▶ ....
b Issued by   **c** Number

Item You Should Note

Clerks of Federal or State courts must now file Form 8300 if more than $10,000 in cash is received as bail for an individual(s) charged with certain criminal offenses. For these purposes, a clerk includes the clerk's office or any other office, department, division, branch, or unit of the court that is authorized to receive bail. If a person receives bail on behalf of a clerk, the clerk is treated as receiving the bail.

If multiple payments are made in cash to satisfy bail and the initial payment does not exceed $10,000, the initial payment and subsequent payments must be aggregated and the information return must be filed by the 15th day after receipt of the payment that causes the aggregate amount to exceed $10,000 in cash. In such cases, the reporting requirement can be satisfied either by sending a single written statement with an aggregate amount listed or by furnishing a copy of each Form 8300 relating to that payer. Payments made to satisfy separate bail requirements are not required to be aggregated. See Treasury Regulations section 1.6050I-2.

Casinos must file Form 8300 for nongaming activities (restaurants, shops, etc.).

General Instructions

Who must file.—Each person engaged in a trade or business who, in the course of that trade or business, receives more than $10,000 in cash in one transaction or in two or more related transactions, must file Form 8300. Any transactions conducted between a payer (or its agent) and the recipient in a 24-hour period are related transactions. Transactions are considered related even if they occur over a period of more than 24 hours if the recipient knows, or has reason to know, that each transaction is one of a series of connected transactions.

Keep a copy of each Form 8300 for 5 years from the date you file it.

Voluntary use of Form 8300.—Form 8300 may be filed voluntarily for any suspicious transaction (see **Definitions**), even if the total amount does not exceed $10,000.

Exceptions.—Cash is not required to be reported if it is received:

● By a financial institution required to file **Form 4789,** Currency Transaction Report.

● By a casino required to file (or exempt from filing) **Form 8362,** Currency Transaction Report by Casinos, if the cash is received as part of its gaming business.

● By an agent who receives the cash from a principal, if the agent uses all of the cash within 15 days in a second transaction that is reportable on Form 8300 or on Form 4789, and discloses all the information necessary to complete Part II of Form 8300 or Form 4789 to the recipient of the cash in the second transaction.

● In a transaction occurring entirely outside the United States. See **Pub. 1544,** Reporting Cash Payments Over $10,000 (Received in a Trade or Business),

regarding transactions occurring in Puerto Rico, the Virgin Islands, and territories and possessions of the United States.

● In a transaction that is not in the course of a person's trade or business.

When to file.—File Form 8300 by the 15th day after the date the cash was received. If that date falls on a Saturday, Sunday, or legal holiday, file the form on the next business day.

Where to file.—File the form with the Internal Revenue Service, Detroit Computing Center, P.O. Box 32621, Detroit, MI 48232, or hand carry it to your local IRS office.

Statement to be provided.—You must give a written statement to each person named on a required Form 8300 on or before January 31 of the year following the calendar year in which the cash is received. The statement must show the name, telephone number, and address of the information contact for the business, the aggregate amount of reportable cash received, and that the information was furnished to the IRS. Keep a copy of the statement for your records.

Multiple payments.—If you receive more than one cash payment for a single transaction or for related transactions, you must report the multiple payments any time you receive a total amount that exceeds $10,000 within any 12-month period. Submit the report within 15 days of the date you receive the payment that causes the total amount to exceed $10,000. If more than one report is required within 15 days, you may file a combined report. File the combined report no later than the date the earliest report, if filed separately, would have to be filed.

Taxpayer identification number (TIN).—You must furnish the correct TIN of the person or persons from whom you receive the cash and, if applicable, the person or persons on whose behalf the transaction is being conducted. **You may be subject to penalties for an incorrect or missing TIN.**

The TIN for an individual (including a sole proprietorship) is the individual's social security number (SSN). For certain resident aliens who are not eligible to get an SSN and nonresident aliens who are required to file tax returns, it is an IRS Individual Taxpayer Identification Number (ITIN). For other persons, including corporations, partnerships, and estates, it is the employer identification number.

If you have requested but are not able to get a TIN for one or more of the parties to a transaction within 15 days following the transaction, file the report and attach a statement explaining why the TIN is not included.

Exception: *You are not required to provide the TIN of a person who is a nonresident alien individual or a foreign organization **if** that person does not have income effectively connected with the conduct of a U.S. trade or business **and** does not have an office or place of business, or fiscal or paying agent, in the United States. See Pub. 1544 for more information.*

Penalties.—You may be subject to penalties if you fail to file a correct and complete Form 8300 on time and you cannot show that the failure was due to reasonable cause. You may also be subject to penalties if you fail to furnish timely a correct and complete statement to each person named in a required report. A minimum penalty of $25,000 may be imposed if the failure is due to an intentional disregard of the cash reporting requirements.

Penalties may also be imposed for causing, or attempting to cause, a trade or business to fail to file a required report; for causing, or attempting to cause, a trade or business to file a required report containing a material omission or misstatement of fact; or for structuring, or attempting to structure, transactions to avoid the reporting requirements. These violations may also be subject to criminal prosecution which, upon conviction, may result in imprisonment of up to 5 years or fines of up to $250,000 for individuals and $500,000 for corporations or both.

Definitions

Cash.—The term "cash" means the following:

● U.S. and foreign coin and currency received in any transaction.

● A cashier's check, money order, bank draft, or traveler's check having a face amount of $10,000 or less that is received in a **designated reporting transaction** (defined below), or that is received in any transaction in which the recipient knows that the instrument is being used in an attempt to avoid the reporting of the transaction under section 6050I.

Note: *Cash does not include a check drawn on the payer's own account, such as a personal check, regardless of the amount.*

Designated reporting transaction.—A retail sale (or the receipt of funds by a broker or other intermediary in connection with a retail sale) of a consumer durable, a collectible, or a travel or entertainment activity.

Retail sale.—Any sale (whether or not the sale is for resale or for any other purpose) made in the course of a trade or business if that trade or business principally consists of making sales to ultimate consumers.

Consumer durable.—An item of tangible personal property of a type that, under ordinary usage, can reasonably be expected to remain useful for at least 1 year, and that has a sales price of more than $10,000.

Collectible.—Any work of art, rug, antique, metal, gem, stamp, coin, etc.

Travel or entertainment activity.—An item of travel or entertainment that pertains to a single trip or event if the combined sales price of the item and all other items relating to the same trip or event that are sold in the same transaction (or related transactions) exceeds $10,000.

Exceptions.—A cashier's check, money order, bank draft, or traveler's check is not considered received in a designated reporting transaction if it constitutes the proceeds of a bank loan or if it is received as a payment on certain promissory notes, installment sales contracts, or down payment plans. See Pub. 1544 for more information.

Person.—An individual, corporation, partnership, trust, estate, association, or company.

Recipient.—The person receiving the cash. Each branch or other unit of a person's trade or business is considered a separate recipient unless the branch receiving the cash (or a central office linking the branches), knows or has reason to know the identity of payers making cash payments to other branches.

Transaction.—Includes the purchase of property or services, the payment of debt, the exchange of a negotiable instrument for cash, and the receipt of cash to be held in escrow or trust. A single transaction may not be broken into multiple transactions to avoid reporting.

Suspicious transaction.—A transaction in which it appears that a person is attempting to cause Form 8300 not to be filed, or to file a false or incomplete form. The term also includes any transaction in which there is an indication of possible illegal activity.

Specific Instructions

You must complete all parts. However, you may skip Part II if the individual named in Part I is conducting the transaction on his or her behalf only.

Item 1.—If you are amending a prior report, check box 1a. Complete the appropriate items with the correct or amended information only. Complete all of Part IV. Staple a copy of the original report to the amended report.

To voluntarily report a suspicious transaction (see **Definitions**), check box 1b. You may also telephone your local IRS Criminal Investigation Division or call 1-800-800-2877.

Part I

Item 2.—If two or more individuals conducted the transaction you are reporting, check the box and complete Part I for any one of the individuals. Provide the same information for the other individual(s) on the back of the form. If more than three individuals are involved, provide the same information on additional sheets of paper and attach them to this form.

Item 6.—Enter the taxpayer identification number (TIN) of the individual named. See **Taxpayer identification number (TIN)** under **General Instructions** for more information.

Item 8.—Enter eight numerals for the date of birth of the individual named. For example, if the individual's birth date is July 6, 1960, enter 07 06 1960.

Item 13.—Fully describe the nature of the occupation, profession, or business (for example, "plumber," "attorney," or "automobile dealer"). Do not use general or nondescriptive terms such as "businessman" or "self-employed."

Item 14.—You must verify the name and address of the named individual(s). Verification must be made by examination of a document normally accepted as a means of identification when cashing checks (for example, a driver's license, passport, alien registration card, or other official document). In item 14a, enter the type of document examined. In item 14b, identify the issuer of the document. In item 14c, enter the document's number. For example, if the individual has a Utah driver's license, enter "driver's license" in item 14a, "Utah" in item 14b, and the number appearing on the license in item 14c.

Part II

Item 15.—If the transaction is being conducted on behalf of more than one person (including husband and wife or parent and child), check the box and complete Part II for any one of the persons. Provide the same information for the other person(s) on the back of the form. If more than three persons are involved, provide the same information on additional sheets of paper and attach them to this form.

Items 16 through 19.—If the person on whose behalf the transaction is being conducted is an individual, complete items 16, 17, and 18. Enter his or her TIN in item 19. If the individual is a sole proprietor and has an employer identification number (EIN), you must enter both the SSN and EIN in item 19. If the person is an organization, put its name as shown on required tax filings in item 16 and its EIN in item 19.

Item 20.—If a sole proprietor or organization named in items 16 through 18 is doing business under a name other than that entered in item 16 (e.g., a "trade" or "doing business as (DBA)" name), enter it here.

Item 27.—If the person is **NOT** required to furnish a TIN (see **Taxpayer identification number (TIN)** under **General Instructions**), complete this item. Enter a description of the type of official document issued to that person in item 27a (for example, "passport"), the country that issued the document in item 27b, and the document's number in item 27c.

Part III

Item 28.—Enter the date you received the cash. If you received the cash in more than one payment, enter the date you received the payment that caused the combined amount to exceed $10,000. See **Multiple payments** under **General Instructions** for more information.

Item 30.—Check this box if the amount shown in item 29 was received in more than one payment (for example, as installment payments or payments on related transactions).

Item 31.—Enter the total price of the property, services, amount of cash exchanged, etc. (for example, the total cost

of a vehicle purchased, cost of catering service, exchange of currency) if different from the amount shown in item 29.

Item 32.—Enter the dollar amount of each form of cash received. Show foreign currency amounts in U.S. dollar equivalent at a fair market rate of exchange available to the public. **The sum of the amounts must equal item 29.** For cashier's check, money order, bank draft, or traveler's check, provide the name of the issuer and the serial number of each instrument. Names of all issuers and all serial numbers involved must be provided. If necessary, provide this information on additional sheets of paper and attach them to this form.

Item 33.—Check the appropriate box(es) that describe the transaction. If the transaction is not specified in boxes a–i, check box j and briefly describe the transaction (for example, car lease, boat lease, house lease, aircraft rental).

Part IV

Item 36.—If you are a sole proprietorship, you must enter your SSN. If your business also has an EIN, you must provide the EIN as well. All other business entities must enter an EIN.

Item 41.—Fully describe the nature of your business, for example, "attorney," "jewelry dealer." Do not use general or nondescriptive terms such as "business" or "store."

Item 42.—This form must be signed by an individual who has been authorized to do so for the business that received the cash.

Paperwork Reduction Act Notice

The requested information is useful in criminal, tax, and regulatory investigations, for instance, by directing the Federal Government's attention to unusual or questionable transactions. Trades or businesses are required to provide the information under 26 U.S.C. 6050I.

You are not required to provide the information requested on a form that is subject to the Paperwork Reduction Act unless the form displays a valid OMB control number. Books or records relating to a form or its instructions must be retained as long as their contents may become material in the administration of any Internal Revenue law. Generally, tax returns and return information are confidential, as required by Code section 6103.

The time needed to complete this form will vary depending on individual circumstances. The estimated average time is 21 minutes. If you have comments concerning the accuracy of this time estimate or suggestions for making this form simpler, you can write to the Tax Forms Committee, Western Area Distribution Center, Rancho Cordova, CA 95743-0001. DO NOT send this form to this office. Instead, see **Where To File** on page 3.